Law, Culture and the Figure of the Girl

This book argues for the critical potential of locating the girl as the subject-position and voice of legal critique.

Law's imaginary is notoriously limited in its ways of thinking through and adjudicating gender violence. This book argues that 'the girl' is a key figure through which to understand, theorise, and challenge law's relation to this violence. *Law, Culture and the Figure of the Girl* explains the meaning and significance of the figure of the girl to legal, political, and critical projects centred on trauma and responsibility. The book offers new readings of exemplary cultural texts that thematically deal with law's adjudication of violence against girls, emphasising the ways these texts challenge dominant ways of thinking and doing law, jurisdiction, violence, race, and gender. The book also explores radical cultural figurations of the girl in fiction, films, and TV series and demonstrates the critical potential of these works in understanding and providing counter-narratives to dominant legal and cultural imaginaries. These works provide ways not only to critique existing law but to theorise emergent forms of law-making.

This book will be of interest to scholars in the areas of cultural legal studies, law and literature, feminist legal studies, and cultural studies. It will also be suitable as a prescribed text for upper undergraduate classes and graduate studies in the disciplines of law, legal studies, cultural studies, and criminology.

Honni van Rijswijk is a Senior Lecturer in the Faculty of Law at the University of Technology Sydney, Australia.

Law, Culture and the Figure of the Girl

Genre and Gender Violence

Honni van Rijswijk

Routledge
Taylor & Francis Group
a GlassHouse Book

First published 2025
by Routledge
4 Park Square, Milton Park, Abingdon, Oxon OX14 4RN

and by Routledge
605 Third Avenue, New York, NY 10158

Routledge is an imprint of the Taylor & Francis Group, an informa business

A GlassHouse book

British Library Cataloguing-in-Publication Data
A catalogue record for this book is available from the British Library

Library of Congress Cataloging-in-Publication Data
Names: Rijswijk, Honni van, author.
Title: Law, culture and the figure of the girl : genre and gender violence / Honni van Rijswijk.
Description: Abingdon, Oxon [UK] ; New York, NY : Routledge, 2025. | Includes bibliographical references and index.
Identifiers: LCCN 2024030181 (print) | LCCN 2024030182 (ebook) | ISBN 9780367193515 (hardback) | ISBN 9781032902852 (paperback) | ISBN 9780429263675 (ebook)
Subjects: LCSH: Women—Violence against—Law and legislation. | Women—Crimes against—Law and legislation. | Gender-based violence. | Feminist jurisprudence. | Culture and law. | Group identity.
Classification: LCC K5191.W65 R55 2025 (print) | LCC K5191. W65 (ebook) | DDC 345/.025082—dc23/eng/20240714
LC record available at https://lccn.loc.gov/2024030181
LC ebook record available at https://lccn.loc.gov/2024030182

ISBN: 978-0-367-19351-5 (hbk)
ISBN: 978-1-032-90285-2 (pbk)
ISBN: 978-0-429-26367-5 (ebk)

DOI: 10.4324/9780429263675

Typeset in Sabon
by Apex CoVantage, LLC

This book is dedicated to Laura, Anika and Dashi

Contents

Acknowledgements

I would like to thank my friends and colleagues, past and present, who have helped me develop these ideas over the years: Thalia Anthony, Maria Aristodemou, Olivia Barr, Christine Black, Tasha Buttler, Emily Clark, Karen Crawley, Penny Crofts, Maria Drakopoulous, Maureen Fadam, Elizabeth Freeman, Peter Goodrich, Melissa Hardie, Laura Joseph, Rosanne Kennedy, Kara McKinney, Deborah Kimmey, Kate Lilley, Kate Livett, Trish Luker, Bill MacNeil, Desmond Manderson, Elizabeth McMahon, Stewart Motha, Greta Olson, Jacqueline Rule, Alecia Simmonds, Jill Stauffer, Karin van Marle, Anthea Vogl, Anne Wagner, Yvette Wajon, Robin West, and Alison Young.

Notes on Terms

First Nations People

I have used the term First Nations people as a sign of respect and acknowledgement of the unceded sovereignty of the peoples whose cultures and communities predate the British invasion and occupation of the lands that have come to be known as 'Australia.' I retain the imposed terms 'Aboriginal' and 'Indigenous' only in relation to quotes in historical material and in relation to the formal names of legacy entities and institutions such as the 'Aboriginal Protectors' or the 'Royal Commission into Aboriginal Deaths in Custody.'

On 'Girl' and 'Woman'

I use 'girl' and 'woman' here and throughout this book as names people call themselves and also as categories of feminist analysis. Neither is a neutral, biological, or predetermined category; girls and women are people who identify as girls and women. Within feminist scholarship, 'girl' and 'woman' are not neutral biological descriptors but concepts that carry a range of legal, religious, political, and cultural meanings.

On 'Gender Violence'

Law, Culture and the Girl is concerned with the harm of sexual violence and how this connects to other structural issues of violence. The title refers to 'gender violence' rather than 'sexual violence' since one of the main arguments of the book is that harms are interconnected, and the term 'gender violence' points to the wider structural connections beyond the conduct or event of sexual violence as it is usually interpreted. However, it is important to note the context of the term 'gender violence.' The radical feminist paradigm shift on violence against women in the 1970s and 1980s was to reframe men's violence against women not as an isolated anomaly but as part of an 'over-conformity with a culturally honoured definition of masculinity that rewarded the successful use of violence to achieve domination over others'

(Messner, 2016, p. 59). However, there was a subsequent backlash against this framework by those who saw this approach as 'guilt-imposing, anti-male monologues that shut off conversation, rather than as openings for dialogue to engage and ask men to change themselves and their communities' (Messner, 2016, p. 60; Messner et al., 2015). So in the 1990s, the focus switched from a political response to anti-rape pedagogies intended to appease or appeal to—rather than alienate—boys and men (Flood, 2018, 2020). Since the early 2000s, the hegemonic approach to rape prevention has recast 'violence against women' as 'gender-based violence.' The advantages of this approach include opening space for thinking about the connections between violence against women and violence against sexual minorities, sexual assaults of boys and men, and gender-based bullying and stereotypes. This new language of gender may enable new lines of inquiry about the construction—and reformation—of masculinity, as well as opening up an exploration of how patriarchy harms not only women but also men and gender-diverse people. The term also encourages a view of harms as interconnected, as extending beyond a specific identity category. But the approach is also problematic because it potentially occludes the nature of this violence—it decentres women, the majority of the victims of violence, as well as sidelining the fact that most of this violence is in fact committed by men.

Bibliography

Flood, M. (2018) *Engaging Men and Boys in Violence Prevention.* London: Palgrave Macmillan.

Flood, M. (2020) 'Sexual Violence Prevention with Men and Boys as a Social Justice Issue.' In L. M. Orchowski and A. Berkowitz (Eds.), *Engaging Boys and Men in Sexual Assault Prevention: Theory, Research and Practice.* London: Elsevier.

Messner, M. (2016) 'Getting Consent "Right": Sexual Assault Law Reform in New South Wales.' *Australian Feminist Law Journal*, 42(1), pp. 58–70.

Messner, M., Greenberg, M. A., and Peretz, T. (2015) *Some Men: Feminist Allies and the Movement to End Violence Against Women.* New York: Oxford University Press.

Chapter 1

The Figure of the Girl

Introduction: The Figure of the Girl in Legal and Cultural Narratives

The figure of the child is fundamental to the contemporary juridico-political imagination. This figure is instrumental in national projects and state narratives, invoked in contexts ranging from the moral panics of the 1990s to the recent the Northern Territory Intervention.[1] In these varied contexts, the child is used to justify legal intervention into and adjudication of violence, thus facilitating increases in the state's jurisdictions. The impact of these approaches, especially under neoliberalism, have been critiqued by a number of scholars.[2] In political and philosophical analyses of law, the figure of the child is used to mark human futurity and potential. This book shifts the critical emphasis from 'the child' of the neoliberal imaginary to 'the girl,' investigating how focusing on the figure of the girl can challenge law's adjudications of violence. Most significantly, gendering the child figure makes not only gender but race and class central to the critique and reimagining of law and justice—the radical imaginaries examined here foreground how 'the child' circulating in the neoliberal imaginary is always gendered and

1 *Northern Territory National Emergency Response Act 2007* (Cth) No. 129 (NTNERA); *Family, Community Services, Indigenous Affairs and Other Legislation Amendment (Northern Territory National Emergency Response and Other Measures) Act 2007* (Cth) No. 128; *Social Security and Other Legislation Amendment (Welfare Payment Reform) Act 2007* (Cth) No. 130; *Families, Community Services and Indigenous Affairs and Other Legislation Amendment (Northern Territory National Emergency Response and Other Measures) Act 2007* (Cth) No. 128; *Appropriation (Northern Territory National Emergency Response) Act (No. 1) 2007* (Cth) No. 126 and *Appropriation (Northern Territory National Emergency Response) Act (No. 2) 2007* (Cth) No. 127. I use the phrase 'the Northern Territory Intervention' or 'the Intervention' to refer to this regime.

2 See e.g., James and Prout, 2015; Stephens, 1995; Faulkner, 2023, 2011, 2014; Cree et al., 2016; Breslow, 2021; Sheldon, 2016; Harkins, 2020. Queer scholars have pushed back against the state's instrumentalisation of the child by arguing that queerness itself radically disrupts these teleological, futuristic imaginaries, as does the figure of the queer child (Edelman, 2004; Stockton, 2009; Bruhm and Hurley, 2004; Halberstam, 2005).

DOI: 10.4324/9780429263675-1

always racialised. This project aims to unpack the cultural-legal imaginary of sexual violence: the effects of liberal law's narratives of sexual violence, and the cultural narratives that produce and support them. The readings in this book will show how 'the girl' is a productive, liminal figure that disrupts the artificial distinction between ruptures of extremity, and the violence of the everyday. The girl is also an inherently temporal figure, which connects past, present, and future violence in poignant ways. By reading key cultural figurations of 'the girl' in fiction, poetry, films, and plays, alongside figurations of girls in legal and quasi-legal texts, this project argues, first, that the girl is a key figure through which to understand law's relation to violence; and second, that the girl can be a productive figure through which to theorise and reimagine law's relation to violence.

Law's imaginary is notoriously limited in its ways of thinking through and adjudicating gender violence. In *Law, Culture and the Figure of the Girl*, I critique and reimagine law's frameworks through encounters with cultural texts. *Law, Culture and the Figure of the Girl* offers new readings of exemplary cultural texts that thematically deal with law's adjudication of violence against girls, emphasising the ways these texts challenge dominant ways of thinking and doing law, jurisdiction, violence, race, and gender. I analyse these works as a way to not only critique existing law and culture but to understand emergent forms of law-making: these cultural works are sites in which new law is created by resistant creators, often speaking from the margins of society. *Law, Culture and the Figure of the Girl* provides new readings of both legal and literary texts, using cultural texts as sites of both critique and theorisation. This book argues for the value of thinking about legal transformation through the lens of literary and popular culture. I argue for the centrality of the cultural imaginary to legal theorisation, and its interpretive potential in understanding the roles of gender and violence in the dominant neoliberal imaginary.

Our contemporary, neoliberal moment is marked by the failure of modern institutions, including legal institutions, to provide proper frameworks of accountability for harm. The main legal and political theories through which we try to understand this collapse emerge from the same historical processes as the institutions that are so inadequate. It is difficult, even impossible, then, to evaluate our contemporary legal terrain through the use of analytical categories that were created in an earlier time. Those categories serve the failing institutions that they produced but are redundant in diagnosing the problems with these institutions and aren't capable of providing frameworks for the way forward. Therefore, in this book, I turn to forms of popular and literary culture (the novels of Alexis Wright, horror films, coming-of-age TV series) that are less bound to the normative reasoning, categories, and imaginaries of neoliberal law and the neoliberal political economy (and less bound to late capitalism, patriarchy, and colonialism). These readings foreground the deep connections that exist between neoliberalism, patriarchy, and settler colonialism, which are latent but disguised in our mainstream culture and in neoliberal law.

Law, Culture and the Figure of the Girl turns to popular and literary representations to theorise new juridical approaches to gender violence. These works centre the figure of the girl, and the associated narratives of violation, generation, family, and futurity. The readings of these texts challenge law's practices of representation and the underlying assumptions upon which legal myths continue: assumptions about the kinds of lives that our juridico-political worlds make possible. Girls and women are subjected to relentless levels of gender violence, a phenomenon so normalised that it is challenging for feminists and social/political movements to effectively name all the harms, let alone address them. This violence occurs in the regulated spaces of institutions—schools, workplaces, sports training centres—as well as in the less regulated domain of the family and in the unregulated 'private' spaces of interpersonal relationships. The law has totally failed in preventing and adjudicating this violence.[3] Law is so ineffective that in a recent UK report on the policing of sexual violence, one police officer stated: 'If you look at our performance around rape, serious sexual offences, the detection rate is so low you may as well say it's legal in London' (Baroness Casey Review, 2023, p. 174).[4] The tolerance for this continuing, relentless violence is somewhat baffling—and yet, perhaps not, since gender violence is also the logical endpoint of our racist, sexist, colonial, and late-capitalist structures. Gender harm is, in fact, normal, given our political and material contexts. Further, there is law's paradox regarding gender violence: legal interventions that have been made with the prevention of gender violence as their justification have frequently caused further violence to vulnerable communities (First Nations, Black, non-white, trans, LGBTQUIA, poor) twinned with law's manifest failure to prevent or remedy gendered violence. Nonetheless, the law remains what Carol Smart (1989, p. 160) described as a 'siren call' for many feminists.' That is, much feminist legal advocacy remains attached to working through the law to achieve social and political transformations while recognising that the adversarial legal system, and its specific protocols and conventions, harms survivors and fails to deliver justice. This commitment to law has, however, been increasingly challenged in recent years by Black and

3 See e.g., Halley et al., 2018; Temkin et al., 2017; Carline and Easteal, 2014; McGlynn, 2010; Deer, 2015; Estrich, 2014; Gray, 2016; Henry and Powell, 2017; Simić, 2018; Russell, 2013, 2016; Russell and Conaghan, 2023; Serisier, 2018. Law's inadequacies in dealing with rape are well-documented. Victims often find themselves trapped in Kafkaesque processes, with their complaints recorded but not acted upon (Leigh Gilmore, 2023).

4 Baronness Louise Casey conducted a year-long investigation into Britain's largest police force, concluding with a 363-page report (Baroness Casey Review, 2023). The Metropolitan Police was found to be institutionally racist, sexist, and homophobic, with a shockingly low detection rate for rape and serious sexual offenses.

abolitionist feminist critics, who caution against calling on the powers of the state to respond to sexual and domestic violence, recognising that a carceral approach will harm the most vulnerable women and the men and children in their lives (Bumiller, 2008; Carlton and Russell, 2018).

Theorising justice through exemplary cultural works encourages an interrogation of the concepts underlying existing and inadequate legal and social frameworks of responsibility for sexual violence—a movement away, especially, from the existing fetishisation of suffering that is so prominent under our current modes of living, where sexual violence is so normal and normalised. I propose these readings as ways of theorising new legalities regarding the adjudication of gender violence: to provide new frameworks, metaphors, and narratives to judge harms and law's relationship to these harms. These works point to emergent ways of understanding and creating laws beyond the (failed, problematic) neoliberal legal imaginary.

The *Bildungsroman* of the Traumatised Girl

Law, Culture and the Figure of the Girl examines the figure of the girl in the dominant cultural imagination, where the girl is not only a child but a young woman—a daughter, an intern, an ingenue, an aspiring actress, graduate journalist, or young medical professional, still in the act of becoming. A young woman is a 'girl' in these representations because she is infantilised as part of a certain form of sexualisation, but also as part of a developmental narrative that is more complex in its origins and what it is doing. Novelist Emily St. John Mandel has explored the trend of novel titles that included 'girl' in them, which dominated the mid-2010s using Goodreads data; she found 810 popular books with 'girl' in the title, excluding children's and young adult literature. Mandel noted that in 65% of the books, the 'girl' was actually an adult woman, not an adolescent or child. Her editor, Jennifer Jackson, suggested that using 'girl' instead of 'woman' might evoke a sense of vulnerability, raising the stakes of the narrative (Brady, 2016, n.p.).

The *bildungsroman* was originally considered a nineteenth-century literary genre that centred on the development and education of a protagonist, traditionally a young man from the provinces, who seeks his fortune in the city. Through a series of obstacles and didactic worldly experiences, he eventually reconciles with society, moving from immaturity to maturity, social exclusion to social inclusion, ignorance to understanding. This conventional narrative framework, however, encompasses several key variants. In one variation, a young woman undergoes a process of worldly or sentimental education and becomes reconciled to her destiny, often through marriage; another variant involves a young man or woman achieving success as a writer or artist through a blend of aesthetic, worldly, and sentimental education (Frow et al., 2020, p. 1905). Stephanie Ansley Hershinow pushes the timeline for the *bildungsroman* back to the eighteenth century, to Samuel Richardson's

Pamela (1740) and *Clarissa* (1748) (Hershinow, 2019, p. 11, cited in Frow et al., 2020, p. 1905). Hershinow's analysis extends to contemporary fiction, film, and television, emphasising continuities within the *bildungsroman* across different periods and media, from the eighteenth century to the present (Hershinow, 2019, p. 11, cited in Frow et al., 2020, p. 1905). So the girl is a child but also a young woman, usually a young woman in the crisis of becoming. But I argue that her *bildungsroman* is not the traditional movement from uncivilised child to civilised citizen through the act of making art, joining a profession or travelling far from home; those things may happen, but the focus of the girl's *bildungsroman* in mainstream culture, from the eighteenth century to the present, is on becoming through suffering/subjugation/sexual violence.

The figure of the suffering girl is an overdetermined fetish in the mainstream. Examples abound from high and low culture, from the sex crimes that permeate the Bible to contemporary culture, where almost every popular thriller or mystery opens with or centres on the violated body of a girl (see for example Larsson, *The Girl with The Dragon Tattoo*, 2005; Flynn, *Sharp Objects* 2006; Flynn, *Gone Girl* 2013); French, *In the Woods* 2007; Hawkins, *The Girl on the Train* 2015). For example, in the highly popular novel *Room* (2010), by Emma Donahue, the protagonist is the young son of a girl who was kidnapped and imprisoned in a basement and raped; conceived through sexual violence and born in the basement, the young boy knows nothing of the outside world. Both the novel and the film are a carnival of suffering, lingering on tropes of sexual violence, imprisonment, and psychological torture. When the young woman and her son escape the basement, the narrative perspective shifts to the young woman, who only truly expresses herself after a suicide attempt: her suffering becomes her primary means of communication.

The aesthetics and logics that position the girl as an overdetermined figure of suffering are not just limited to the girl as child or adolescent; they also inflect the young woman's *bildungsroman*, even where she is 'out in the world' in a professional capacity. This metonymic/synecdochal relationship between girl and woman is iconically embodied by the actress Elisabeth Moss. With her small stature and wide eyes, Moss is childlike in appearance and is consistently cast as characters who are always-already vulnerable and subjugated. In the series *Mad Man* (2007–2015), Moss's character Peggy Olsen has an iconic *bildungsroman* arc, including an unwanted pregnancy from a sexually ambiguous encounter with a senior member of her workplace, followed by a mental breakdown. Olsen ultimately gains some agency by navigating the extreme sexism of her workplace to move from the position of a secretary to an advertising executive. In *Shining Girls* (2022), Moss plays a character who deals with a serial killer who can time-travel to hunt girls, emphasising the impossibility of escape. In *Top of the Lake* (2013) and its sequel *Top of the Lake: China Girl* (2017), Moss portrays a detective investigating cases involving sexual violence against a 12-year-old girl and then victims of sex trafficking. The origin story of the detective Moss plays is that she was gang-raped as a teenager, followed by a forced pregnancy/birth. In the TV series *The Handmaid's Tale* (2017–), Moss plays June, a young woman whose sole purpose is to be subjected to forced pregnancy and birth in a future dystopia. In *The Invisible Man* (2020), Moss is ruthlessly pursued by a man who has developed the technology to make himself invisible. These roles often cast Moss as the ultimate, most abject victim, emphasising societal anxieties about female vulnerability. Moreover, these series frequently feature scenes that linger over the suffering of girls and young women—long shots of dead girls at crime scenes or on autopsy tables, shots that spend time focusing on their wounds and underscoring the excessiveness of the violence inflicted. By embodying these roles as the suffering girl/woman, Moss has become a powerful symbol of abjection, where the visual and narrative focus on female suffering underscores the broader cultural practices that normalise and reinforce the subjugation of girls; as she performs in more and more similar roles, the association with abjection is reinforced and carried to the next performance. She has come to figure the *bildungsroman* of girls as essentially subjugated by sexual violence.

Such depictions of sexual violence as the *bildungsroman* of girls and its significance within the wider cultural framework of sexual violence are the focus of this book. The thematic focus on sexual violence in stories about girls and young women is partly due to the depressingly pervasive nature of sexual violence in the lives of girls and young women—in their families, in schools, colleges, universities, and police and military training centres—with one in two women in the US reporting unwanted sexual contact at some point in their lifetime and girls/young women being the demographic most at risk (Centers for Disease Control and Prevention, 2021). Associated with this harm are related gender harms. Jack Halberstam, in *Female Masculinity*, observes that female adolescence represents a critical period of coming of age in a male-dominated society; while adolescence for boys is often celebrated as a rite of passage, symbolising an ascension to some form of social power, for girls, this stage is marked by lessons in restraint, punishment, and repression (Halberstam, 1998, p. 6). Simone de Beauvoir points out that puberty is experienced differently by each sex: virility for boys and femininity for girls, with femininity being associated with alterity and inferiority, thus its revelation is met with shame (de Beauvoir 1993, p. 329). Furthermore, Beauvoir highlights a patriarchal perspective that views a young girl's emerging sexuality as positioning her as 'consenting prey,' both sexually attractive and dangerous (de Beauvoir 1993, p. 335). There are real forces, then, that culture is reflecting in its depiction of subjugated girls, but there is also excess here, and these representations themselves reinforce the trope of the girl as innately subjugated and in need of rescue. Portrayals such as Moss's characters or of girls in novels such as *Room* also promote the powerful and damaging ideology that victims and survivors communicate mainly, if not entirely, through their suffering. They are not considered authorities on justice; rather, the girl's suffering is left to speak for her, silencing her actual voice. In the context of adjudicating sexual violence, whether within or outside the law, the figure of the girl often calls upon the state or men to assert jurisdiction over women's harms, thereby reinforcing patriarchal control over female bodies and experiences. In the different context of transitional justice, Rosanne Kennedy and Robert Meister have argued that legal and cultural texts that demand an affective response can actively negate possibilities of justice. For Kennedy, some harms are experienced as 'scenes of suffering' rather than as 'scenes of injustice' (Kennedy, 2011, p. 270), the focus on pain and empathy thereby foreclosing the development of a proper and subtle concept of responsibility in legal and political domains. For Meister, the 'role of this "melodrama's" audience is not to struggle but to feel' (Meister, 2011, p. 70). When a text invites a response from the reader or viewer predominantly in the realm of feeling, it forgoes the possibility of justice. These popular texts implicitly call for justice through the assumption that the sign of the wounded or suffering girl is communication in itself, with the question of justice not raised apart from the affective response of the reader or audience; the audience's feelings of loss and empathy for the suffering of the girl stand in for justice.

In mainstream culture, representations of girls become legible through dominant frameworks—late capital, structural racism, colonialism, patriarchy. This dominant 'girl' figure has little to do with the lived experience of actual girls, especially trans girls, non-white girls, and poor girls. Girls are often depicted in visual media and stories as 'objects to be seen and rescued' (Hesford, 2011, p. 130), implying that their vulnerability not only enables the display of heroism by others but also traps them in a constant state of danger. These portrayals condition audiences to view such vulnerability and peril as an inevitable aspect of girls' lives (Marshall and Gilmore, 2015). Their vulnerability enables others to act heroically, while the girls themselves remain persistently trapped in dangerous material conditions and entrenched visual and narrative practices. These depictions condition audiences to perceive this vulnerability and peril as the girls' unchangeable destiny (Marshall and Gilmore, 2015, p. 95). Representations of girls also frequently emblematise social anxiety about neoliberalism—symbolising the neoliberal insistence that girls invest in themselves as sites of human capital while also acting as the invisible infrastructure supporting neoliberal structures (Lamm, 2015, p. 115). Lamm argues that historically and culturally, girls have been molded to embody specific roles within neoliberalism, roles designed to mitigate the harsh effects of capitalism. Drawing on recent developments in girl studies and feminist theory, Lamm contends that these roles often arise from a long-standing practice of equating girls with commodification. This 'girlphobic' perspective is prevalent in both pro-capitalist and anti-capitalist discussions. In anti-capitalist critiques, the engagement of girls with capitalist culture is often criticised as emblematic of capitalism's pervasive influence. Critics use images of girls, such as pop stars, to highlight the trivialisation of significant social values, yet these criticisms seldom address the deeper issue of girls being commodified (Warren-Crow, 2014, pp. 10–11). Additionally, the modern marketing of empowerment to girls globally, while seemingly positive, underscores their perceived lower societal value by suggesting that overcoming devaluation is an aspiration rather than a fundamental right (Lamm, 2015, p. 112).

In feminist discourses, the figure of the girl has become a powerful symbol with multiple roles. Historically, literature has portrayed the girl as a disruptor within various systems, such as the legal machinery in Franz Kafka's *The Trial* and the logical constructs in Lewis Carroll's Alice stories; however, she has also been depicted problematically as both a victim and an agent of capitalist exploitation (Tiqqun, 2012). She is portrayed as a challenger of late capitalism and its temporality (Freeman, 2000) and more negatively as the reinforcer of heteronormativity and capitalism through the commercialised 'Girl Power' movement of the late 1990s (McRobbie, 2008). The field of 'girlhood studies,' emerging in the early 2000s, examines the psychological and social growth of girls in various global contexts. In these studies, the figure of the girl shifts between reflecting actual experiences of young women and acting as a screen for imposed interpretations, highlighting her as a symbol subject to constant change, especially in how her development is studied in social sciences. The concept of 'girlism' has risen to prominence in popular culture, exemplified by phenomena such as Lena Dunham's HBO series *Girls* and the Riot Grrrl punk movement.

The genre of the *bildungsroman* trauma novel reflects the grim reality of sexual violence's pervasiveness. However, it also exhibits an excess, where the narratives and aesthetics instrumentalise the figure of the girl for purposes unrelated to her point of view or best interests. There is a strong literary tradition where narratives, tropes, and 'scenes' of sexual violence centring the figure of the violated girl are instrumentalised—where the figure is used to thematise 'wider' legal, political, and national questions. This approach is exemplified by Nobel Laureate J. M. Coetzee's literary novel *Disgrace*, which, since it first appeared in 1999, has attracted wide readership and scholarly attention (Coetzee, 1999). Set in post-apartheid South Africa, the novel follows Prof. David Lurie as he encounters personal 'disgrace,' first because of his sexual exploitation of one of his students, Melanie, and second, after a group of men sexually assault his daughter, Lucy, while he is restrained in the next room. Both the novel's theme of transitional justice and Lurie's moral arc rely on the sexual violation of two young women/girls. Lurie is a white, middle-aged South African professor of literature. The violation of Melanie stands in for the institutional violence of which Lurie is part, and his negotiation of this violence is presented as a moral grey area. His daughter's violation figures the national violence of apartheid and the complexities of negotiating a national future out of the violence and disgrace of South

Africa's colonial history. Lurie's refusal to negotiate his public confession of guilt over his abuse of his student leads to his dismissal, and his daughter's refusal to pursue her rapists' capture baffles and angers him. Lucy's bodily integrity is shattered, and she is also geographically placed in proximity with one of her rapists, who is kin to her neighbour. The neighbour is scheming to take over her land, and it is suggested that he encouraged or at least permitted his kin to rape her. Lucy then lives at the nexus of two competing, violent patriarchies: her father's, who has earlier been violent towards Melanie, and her neighbour's. In this small space, her violated body marks the intersection of historical and contemporary patriarchal and racial violence. Each of these characters is hyperbolically vulnerable, and this vulnerability is key to the novel's critique of political violence. While there are critical and political 'pay offs' to the use of these figures in the novel, the continued use of the figure of a raped woman in literary and cultural projects to ground critiques of colonial, racist, and political violence is itself not only a tired cliché (McClintock, 1995) but politically and critically problematic.

Lucy refuses to report the rape to the police, she refuses to leave, and she refuses to do anything about the pregnancy that results from the rape. She invokes the language of privacy: 'as far as I am concerned, what happened to me is a purely private matter. In another time, in another place it might be held to be a public matter. But in this place, at this time, it is not' (Coetzee, 1999, p. 112). 'I don't act in terms of abstractions,' Lucy declares (Coetzee, 1999, p. 112), ironically when her character is most abject and most abstracted as the sign of South Africa's post-apartheid sha me and complexity. David is stunned by Lucy's refusals. David thinks that if Lucy moved away and aborted the foetus, restoring bodily integrity and achieving spatial distance from her violators, she would be safe: that she can somehow be made invulnerable by a reversal of the processes she has endured, by achieving geographic distance and by removing the foetus that compromises her physical integrity. He doesn't understand Lucy's argument that she will never feel safe again. He doesn't understand political reality, gendered and raced realities, and the realities of violence. The 'journey' of the book is David's gradual comprehension. At the beginning, David refuses to be drawn into the political consequences of what he thinks of as the 'private' act of 'seducing' Melanie. By the end of the book, he has been drawn into his daughter's life, in which the distinctions between private and public violence have broken down. Here Lucy is a figure for South Africa, and the fact that she can never be rendered whole shows the falsity of the logic that draws a clear line between a period 'before' and a period 'after' apartheid, as though each temporal space were a neat parallel of the other, where all the violence of the earlier period is made whole in the latter.

The book is focalised through David's point of view, and his daughter's experience matters in the novel because it is experienced as his trauma: her rape, pregnancy, and refusal to do anything 'active' about this (again, breaking down the dualism of activity/passivity), is figured as a 'violence' to David's expectations of right to his daughter and his women: a right that he and his laws will protect her, which they do not and cannot, and which protection she refuses. The novel represents a breakdown in neoliberal logics following the end of apartheid, simultaneously revealing what has always been there, but mostly not experienced by, white South Africans. The novel does this over the body of a young white woman, and at the end of the novel, she is a figure of complete abjection: pregnant by her rapists and increasingly under their dominion. The figure of the subjugated young woman becomes the structuring metaphor for continuing racism, war, and disaster. The novel is generally interpreted by critics as a critique of nation and history (Attwell, 2015; Gallagher, 2002; Attridge, 2004; Barnard, 2003; Marais, 2011).

Some writers, however, have pushed against this instrumentalisation of sexual violence; they still represent the significance of the violence of continuing colonialism, patriarchy, and late capitalism, but rather than the violated girl 'standing in' for these other harms, they are conscious of how these harms are interconnected, with sexual violence more than mere 'background.' Written in 2003, McBride's debut novel *A Girl Is a Half-formed Thing* wasn't published until 2013 by the then newly established Galley Beggar Press, which aimed to foster unconventional, challenging writing. *A Girl Is a Half-formed Thing* has since won the inaugural Goldsmiths Prize for fiction which expands the novel form as well as the Bailey's Prize for Women's Fiction (formerly the Orange Prise). Set in Ireland, in an undetermined time and place, *A Girl is a Half-formed Thing* is a story of a nameless girl who has been sexually abused by her uncle. The violence shatters her, transforming her into a 'half-formed thing.' The novel refutes an 'event-based' reading of sexual violence; rather, sexual violence is a structure produced by patriarchy and colonialism. In its fragmentation, the narrative enacts the difficulty of finding frameworks and language with which to make traumatic experience intelligible while at the same time refusing the myth that trauma is unspeakable or unable to be represented. McBride represents this fragmentation through experimental linguistic and narrative strategies. After being raped, Girl remarks that '[h]e knows something I don't. About me' (McBride, 2013, p. 53). Girl is suspended at half-formation, 'splinter[ed]' by epistemological and physical violence; she observes that 'fucking' 'stitch[es] up my eyes and sew[s] up my mouth' (McBride, 2013, p. 43). Girl's ultimate suicide comprises a total rejection of the world, of the sexual violence inflicted upon her and of the colonial and patriarchal world, an act constituting rebellion, as well as self-obliteration: 'there's no way for this. Not a single way. Out' (McBride, 2013, p. 127). Gendered violence is bound up with epistemic violence in the novel, particularly through the power of naming (Darling, 2021). This opposes Cathy Caruth's theory of survivors speaking through the wound, where the language of trauma somehow 'defies, even as it claims, our understanding' (Caruth, 1996, p. 4). A number of texts examined in this book similarly push against the trope of the wound that speaks for the survivor—in Chapter 3, this trope is reinvented in contemporary revenge films, and in Chapter 4, novelist Alexis Wright rejects the trauma framework in favour of interpreting sexual violence as the effect of colonialism. These cultural texts take up the question of how to write 'about' sexual violence in innovative ways, deconstructing both this violence and the figure of the girl in the process.

Law, Culture and the Figure of the Girl is primarily concerned with representations of girls rather than girls themselves. While I cite some empirical evidence about what is happening to actual girls, my main focus is how practices of representation support, produce, or challenge violence. The focus is on very recent texts, roughly from 2000 onwards, but draws on a literary tradition that is much older. We can think of this literary tradition as being written from a position of complexity or near impossibility—a tradition that uses the figure of the girl as a seemingly solid character (for example, using first-person focalisation that seems to firm up the idea of a 'girl') but then unravels or deconstructs the apparent solidity of this figure into political, social, and legal worlds. Examples in this tradition include Harriet Jacobs's *Incidents in the Life of a Slave Girl* (1861), Dorothy Allison's *Bastard Out of Carolina* (1992), Sapphire's *Push/Precious* (1996), and Toni Morrison's *The Bluest Eye* (1970). Scholars have shown how these books use the figure of the girl and themes of sexual violence in ways where that figure is deconstructed and demonstrated to show a critique of material conditions including racism, law, and neoliberalism—while still insisting that the point of view of the marginalised girl is the legitimate position from which to adjudicate justice, that is, the girl is not instrumentalised as in novels such as *Disgrace* (1999).[5]

The Role of Culture in Reframing Gender Violence

In an era of increased attentiveness to sexual violence, *Law, Culture and the Figure of the Girl* critiques the law and culture of sexual violence through the voice and point of view of 'the girl,' as she is imagined in the dominant imaginary and reimagined in resistant imaginaries. *Law, Culture and the Figure of the Girl* is part of the cultural legal studies movement, a critical movement that uses cultural representations as sites of legal critique and legal theorising. Narratives on the development of cultural legal studies emphasise its roots in several related fields over the decades. It began with 'law and literature' in the 1970s, evolved into 'critical legal studies' in the 1980s, and expanded to

5 For readings of texts in this tradition, see e.g., Gilmore, 2017, Gilmore and Marshall 2019; Harkins, 2003, 2007, 2009.

include ‘law and film’ and ‘law and popular culture’ starting in the 1990s.[6] In the twenty-first century, this method now positions questions of genre, narrative, and aesthetics not only as modes of critique but also as modes for the radical reinvention of law, as a way to theorise emergent legal forms. These readings of genre include established genres (*bildungsroman*, horror, documentary genres, realism) and also new, hybrid genres exemplified by the imaginative works discussed. Law’s narratives and figures, as well as what we might more widely think of as its practices of representation, produce social, economic, and political realities. Literary jurisprudence encourages a broader understanding of what constitutes ‘law’ and legal thinking, to include theories produced in cultural domains.

Law, Culture and the Figure of the Girl considers how the figure of girl provides a subject position from which to resist and recreate juridical and political spaces—especially in the context of forms of judgment about sexual violence, which takes place not only in legal spaces but in social and cultural domains as well. Radical readings of figurations of the girl give us an understanding of how the girl is mobilised in conservative/dominant representations and also how the figure can provide an innovative site for critique and reinvention. In *Law, Culture and the Figure of the Girl*, I critique and reimagine law’s frameworks as well as our dominant cultural imaginary through encounters with novels, films, and TV shows. *Law, Culture and the Figure of the Girl* offers new readings of exemplary cultural texts that thematically deal with violence against girls, emphasising the ways they challenge dominant ways of thinking and doing law, jurisdiction, violence, race, and gender. These readings reveal the fragility of categories and narratives of identity and truth upon which law relies. These readings also undo logics that law takes as axiomatic. *Law, Culture and the Figure of the Girl* forms part of an emerging transnational, interdisciplinary jurisprudence, based on an engagement between critical legal studies and studies in law and literature.

Law is the nomos within which we live, a genre that is deeply political but cannot be reduced to politics (Cover, 1983, pp. 12–19). Law is not only shaped by its institutional framework but also through cultural texts. These cultural representations do not merely *reflect* an external legal reality found in texts, institutions, and officials but rather *produce* legality, including its ‘ocular and spectacular dimensions’ (Giddens et al., 2024, p. 3). For Giddens, Crawley, and Peters, ‘representational legality’ encompasses the genre influences on audience reactions and the emotional and psychological engagement

6 Different accounts of this emergence are articulated in Crawley, Giddens and Peters (2024). See also Crawley and Peters (2018), Giddens (2018); Sarat (2001); Binder and Weisberg (2000), Coombe (1999), Cover (1993), Ewick and Silbey (1998), Kahn (2008), Leonard (1995), Mezey (2003). Many of the early predecessors in this area have worked primarily in anthropology and American studies. E.g., Clifford (1988), Geertz (1983).

of spectators (Giddens et al., 2024, p. 3). These dimensions reveal how law is enacted, enforced, and experienced, highlighting the complex interplay between legal constructs and the subjective experiences of legal subjects.[7] This approach encompasses a wide range of texts and objects that make up 'culture' in its most expansive definition, illustrating the multifaceted ways in which law intersects with cultural expressions. For Giddens, Crawley, and Peters, cultural legal studies has generated two important effects: First, cultural legal studies challenges traditional views on legal sources by debunking the longstanding Western belief that law originates from or is backed by a sovereign or state, instead arguing that law is discovered through its representation; second, since this approach asserts that the essence of law is inherently tied to how it is represented, law is seen as fluid and dependent on its portrayal rather than having any inherent, predetermined shape or structure (2024, pp. 1–2). Consequently, law does not possess a fixed, tangible, or objective existence—it is continually emerging, evolving, and being shaped through its interactions, intertwined with the ways it is represented and perceived. The representational nature of law reflects a conceptual shift from the traditional notion of law to the broader concept of *legality*. Legality includes not only the operation of law but also the pervasive presence of legal forms in political, social, and economic spheres. It involves the application of legal concepts, practices, and methods to key aspects of life, thereby subjecting them to a knowledge framework structured by these juridical forms. This influence extends to the disciplinary modes of life, highlighting how legal norms permeate and shape societal behaviours and institutions (Crawley and Peters, 2018, p. 6). This is an extremely optimistic and hopeful methodology: instead of regarding law as staid, innately conservative and infinitely captured by neoliberalism, patriarchy, and colonialism, we see the potential of *legality*—of new, responsive, and radical ways of making law.

Desmond Manderson's emphasis on literature's incompletion, its pluralism, its excesses of signification and its interpretative openness reminds us that justice is not an ideal so much as an experience or a process (Manderson, 2012). In William MacNeil's *Lex Populi*, a foundational text of cultural legal studies, 'popular' or 'normal' culture is recognised for its contributions to discussions on law and legal theory. These perspectives challenge the traditional focus in jurisprudence on abstract universals and state forms, positing that popular culture's insights into law cannot be simplified to mere direct transmissions absorbed by the audience (MacNeil, 2007). MacNeil's legal analyses also demonstrate that the goal of critique is not simply to reveal the hidden ideological forces or power within law's rational facade. Instead, the focus is on understanding how the very essence of legality is shaped by

7 On the relationship between law, culture and affect, see Young, 2010; Buchanan and Johnson, 2009, p. 33; Hickey-Moody and Malins, 2008; Sedgwick, 2003.

desire or *jouissance* (MacNeil, 2007, p. 20). Practices of representation have implications for the 'deep structures' of the juridical imaginary (MacNeil, 2012, p. 27), and 'questions of form, style, and genre' require interrogation to avoid the 'romantic fantasy' of a simple, thematic approach to law and literature (Manderson, 2012, pp. 10, 17). In postcolonial contexts, a focus on genre and its distinct components of representation help us move beyond the problematic model of 'sentimental' or 'humanitarian reading' criticised by Joseph Slaughter (see also work by Antaki, Meister, and Kahn). It also builds on feminist critical legal approaches to law and culture (put forward by scholars including West, Murray and Esser, van Marle and Aristemou) and that examine the role of representation, affect, and imagination in the ongoing dominance of legal concepts from sovereignty to captivity (addressed in the recent work of Motha, Tuitt, Kennedy, and Genovese).

Law's Claim to Jurisdiction Over Gender Violence

The issue of control over representation is key to questions of power, and this is the case within the domain of legal representation. Walter Benjamin and Jacques Derrida are helpful in thinking about the ways in which the law's adjudication of violence—here, my focus is sexual violence—acts to support state violence and power, as well as producing norms that carry their own violence. In his essay 'Critique of Violence' (1968) Walter Benjamin provides one account of the ways in which violence is taken up in the domain of law (not violence 'as such'), arguing that violence operates in the legal domain as a concept produced by law and one that organises particular logics in which the law is invested. In this essay, Benjamin provides an exposition of the logics of natural and positivist law, which are organised by 'means' and 'ends,'; he argues that law does not exclude or stop violence but rather produces categories of violence (i.e., violence sanctioned by law and violence that is not sanctioned) (1968, p 279). The critique of violence as it operates in this domain requires a 'historico-philosophical view of law' in order to properly historicise and contextualise the production of these logics. This is why 'the critique of violence is the philosophy of its history' (Benjamin, 1968, p. 299)—legal violence is a concept haunted by different logics. If tracked as a figure produced across Western legal philosophy, 'violence' as a concept is destabilised—is not self-evident—and becomes a concept that shores up or organises different logics at different historical moments, naturalising different world-views. Benjamin argues that the law represents itself as mediating and adjudicating violence, and this is power-making (1968, p. 293). Benjamin's account demonstrates how violence becomes instrumental in shoring up the law's processes. For Benjamin, modern law comes from continuing acts of genocidal exclusion, and such violence is required for the continuing formation of the state: 'All violence as a means is either lawmaking or law-preserving' and is 'implicated in the problematic nature of law itself'

(1968, p. 115). Law asserts an exclusive role in the adjudication of violence, thereby establishing its own unique authority, and thereby either 'making' or 'preserving' itself. Law's claim to an exclusive role in adjudicating violence has been central to the production of law's authority in modernity, and central, too, to modernist politico-philosophical analyses of law's authority. As well as the norm-producing nature of these representations, violence here is operating in the context of the law, in ways that shore up the law's logics and authority.

Jacques Derrida continues Benjamin's argument by arguing that the adjudication of violence in the law becomes instrumental in supporting the law's claim to authority: its adjudication is '*said* to found the law or state' (Benajamin, 1968, p. 31, emphasis mine). Derrida considers 'law,' 'justice,' and 'morality' within the schema of violence: violence is an operating idea that organises these concepts and naturalises a particular, liberal world-view. The paradox is that law claims it is adjudicating violence, but in doing so, it is justifying its own infliction of violence. We see this vividly in law's adjudication of sexual violence and its harmful effects on all victim-survivors but especially on First Nations victim-survivors as explored in Chapter 4. The key for Derrida is that the concept of law's 'origins' is abstract, not historical—the moment of origins 'always takes place and never takes place' (Derrida, 1992, p. 31). These are not Rousseauan origins but rather a continuing, animating concept: for Derrida, origins are about moments of 'emergence,' 'foundation,' 'iterability' (1992, p. 43). While these moments are neither inherently 'just nor unjust,' they are *represented as* just through a 'discourse of self-legitimation' (Derrida, 1992, p. 36). What emerges in these different accounts are thematics of 'justice,' determined by various parties, which Jacques Derrida characterises as instances of 'performative force,' which 'is always an interpretative force' (1992, p. 13) and inherently violent. While these moments are neither inherently 'just nor unjust,' they are represented as just through a 'discourse of self-legitimation' (Derrida, 1992, p. 36). This control over the means of representation is crucial, both to the 'emergence of justice' (Derrida, 1992, p. 13) and the emergence of the legal violence that is inherent in this representation. We see a succession of these 'originary' and constitutive moments. Legal origins are suspect: we should sense that they are really assertions of power and accompanied by violence.

Through an insistence on singular doctrine and singular authority, we can think of law's representational practice, and indeed of its genre, as a distinct form of realism. Law excludes other genres and representational practices in its adjudications. Law is also aggressive in its assertion of an exclusive jurisdiction over violence; implicitly claiming that law alone can access the truth and repair harms. In doing so, law's assertion of jurisdiction over representation excludes the possibility of other genres and practices of representation responding to violence. State law's assertions of jurisdiction and right to judgment have a significant formal component. State law asserts an exclusive claim to truths about sexual violence that it alone can resolve. Through an insistence on singular doctrine and singular authority, we can think of law's representational practice, and indeed of its genre, as a form of aggressive realism, one that excludes other genres and representational practices in its adjudications, as I have argued elsewhere (see van Rijswijk, 2019). Law is aggressive in its assertion of an exclusive jurisdiction over sexual violence, making an implied claim that it alone can access the truth and repair harms. Law's assertion of jurisdiction is also representational, excluding other genres and representational practices in responding to violence. In a sense, the subject matter of the adjudication is less important than the fact and means through which law's adjudication takes place. The courts have insisted on a singular authority, represented through specific practices that are presented as universal and normative. In the case of Australia, although created through the particular history of colonisation—a legal system that has been present on Australian territory for just over 200 years, and which exists alongside continuing First Nations laws—this historical contingency is exempt from the legal record. Law is aggressive in its assertion of an exclusive jurisdiction over the subject matter it judges. It is also aggressive in excluding other authorities in making its judgments. For Derrida, this tactic of singularity is at the core of any archive's violence:

> The one guards against the other, it protects itself from the other. . . . It keeps and erases the archive of this injustice that it is, of this violence that it does. . . . The determination of the self as one is violence.
>
> (2006, p. 78)

The 'power' of consignation within the archive lies in the act of 'gathering together signs' in the coordination of 'a single corpus,' which refuses heterogeneity (Derrida, 2006, p. 8). The insistence on singularity is crucial to the vesting of authority. Derrida provides the metaphor of the exterior and interior of the archive and explains that the boundary between them is guarded to preserve this singularity (1996, p. 10). State law speaks with one voice and authority and guards its archive against others: there is 'no archive without outside' (Derrida, 2006, p. 11); its archive is a 'place of election where law and singularity intersect in *privilege*' (Derrida, 2006, p. 8) (emphasis in original).

Moving Beyond the Aggressive Realism of Neoliberal State Law

Literary scholars, including Wai-Chee Dimock and Villishani Cooppan, argue for the efficacy of genre as a mode to challenge the form of the nation-state, as well as the teleological time of modernity. Cooppan emphasises that genre is not merely a reflection of historical or political structures such as capitalism and imperialism, but rather, that genre's 'modalities' can be thought of as the very forms through which capitalism and imperialism are produced (Cooppan, 2009, p. 39). Here, we might also include law's genre and its production of the conditions of continuing colonisation. Law's aggressive realism not only asserts a unique role in adjudicating and creating social conditions; it also insists on a linear, national time, in which there is a distinct break between present and past. One way to reorient the power of the state, Dimock argues, is to change the scale of analysis. She asks the following:

> On what map should we break down this massive corpus into meaning-bearing contexts or units of analysis: the map of a locality, the map of the nation-state, or a map still larger—continental, hemispheric, even planetary in scope?
>
> (2006, p. 488)

The cultural domain provides a space in which to engage with the time and space of violence outside law's frameworks—to refuse to accept the terms of dominant legal, political, and social imaginaries in representing and adjudicating events. Engaging exemplary counter-texts in this mode provides a way to challenge law's forms, not least through experiences of 'affective dissonance' (Antaki, 2013, p. 977). Certain genres and modes have the capacity to introduce a critical framework or sensibility, foregrounding and making visible certain narratives *as* narratives, which would otherwise be experienced as true and real (Antaki, 2013, p. 977). Engaging exemplary counter-texts in these critical and creative modes provides a way to challenge cultural and legal logics, creating spaces that are neither purely legal nor purely literary. Reading genre in this way means moving beyond a thematic reading of cultural texts to examine the influence of form, metaphor, and narrative on legal thinking. Here, genre is understood not merely as a 'stylistic device' but as constituting (and revealing) ways of being (Frow, 2006, p. 2). Genres not only construct 'schematic world[s]' with their own 'definition[s] of space, time, moral ethos, and players' but can reveal something of how worlds—including legal worlds—are created and maintained (Frow, 2006, p. 7). Such a method of critique introduces a degree of self-consciousness into our practices of representation, providing a way to think through subjectivity and authority. The potential of critique focused on the 'problem of genre' (Motha and van Marle, 2013, p. 18) is that it provides a way to challenge law's aggressive realism; it exposes how worlds are created and maintained in ways that appear natural but that are in fact highly intentional and stylised (as produced through the intentional dynamics of colonialism, patriarchy, and neoliberalism). In Chapter 2, my reading of *Dogville*'s use of multiple genres makes possible an aesthetic form of radical legal critique of the ways contract and consent operate in liberal democracies. In Chapter 3, I critically examine the ways feminist filmmakers and writers use the trope of violation within the genre of revenge to rewrite responsibility for sexual violence. In Chapter 4, I examine how First Nations writer Alexis Wright uses genre to destabilise the claims and representational practices of colonial law, including its claim to an exclusive jurisdiction over the adjudication of sexual violence.

The Legacy of #MeToo Under Colonialism

The nature of legal and extra-legal adjudication of sexual violence was shifted by the recent #MeToo movement, but its continuing impact is still debated by feminists. The #MeToo movement was in large part a public, extra-legal response to the inadequacies of neoliberal law in responding to sexual violence. #MeToo purportedly interrogated neoliberal institutions and the operation of gender within it. In particular, #MeToo has shown that gendered harm, including but not limited to the harms of sexual violence and harassment, are a normalised part of the operation of our institutions. But more needs to be done to interrogate and historicise the concepts and institutions with which we are concerned. We need to bring to the forefront that here state law is colonising law. We need to decolonise and historicise the concepts of 'gendered harm' and 'state institutions,' in particular, to understand how these have been understood in recent law and culture, and also how they have failed and even at times been weaponised against women.

'MeToo' Founder Tarana Burke had held 'MeToo' workshops in Alabama from 2007, but in October 2017, the hashtag #MeToo went viral, first in the US and then across the world (Garcia, 2017). This was followed by allegations of sexual violence and sexual harassment against men in high-profile industries, including entertainment, politics, architecture, and higher education: mostly infamously, Harvey Weinstein, the producer and co-founder of the Weinstein company, was accused by a number of women of behaviour ranging from harassment to rape and was subsequently charged criminally as well as fired from his production company; other famous examples have included Mark Halperin (political journalist), Kevin Spacey (actor), Louis C. K (comedian), Matt Lauer (television news anchor), Lorin Stein (literary editor), Richard Meier (architect), and Jorge I. Domiguez (academic) (Carlsen et al., 2018).

#MeToo has been criticised for centring the experiences of white Western women, as have feminist political and legal movements based on redressing sexual violence (Crenshaw, 1991, 2018; de la Garza, 2019; Dougherty and Calafell, 2019; Onwuachi-Willig, 2018), and for reifying white Western women's subjectivity by foregrounding self-disclosure as the primary means of discursive agency (Burke, 2017). Academics and activists have also been critical of parts of the #MeToo movement for its tendency to advocate for harsher carceral punishments for sexual violence, despite the disproportionate impact of this state violence on colonised groups (Mack and McCann, 2018). Questioning whether #MeToo is a white women's movement,

Ashwini Tambe says the answer is 'both yes and no' (Tambe, 2018, p. 199). The subject matter of the movement—the injuries of sexual violence and harassment—clearly go beyond the scope of white women's problems, but in media coverage, Tambe argues, 'it is certainly white women's pain that is centred' (2018, p. 199). Further, the institutional contexts of #MeToo—not only the legal institutions it seeks to side-step, but the wider corporate and cultural liberal institutions #MeToo invokes—carry not only racist but specifically colonial legacies, and these were not sufficiently brought out in either the legal cases or many of the public responses, which tended to rely on the actions of the corporate boards of large, publicly listed companies.

The focus of #MeToo tended to be on institutions such as schools, universities, and corporations. A decolonial praxis requires an expansion to include prisons, policing, healthcare, and 'family welfare' services, among other institutions, to dismantle the 'colonial patriarchy' (Baldry and Cuneen, 2014, p. 1). A significant way to decolonise adjudications of sexual violence is to include an understanding of the role of state violence in shaping sexual violence against First Nations women. State violence is defined broadly to include everything from obvious state arms such as direct police violence and genocide, to the provision or withdrawal of social services, and the covert use of new technologies of citizen surveillance (Torres, 2018). There is a rich critical history which has proven that non-white women and girls are the most vulnerable groups in relation to state violence, due to the intersections of their gender, race, class, and sexuality, resulting in their experiences with physical, sexual, institutional, and state violence (Collins, 2000; Crenshaw, 1991; Richie, 2012). In this context, a decolonial praxis requires an interdisciplinary, anti-racist, intersectional and critical approach. A decolonial feminist methodology understands gendered violence as part of colonial violence (Dougherty and Calafell, 2019). Working toward decolonisation necessitates reconsidering the methods and practices of knowledge production embodied in our scholarship without replicating colonial logics and relations (Mack and Na'Puti, 2019). Although it is reported that finding reliable data on the nature and extent of sexual violence against First Nations Australians is difficult, it is estimated that First Nations women are twelve times more likely to be the victims or survivors of assault than non-First Nations women (McCalman, Bridge, Whiteside, Bainbridge, Tsey and Jorgen, p. 1). A number of factors lead to this appalling statistic, including systemic racism and poverty, and the understandable unwillingness of First Nations women to access state services, including the police, in the context of state violence towards First Nations people—as I will explore in Chapter 4, the recent history of the state's adjudication of sexual violence has included the instrumentalisation of this violence to further subjugate First Nations communities. These colonial histories were not perhaps so simply brought out by the individual call-and-response approach of much of #MeToo, but require attention to specific structures and histories of power in Australian political and legal life—of processes that have combined, at their limits, to criminalise, impoverish, and kill First Nations women. This means considering sexual violence in the context of a number of domains: the 'Northern Territory Intervention,' the Stolen Generations, the Royal Commission Into Institutional Responses to Child Sexual Abuse, and First Nations deaths in custody. Sexual violence needs to be understood in two key ways: (1) alongside other continuing colonial harms and (2) alongside the state's refusal to acknowledge First Nations sovereignty, which means reframing what is meant by 'sexual violence' and 'sexual harassment' from an isolated, individual experience of subjection to one that foregrounds the sovereignty of First Nations women whose laws have survived despite the injuries of the colonial past and present. We need a radical rethinking of legal and political categories of injury, reparation, sovereignty, and law. Essentially, we need to reframe sexual violence to view it fundamentally as an issue of First Nations sovereignty. Indeed, sexual violence understood in the colonial context should be extended intersectionally beyond the framework of 'harm to the person' that dominates legal and cultural domains—instead, sexual violence should be conceptually revised to include damage to First Nations sovereignty and law. For First Nations women, sexual violence can only be made sense of against the background of state violence. We need to unpack assumptions by deconstructing the nature of 'sexual violence,' 'sexual harassment,' and 'sexual harm,' to reconceptualise the nature of 'harm' in colonialised spaces. It simply does not make sense to separate out sexual acts as pinpoints of harm, as though these could be separated from a network of harms of sovereignty and intergenerational harm.

The Genre of 'Speaking Out'

#MeToo drew from the established feminist genre of 'speaking out.' In the wake of the #MeToo movement, survivors are re-evaluating and rewriting the narratives and tropes of sexual violence in light of this newly foregrounded genre. For Leigh Gilmore, this collective body of work represents a new genre of fourth-wave rape testimonies: from protest marches and labour strikes to serialised television, personal accounts, and fictional works, these diverse activities and forms serve as testimonies, functioning not only as individual examples but as a wider genre of intersectional feminism and narrative activism, that challenges the established norms of gendered violence (Gilmore, 2023, p. 164). Since #MeToo shifts the power relations of responses to sexual violence from he said/she said to one where survivors are in relation to each other, this genre is potentially 'paradigm-shifting,' in that it generates 'collective credibility' (Gilmore, 2023, p. 164). In evaluating the effects of the movement, Leigh Gilmore reframes #MeToo as a breakthrough moment within a longer history of feminist thought and activism, where the creation of community and the sharing of stories are at the core of feminist praxis (Gilmore, 2023, p. 3). Part of the #MeToo effect is that it enables 'individual experiences to become legible as a critique of the structures that enable abuse' (Gilmore, 2023, p. 61). This was achieved as the result of a long-standing feminist activist tradition that uses autobiographical narratives to inform, move, and persuade diverse audiences about structural inequalities from Harriet Jacobs's *Incidents in the Life of a Slave Girl*, published in 1861, to Black feminist activist Tarana Burke's work with survivors (Gilmore, 2023, p. 63). By situating #MeToo within the broader context of life writing and survivor narratives, Gilmore's work reframes the movement as a powerful episode of narrative activism within a long-standing intersectional feminist lineage rather than as an exceptional point in time. Gilmore argues that assessing the impact of #MeToo should not be limited to legal or policy changes, where it may often seem lacking.

In *Witnessing Girlhood*, Gilmore and Marshall examine the genealogy of life-writing and how this has shaped the possibilities of justice for survivors of sexual violence. Gilmore and Marshall argue that when women speak out about sexual violence in the present, they benefit and draw from a subgenre of autobiographical writing led by women of colour (Gilmore and Marshall, 2019). In this subgenre, which includes a range of self-representational forms as diverse as slave narratives to memoirs and picture books, the figure and voice of the child witness is used to reveal harm and demand accountability. The authors provide a genealogy of the figure and voice of the child as witness to harm as centred by writers of colour, spanning the period from the mid-nineteenth century to the present day, and thereby re-positioning women of colour as the authorities in crafting this genre (Gilmore and Marshall, 2019, p. 11).[8] A major approach is how life writing uses the 'temporalities of witnessing' to retroactively afford adult language, perspective, and credibility to recounted childhood experiences (Gilmore, 2001, p. 4). Focusing on the child within the history of feminist life writing foregrounds historical continuity of the 'speaking out' genre, following Hartman's method of reading of historical harm in the present. (Hartman, 1997; Gilmore and Marshall, 2019, p. 14). Reconstructing these historical and theoretical trajectories restores an intersectional testimonial history of writing by women of colour about sexual and racist violence.

In *The Limits of Autobiography* (2001) Gilmore shows how writing at the margins of trauma narratives can be productive and create 'an alternative jurisdiction for the self-representation of trauma' (Gilmore, 2001, p. 16), where the subject crosses social, legal, narrative, and psychic boundaries 'to tell complex stories of injury' (Gilmore, 2001, p. 43). Here, jurisdiction is not only as a geographical territory or conceptual domain, but also as 'a

8 On the racialised production of childhood innocence, see also Robin Bernstein, *Racial Innocence: Performing American Childhood from Slavery to Civil Rights* (New York: New York University Press, 2011).

rhetorical and discursive entity' in which judgments are made by authoritative institutions and by publics about what constitutes 'truth' and what is deemed credible (Gilmore, 2017). Although focused on the genealogy arising out of life writing, these narratives are not necessarily autobiographical—they include fictional accounts. What she calls 'limit-case' autobiographical texts allow alternative knowledges to appear and thus offer 'an alternative form of jurisprudence about trauma' (Gilmore, 2001, p. 147). As my comments on law's aggressive realism will show, I'm sceptical of law's claims of an exclusive access to 'truth' or 'reality' and appreciate that the testimonial jurisdiction that Gilmore focuses on seeks to challenge this exclusivity. *Law, Culture and the Figure of the Girl* builds on Gilmore's work in deepening the exploration of jurisdictions that push against law's dominant narratives of sexual violence, as well as those of the dominant culture's. Some of the genres I examine fall within the alternative jurisdictions that Gilmore theorises, and some lie far outside this jurisdiction (for example, the horror film *It Follows*, explored in Chapter 2). In the latter cases, I'm less invested in the truth claims of these representations, and more interested in the texts' investigations into what 'the girl' stands in for (i.e., the deconstruction of that figure).

Oppositional social movements, such as #MeToo, do not necessarily dismantle the systems they challenge, nor do they need to do so to be considered meaningful. It is unreasonable to expect #MeToo to end patriarchy entirely to be deemed valuable, harnessed for future efforts, and recognised for uniting survivors in broader solidarities. Rather, the #MeToo movement offers a new framework for understanding survivor testimony (Gilmore, 2023, p. 180). It shifts the narrative from 'he said/she said' to a more credible standard for discussing and addressing the truth about sexual violence both within and outside law. This is significant since, for Gilmore, the he said/she said trope 'has an astonishing grip on the cultural imagination as a fair standard' (Gilmore, 2017, p. 24). Gilmore contends that the 'he said/she said' trope misrepresents a gendered hierarchy of credibility as a neutral binary. Cultural judgment practices undermine women's status as reliable sources and individuals deserving of justice. Societal norms condition us to believe men more readily, prioritise their futures, and be more concerned about their potential harm, leading to the devaluation of women as truth-tellers. Sexual violence is often minimised as 'not that bad,' 'a case of he said/she said,' or an inevitable result of women entering the workforce, reflecting the belief that women are worth less than men. This pervasive doubt directed at women seems rational and ethical, appearing as common sense. The 'he said/she said' trope allows institutions to sustain cultures of unequal power where abuse thrives, by dismissing women's claims and suppressing the collective knowledge from their testimonies. It introduces hostility into testimonial spaces under the guise of due process, often evoking a rescue response for accused men. This trope falsely suggests that processes biased against women are fair and neutral. While not the only method by which the law silences survivors, the 'he said/

she said' trope exemplifies how legal notions permeate cultural judgment practices, often downplaying scenes of violence and reflecting broader issues in the legal and cultural treatment of sexual violence claims.

As Tanya Serisier explains in her book that critically interrogates the genre of speaking out, *Speaking Out: Rape, Feminism and Narrative Politics*, the #MeToo movement was not the first instance where a movement centred on public speech led to widespread belief in inevitable changes within the political landscape surrounding sexual violence (Serisier, 2018). Tracing through the first speak-outs about rape in the 1970s, through the celebrity-backed movements in the 1980s, and Rebecca Solnit's #YesAllWomen movement in 2014, Serisier argues that each time, feminists optimistically claimed these movements led to a change in public culture but that we should instead see them 'through the analogy of throwing a rock into a pond' (Serisier, 2023, p. 209). There is an immediate impact, Serisier argues, which seems effective, but 'in the absence of anything else happening . . . there is no lasting trace of the disruption' (Serisier, 2023, p. 209). Using this framework, Serisier argues that #MeToo should be interpreted as a 'limit point of speaking out as a political strategy'; it is the most successful example of these speech acts to date and so 'the most complete demonstration of its limits' (Serisier, 2023, p. 210). Considering its limits, Serisier argues that speaking out should not be seen as an end in itself, but rather the starting point of political engagement—a political movement that engages radically with the structures of gender, race, and class (Serisier, 2023, p. 210).

For Tanya Serisier, the 'speaking out' genre highlights the paradox of the #MeToo movement, which merges the undeniable impact of shared storytelling with elements of marginalisation and exclusion, particularly along racial and socioeconomic lines. While the #MeToo movement has provided some benefits by repeatedly sharing experiences, it has also led to the emergence of 'new forms of scepticism and disbelief towards women's accounts' (Serisier, 2018, p. 96). Despite raising awareness about the collective and societal dimensions of sexual violence, the movement has not effectively challenged traditional heterosexual norms or the patriarchal family structure. According to Serisier, #MeToo has created a 'story production' economy, where survivors of sexual violence feel compelled to publicly disclose their personal experiences in order to gain societal empathy and acknowledgment of their humanity. Serisier discusses how the category of 'speaking out' narratives has been influenced by the dominant influence of criminal justice discourses. This means that narratives conforming to conventional and discriminatory notions of 'real rape' have been given prominence in discussions. She particularly scrutinises the criminal trial process, illustrating that a survivor's ability to resist 'sexist narratives that label them as liars or at fault' can hinge on their capacity to effectively utilise other societal narratives related to class and racial distinctions (Serisier, 2018, p. 86). Additionally, she highlights the omission of race in accounts of sexual violence and its connection to the 'history of the criminal justice system's efforts to present itself as colour-blind' (Serisier, 2018, p. 32). Her intention is not to criticise the act of speaking out, but rather to underscore the risk of a political stance that would require survivors to disclose the violence inflicted upon them in order to assert an authoritative speaking position. She argues that a revitalised political approach necessitates the audience's willingness to accept narratives that are 'unconventional and unfamiliar rather than always and inherently understandable' (Serisier, 2018, p. 193), rather than the status quo which requires that narratives conform to the specific 'speaking out' genre. In seeking to reframe the existing, problematic narratives and tropes of sexual violence, what Serisier calls the dominant 'trauma narrative' framework, Serisier turns to Jacques Derrida's theories on genre (Serisier, 2018, p. 32). Serisier argues that the existing trauma narrative foregrounds stories of sexual violence where rape is portrayed as an 'unprecedented act of violence with no biographical parallel' (Serisier, 2018, p. 54). This framework tends to make sexual violence that is pervasive—such as in colonialism—less visible, or even invisible. Serisier advocates for employing 'the law of the "law of genre" to view generic impurity and contamination as a political and narrative resource' (2018, p. 214). This law is exemplified by 'the stories of Black abolitionist feminists who address the violence of the carceral state within the same narratives as interpersonal violence' (Serisier, 2018, p. 214), rather than portraying the state as a rescuer. She asks, 'What kind of vision of feminist narrative and feminist futures might we produce if #BlackLivesMatter was as central to the feminist story of violence as #MeToo?' (Serisier, 2018, p. 215).

Framing Harm: The Eventfulness of Gender Violence

Law, Culture and the Figure of the Girl examines responsibility for gender violence across law and culture—the 'everyday' harms of sexual violence and harassment. Both law and mainstream culture belabour the exceptionality of rape, emphasising and staging its eventfulness. The dominant trope of consent supports this eventfulness, this exceptionality, in that it demands a scene where sex is accepted or denied, rather than seeing sexual violence as a continuation of existing conditions. This framing denies the reality that sexual violence is baked into ordinary life and ordinary institutions. Cvetkovich argues that the way through these problems is not via arguments that equate sexual trauma with other traumas, but rather recognition of 'trauma's specificities and variations' (Cvetkovich, 2003, p. 3). That is, we ought to theorise from the specific, rather than use the specific to supplement a 'universal' theory of justice for sexual violence. In this way, 'trauma challenges common understandings of what constitutes an archive' (Cvetkovich, 2003, p. 7). Both law and mainstream culture fail to acknowledge the claims of everyday violence, the shocks and tolls of racism, gender violence, and poverty on late-capitalist lives (trauma being 'part of the affective language that describes life under capitalism' (Cvetkovich, 2003, p. 19). This understanding of everyday violence is particularly pertinent now, as individual responsibility is being increasingly emphasised across political and legal domains, in contrast to corporate or state responsibilities, as part of a neoliberal shift in the conception of the proper role of the citizen-consumer. To take the claims of this suffering seriously means a radical re-working of culture, as well as law: we need to radically change our frameworks of reference and admit that 'our culture is a factory for the production of so many walking wounded' (Brown, 1995, p. 103). What becomes interesting, then, are the narrative strategies of refusal, and the crafting of its boundaries in resisting the intrusion of everyday trauma within frameworks of responsibility. Cultural representations that push back against dominant forms can be uniquely suited to speak to this specificity. An analysis of these boundaries provides us, as critical scholars, with awareness of those points at which we might press a little harder, to open up categories, to question assumptions about proximity, to keep drawing attention to the arbitrariness of the narratives and divisions that assign responsibility for some kinds of harms while ignoring others. Taking this idea and introducing a specifically gendered element, Theresa O'Keefe argues the case for considering sexual violence as 'a continuum of violence . . . a set of inter-related, interdependent practices that are held together by gendered webs of power, giving rise to and reinforcing a climate of sexual violence' (O'Keefe, 2017, p. 70). Another helpful framework is the concept of slow violence, defined as 'a violence occur[ing] gradually and out of sight, a violence of delayed destruction . . . dispersed across time and space, an attritional violence that is typically not viewed as violence at all' (Nixon, 2011, p. 2). Slow violence has been developed in relation to issues such as race and class-based harms, for example, racist violence (Ward, 2015), police violence (Kramer and Remster, 2022), and climate change (Ahmann, 2018). Tombs and Canning have used the notion of social harms such as climate change and routine deaths caused by large organisations to make an argument for social change and social justice (Canning and Tombs, 2021; Tombs, 2018). These developments focus on making structural harms and social impacts clearer and counteracting the misrecognition and failure to prevent and/or respond appropriately to these harms. We need to connect everyday, 'individual' harm to political power, to land, to decolonisation, to capitalism.

Essentially, though, I am arguing for cultural and literary texts as the sites for new theorisation and legality. They offer a particularity not available even in most theoretical frameworks. For a theory of how to undo eventfulness, we can learn from Anna Burns's Booker Prise–winning novel *Milkman* (Burns, 2018), which tells the story of an 18-year-old girl who is being stalked by a much older married man, who is also a Republican paramilitary (the 'Milkman'). The Milkman's violence towards the narrator is pervasive yet always subject to plausible deniability given the cultural context of acceptable levels of duress from men towards girls: 'Hard to define this stalking thing, this predation' (Burns, 2018, p. 181). The violence comprises 'constant hints, symbolisms, representations, metaphors. He could have meant what I thought he'd meant, but equally, he might not have meant anything' (Burns, 2018, p. 181). The novel shows how this state of knowledge, of lack of knowledge, is an effect of power relations. The novel addresses a number of questions about the relationship of sexual violence to wider political violence, and explores how the relationship between knowledge and power produces the concept of 'consent.' Looking back, the narrator—alternately called 'middle sister,' 'maybe-girlfriend,' and 'daughter'—wonders about the interiority of her young self: 'I did not know intuition and repugnance counted . . . did not know I had a right not to like, not to have to put up with, anybody and everybody coming near' (Burns, 2018, p. 49). Would knowing that she had a preference matter? If she had a right 'not to like,' could she have acted on this right? Or is her very interiority a product of power relations that make this choice a mute issue? The novel is set in 1970s Belfast during the colonial violence known as the Troubles, and the novel shows how the privileging of this political violence potentially obscures the high incidence of gendered violence. This is part of Burns's persistent efforts to undo the pervasive logic of what Maureen E. Ruprecht Fadem calls the 'cruel Belfast ordinary' (2015, p. 140) or Dominick LaCapra's 'reductive contextualism' (1999, p. 725). As Lehner has suggested, Burns refuses any domestication of the Troubles (Lehner, 2014, p. 287), pushing back against recuperative narratives that seek to stress the ongoing nature of 'everyday life' as some sort of separate existence to political violence (Lehner, 2014, p. 273). The novel shows that sexual violence is produced within this wider political context—it is not exceptional, and nor is it incidental background. The protagonist describes 'the drip-drip effect of sexual comments' made by soldiers: '"*Your boot*," they'd say. "*Your box*," they'd say. "*Your suitability for doxiness*." Then, "*What we'd do to your face if . . .*" or something like that' (Burns, 2018, p. 95). The effect of imbricating colonial and sexual violence is to demonstrate that sexual violence is not epiphenomenal to colonialism and vice versa—that is, the novel takes the opposite approach to Coetzee's in *Disgrace*. In this, the novel rejects the narrative that sexual violation is less significant than the political violence and also rejects the normalisation of gender-based violence that sees this violence as an unseen backdrop to everyday life.

Although Burns's narrator describes at least one scene of spectacular violence (the massacre of local dogs), the narrative as a whole focuses on insidious, daily forms of harm. Our cultural history of representing this relentless sexual violence as a 'backdrop' to the eventfulness of, for example, political violence ('the Troubles') makes this violence more difficult to represent. Using new and difficult language, and emphasising interconnectedness, the ways in which one harm forms part of another, Burns's representation of sexual violence rejects the event-based readings of trauma that rely on the

Freudian account of rupture and of the tradition of trauma studies led by Cathy Caruth. Indeed, this is a theme in *Law, Culture and the Girl*—in contemporary rewritings of sexual violence, we see creators reject the trope of the event, of a discrete trauma that demands resolution, in favour of representing sexual violence as embedded in everyday structures. This is critically examined through the framework of consent (in Chapter 2), revenge narratives (in Chapter 3), and sovereignty (in Chapter 4).

In *Law, Culture and the Figure of the Girl*, I show how novels, films, and TV provide new frameworks for harm and culpability—the advantage of using cultural forms in this way is their particularity as opposed to reaching for an abstract theory. For example, Chapter 4: *The Swan Book* uses very different strategies to connect sexual violence with sovereignty. *The Swan Book* is not asking for harms to be witnessed—its imaginary demands a different kind of reading and relation, one that involves a practice of critical undoing. The reader of *The Swan Book* is blocked from a sentimental identification with the victim/survivor of trauma—the figure refuses this kind of readerly identification. The reader is not taken on a journey of healing or resolution. The traumatised subject is not set apart from her environment but shown to be an effect of intersecting processes. The harms of colonisation, late capitalism, and patriarchy call for different kinds of legal and ethical responses from those modelled on the adjudication of rupturing, traumatic events such as war: clear events with a start and a finish. Structural violence has no discrete or extraordinary event but is rather a process of ongoing evisceration.

The Genre of Pornography

Ironically, *Law, Culture and the Figure of the Girl* will not critically examine the most powerful imaginary of the girl as connected to sexual violence, which is, of course, produced through the contemporary genre of online pornography. Nothing that I can write in this scholarly monograph could have even marginal impact on the dominant imaginary of sexual violence compared to the vast volume and impact of online pornography. However, *Law, Culture and the Figure of the Girl* does diagnose, critique, and reimagine the dominant tropes of sexual violence that dominate mainstream culture in ways that overlap with online pornography. Pornography has been a flashpoint for feminist discourses since the 1970s. I'm not an expert in pornography, but I do believe, and my work is premised on, the foundational tenet that representation is not epiphenomenal. Our cultural, social and psychological lives are animated by, and produced by language, narrative, and figuration, as is law. There is a vast literature on the discursive production of legal violence, and of social violence. It's important that we consider pornography in this context; former arguments about pornography are now redundant in the context of the contemporary online pornography environment, which is super-charged not only by increasingly sophisticated technology, but by the aggressive, profit-seeking engine of late-stage capitalism. The scale of the consumption and production of pornography is overwhelming; in particular, pornography exposure is widespread among young people aged 12–20 years (Crabbe et al., 2024; Martellozzo et al., 2016; Peter and Valkenurg, 2016; Henry and Talbot, 2019). The extent of pornography exposure makes it likely pornography is a significant influence on Australian young people's sexual attitudes and behaviours; in particular, pornography plays a role in shaping young people's sexual understandings, expectations, and experiences (Crabbe et al., 2024). There also is evidence that pornography is increasingly dominated by fantasies of violence against women (Purcell, 2012; Carrotte et al., 2020). Pornography consumption is associated with sexual violence (Crabbe et al., 2024; Fisher et al., 2013; Tarzia and Tyler, 2021; Purcell, 2012; Antevska and Gavey, 2015). Pornography is also associated with a range of related harmful attitudes, behaviours, and experiences, including more sexually objectifying and stereotypic gender views of women (Peter and Valkenburg, 2007; Peter and Valkenburg 2009), rape myth acceptance (Malamuth et al., 2012), sexual coercion and aggression (Marston and Lewis, 2014; Ybarra et al., 2011). Further, online spaces themselves have become sites of sexual violence through acts including revenge porn. Given that young men aged 15–19 years are the demographic most likely to perpetrate sexual violence, and young women of that age group are the most likely to be victims of sexual violence (Australian Institute of Health and Welfare, 2020), and pornography use is associated with both perpetration and victimisation (Wright et al., 2015), Michael Flood argues that violence prevention efforts should include increased attention to reducing pornography's potential harms.

Perhaps not unrelatedly, the first nationally representative research into the prevalence of child sexual offending behaviours and attitudes has shed unprecedented light on sexually abusive behaviours and feelings among Australian men. The largest study of its kind ever undertaken globally, *Identifying and understanding child sexual offending behaviour and attitudes among Australian men*, measures the prevalence of risk behaviours and attitudes regarding child sexual offending among a representative sample of 1,945 Australian men aged 18 to over 65. The study reveals that, of the community sample surveyed, one in five Australian men reported sexual feelings towards children and/or have sexually offended against children, with one-third of those who have thoughts towards children motivated to access help.

Keywords: The Girl, Consent, Revenge, and Sovereignty

Law, Culture and the Figure of the Girl critically examines the ways in which contemporary feminist creators use the figure of the girl to critique existing structures and envision new forms of legality and justice. The utter failure of the law to provide justice to victims of sexual assault and sexual harassment—through inadequate reporting mechanisms, low conviction rates, and re-traumatising processes—is well-documented. Further, there are notable extra-legal failures, such as institutions' inability to prevent and address sexual violence and the perpetuation of toxic environments or 'rape cultures.' How, then, are contemporary feminist imaginaries engaging in extra-legal responses to these legal and social failures? I explore the ways in which these cultural imaginaries relate to the law and how they also go beyond law to incorporate qualities including vengeance, forgiveness, tragedy, and contract in their concepts of justice. These imaginaries position themselves as alternatives to state law, proposing new frameworks and vocabularies.

Against the legal, political, and cultural overdetermination of the figure of the raped child/woman, resistant writers and filmmakers navigate responsibility for sexual violence. These cultural works challenge legal thinking and related concepts of responsibility, violence, and justice. I consider how a selection of exemplary cultural texts focused on the girl offer a new aesthetics of responsibility for suffering: a movement away from an emphasis on suffering and towards one of responsibility. It is through these exemplary cultural works that we can encourage an interrogation of concepts underlying both legal and mainstream cultural frameworks of responsibility. Their works rely on the figure of the girl to rewrite genres of colonial imaginaries and of settler laws. These books do not tell stories of trauma and its resolution; rather, they 'undo' the figure of the girl and imagine harms to the girl as harms to laws and sovereignties beyond the state, thereby positioning the girl at the centre of political and legal claims that are different to the genres of the state (these genres include aggressive realism and, as I will explore in Chapter 4, sentimentality).

The chapters in this volume critically engage with the figure of the girl as a central trope in understanding and challenging cultural and legal narratives surrounding consent, revenge, and colonial authority. By focusing on the experiences, representations, and symbolic significance of the girl, these chapters reveal how this figure is instrumentalised within various frameworks of power and justice. The book argues that the figure of the girl serves as a powerful focal point for exploring the failures of legal systems and the possibilities for extra-legal forms of justice. By transforming the girl from a passive victim to an active agent of change, contemporary feminist creators challenge dominant cultural and legal paradigms. These narratives propose alternative frameworks for understanding and addressing sexual violence, emphasising the need for radical transformation of our material conditions and social structures. *Law, Culture and the Figure of the Girl* ultimately calls for a reimagining of justice that transcends the limitations of the law and addresses the root causes of violence and inequality.

In 1976, Raymond Williams published *Keywords: A Vocabulary of Culture and Society*, a seminal work that has profoundly influenced cultural and social analysis. Williams's aim was to trace the meanings and historical shifts of key terms that shape our understanding of culture and society. *Keywords* not only provided a detailed account of the etymology and changing meanings of words but also highlighted their significance in contemporary cultural and social contexts. The enduring impact of *Keywords* lies in its interdisciplinary approach and its critical examination of language as an active agent in constructing and deconstructing societal norms and ideologies. Williams's method involved examining how the meaning of strategically chosen keywords have evolved over time and how these changes reflect broader social, cultural, and political transformations. He drew from various fields, including literature, sociology, politics, and history, to offer a comprehensive understanding of each term. By doing so, Williams encouraged readers to think critically about language and its role in shaping cultural and social realities. The influence of Williams' *Keywords* has extended far beyond its initial publication, inspiring a variety of contemporary scholarly projects that adopt and adapt his methodology to new contexts and fields. *New Keywords: A Revised Vocabulary of Culture and Society* (ed. by Bennett et al., 2005) revisits and updates Williams' original entries while adding new terms relevant to contemporary cultural studies, reflecting changes in the social and cultural landscape since Williams's time and addressing new theoretical developments and social issues. In the context of American cultural studies, *Keywords for American Cultural Studies* (ed. by Burgett and Hendler, 2020) adapts Williams's approach to examine terms including 'democracy,' 'diversity,' and 'public.' *Keywords for Disability Studies* (ed. by Adams et al., 2005) examines critical terms such as 'access,' 'care,' 'independence,' and 'normal' and provides a comprehensive vocabulary for understanding disability from multiple disciplinary perspectives. Environmental studies have also benefited from the 'keywords' methodology: *Keywords for Environmental Studies* (ed. by Adamson et al., 2016) organises its entries around environmental terms like 'sustainability,' 'biodiversity,' 'justice,' and 'resilience.' In the field of children's literature, *Keywords for Children's Literature* (ed. by Nel and Paul) brings together key terms related to the study and analysis of literature for children. Entries such as 'adaptation,' 'multiculturalism,' and 'trauma' are explored in terms of their significance within the context of children's literature. Finally, a special issue of *Differences: A Journal of Feminist Cultural Studies*, included keywords '#MeToo,' 'Solidarity,' 'Mother,' 'Sex Offender,' 'Paedophile,' 'Consent,' 'Testimony,' and 'Trigger Warnings' (*Differences*, 2019).

In the spirit of the *Keywords* tradition, *Law, Culture and the Figure of the Girl* is organised by four keywords that I argue are central to the legal and cultural imaginaries of gender violence. *Law, Culture and the Figure of the Girl* is organised by one main keyword—the girl—which structures the book, and then each chapter is organised by a keyword that is central to the concerns of representation and sexual violence in the present: 'Consent' (Chapter 2), 'Revenge' (Chapter 3), and 'Sovereignty' (Chapter 4). I chose these keywords for their significance in legal and cultural imaginaries—for their diagnostic potential, as well as the potential they hold for reimagining legalities. I regard these keywords as either an obstacle to us fully seeing the interconnectedness of gender violence ('Consent') or concepts that facilitate ways through to foregrounding this interconnectedness ('Revenge' and 'Sovereignty').

Consent (Chapter 2)

The chapter titled '(Undoing) The Bildungsroman of Consent' critically explores the figure of the girl within the frameworks of consent in both legal and cultural discourses. It argues that the concept of consent, deeply embedded in modern societal and legal structures, is used to uphold systems of power and control. The *bildungsroman* genre, which focuses on the moral and existential development of young women through scenes of desire and sexual violence, is identified as a significant influence. Classic examples include Samuel Richardson's *Pamela* and *Clarissa*, where the protagonists' encounters with sexual violence are central to their development and the narrative itself (Richardson, 1740, 1748). This historical context sets the stage for understanding how contemporary cultural narratives continue to position sexual violence as a formative experience for young women. This chapter presents a nuanced analysis of how the girl is constructed as a subject within these frameworks. The chapter critically examines the didactic approach to consent that has gained prominence in recent years, especially in Australia. Legal reforms and educational programs aim to clarify definitions of consent and teach young people about consent to combat rape culture. This approach, however, is criticised for its limitations. The chapter references works such as Jess Hill's documentary *Asking for It: Creating Consent Culture* (2023) and Chanel Contos's book *Consent Laid Bare* (2023), which highlight complexities and nuances that go beyond the didactic framework. Through an analysis of the films *Dogville* (2003) and *It Follows* (2014), the chapter explores how the aesthetic and emotional dimensions of contract and consent are used to sustain the subordination of girls and women. These cultural texts critique the notion that mere affirmation of consent can address the deep-seated power imbalances in interpersonal dynamics.

Revenge (Chapter 3)

This chapter examines how contemporary feminist creators employ the figure of the girl to critique the failures of legal systems and envision new forms of justice that go beyond traditional boundaries. By analysing works including *Promising Young Woman* (2020) and *The Nightingale* (2020), the chapter explores how these narratives reclaim the girl's voice and agency, transforming her from a passive victim to an active agent of justice, and also how reclaiming agency alone is not the answer. These texts challenge the simplistic notion of revenge as purely retributive justice and propose more complex and nuanced approaches to addressing harm, incorporating elements of tragedy, forgiveness, and social contract reimagining.

Sovereignty (Chapter 4)

This chapter critically examines legal 'scenes' in which the child figure is at the centre—providing new readings of significant interventions, programs of protection, and programs of control, as well as the narratives that underlie these scenes. I argue that the figure of the girl is central to a number of interventions in which law is called to—or asserts a role in—the adjudication of violence and is therefore a significant figure in constituting the authority and legitimacy of law, especially during time of crisis. The chapter critically examines how legal and cultural narratives instrumentalise the figure of the vulnerable First Nations child to justify state intervention and perpetuate colonial violence. Through a detailed analysis of Alexis Wright's novels, the chapter reveals how these works deconstruct the myths and figures of state law, providing new frameworks for understanding and addressing the ongoing harms inflicted by colonial policies. Wright's novels highlight the fragility of legal categories and the interconnectedness of different forms of violence, emphasising the need for a radical reimagining of law and justice from the perspective of the most vulnerable.

Bibliography

Adams, R., Reiss, B., and Serlin, D. (Eds.) (2015) *Keywords for Disability Studies*. New York: New York University Press.

Adamson, J., Gleason, W. A., and Pellow, D. N. (Eds.) (2016) *Keywords for Environmental Studies*. New York.: New York University Press.

Ahmann, C. (2018) '"It's Exhausting to Create an Event Out of Nothing': Slow Violence and the Manipulation of Time.' *Cultural Anthropology*, 33, p. 142.

Ahmed, S. (2014) *The Cultural Politics of Emotion*, 2nd ed. Edinburgh: Edinburgh University Press.

Anker, E. S., and Meyler, B. (Eds.) (2017) *New Directions in Law and Literature*. New York: Oxford University Press.

Antaki, M. (2013) 'Genre, Critique, and Human Rights.' *University of Toronto Quarterly*, 82(4), pp. 974–996.

Antevska, A., and Gavey, N. (2015) '"Out of Sight and Out of Mind": Detachment and Men's Consumption of Male Sexual Dominance and Female Submission in Pornography.' *Men Masculinities*, 18(5).

Attridge, D. (2004) *J.M. Coetzee and the Ethics of Reading: Literature in the Event*. Chicago: University of Chicago Press.

Attwell, D. (2015) *J.M. Coetzee and the Life of Writing: Face-to-Face with Time*. New York: Viking.

Australian Institute of Health and Welfare (2020) *Sexual Assault in Australia. Cat. no. FDV 5*. Canberra: AIHW.

Baldry, E., and Cuneen, C. (2014) 'Imprisoned Indigenous Women and the Shadow of Colonial Patriarcy.' *Australian and New Zealand Journal of Criminology*, pp. 1–23.

Barnard, R. (2003) *Apartheid and Beyond: South African Writers and the Politics of Place*. Oxford: Oxford University Press.
Baroness Casey Review (2023) 'The Baroness Casey Review: Final Report.' *Metropolitan Police*. Available at: www.met.police.uk/police-forces/metropolitan-police/areas/about-us/about-the-met/bcr/baroness-casey-review/
Beauvoir, S. de, and Parshley, H. M. (1993). *The Second Sex*. New York: Alfred A. Knopf.
Benjamin, W. (1968) *Illuminations*, 1st ed. New York: Harcourt, Brace & World.
Bennett, T., Grossberg, L., and Morris, M. (Eds.) (2005) *New Keywords: A Revised Vocabulary of Culture and Society*. Malden, MA: Blackwell Publishing.
Binder, G., and Weisberg, R. (2000) *Literary Criticisms of Law*. Princeton: Princeton University Press.
Brady, T. (2016, October 28) 'Why Are So Many Books Now Called "The Girl . . ."?' *Time*. Available at: https://time.com/4551310/girl-book-titles/ (Accessed: 8 June 2024).
Breslow, J. (2021) *Ambivalent Childhoods: Speculative Futures and the Psychic Life of the Child*. Minneapolis: University of Minnesota Press.
Brown, W. (1995) *States of Injury: Power and Freedom in Late Modernity*. Princeton: Princeton University Press.
Bruhm, S., and Hurley, N. (Eds.) (2004) *Curiouser: On the Queerness of Children*. Minneapolis: University of Minnesota Press.
Buchanan, R., and Johnson, R. (2009) 'Strange Encounters: Exploring Law and Film in the Affective Register.' In A. Sarat (Ed.), *Studies in Law, Politics and Society: A Special Symposium Issue on Law and Film*, vol. 46. Bradford: Emerald, p. 33.
Bumiller, K. (2008) *In an Abusive State: How Neoliberalism Appropriated the Feminist Movement against Sexual Violence*. Durham: Duke University Press.
Burgett, B., and Hendler, G. (2020) *Keywords for American Cultural Studies*, 3rd ed. New York: New York University Press.
Burke, T. (2017, November 9) '#MeToo Was Started for Black and Brown Women and Girls. They Are Still Being Ignored.' *Washington Post* (Accessed: 22 May 2022).
Burns, A. (2018) *Milkman*. London: Faber & Faber.
Butler, J. (2016) *Frames of War: When Is Life Grievable*? New York: Verso.
Canning, V., and Tombs, S. (2021) *From Social Harm to Zemiology: A Critical Introduction*, 1st ed. London: Routledge.
Carline, A., and Easteal, P. (2014) *Shadows of the Law: The Legal Contexts of Ineffective Rape Prosecution*. London: Routledge.
Carlsen, A., Salam, M., Miller, C. C., Lu, D., Ngu, A., Patel, J. K., and Wichter, Z. (2018, October 23) 'Me Too Brought Down 201 Powerful Men. Nearly Half of Their Replacements Are Women.' *The New York Times*. Available at: www.nytimes.com/interactive/2018/10/23/us/metoo-replacements.html (Accessed: 12 December 2023).
Carlton, B., and Russell, E. K. (2018) *Resisting Carceral Violence: Women's Imprisonment and the Politics of Abolition*. London: Springer International Publishing.
Carrotte, E. R., et al. (2020) 'Sexual Behaviors and Violence in Pornography: Systematic Review and Narrative Synthesis of Video Content Analyses.' *Journal of Medical Internet Research*, 22(5), pp. e16702–e16702.
Caruth, C. (1996) *Unclaimed Experience: Trauma, Narrative, and History*. Baltimore: Johns Hopkins University Press.
Centers for Disease Control and Prevention (CDC). (2021) *National Intimate Partner and Sexual Violence Survey (NISVS): An Overview*. Available at: www.cdc.gov/nisvs/about/index.html (Accessed: 8 June 2024).
Champion, J. (2013) *Top of the Lake*. BBC Two, UKTV and Sundance Channel.
Champion, J. (2017) *Top of the Lake: China Girl*. BBC Two, UKTV and Sundance Channel.

Clifford, J. (1988) *The Predicament of Culture: Twentieth-Century Ethnography, Literature, and Art*. Cambridge: Harvard University Press.
Coetzee, J. M. (1999) *Disgrace*. London: Martin Secker & Warburg Ltd.
Collins, P. H. (2000) *Black Feminist Thought: Knowledge,Consciousness, and the Politics of Empowerment*. New York: Routledge.
Coombe, R. J. (1999) *The Cultural Life of Intellectual Properties: Authorship, Appropriation and the Law*. Durham: Duke University Press.
Cooppan, V. (2009) *Worlds Within: National Narratives and Global Connections in Postcolonial Writing*, 1st ed. Stanford: Stanford University Press.
Cover, R. M. (1983) 'Foreword: Nomos and Narrative.' *Harvard Law Review*, 4, pp. 12–19.
Cover, R. M. (1993) *Narrative, Violence, and the Law: The Essays of Robert M. Cover*. Edited by Martha Minow et al. Ann Arbor: University of Michigan Press.
Crabbe, M., Adams, K., and Flood, M. (2024) 'Pornography Exposure and Access Among Young Australians: A Cross-Sectional Study.' *Australian and New Zealand Journal of Public Health*, 88(3), p. 10013.
Crawley, K., Giddens, T., and Peters, T. (2024) *The Routledge Handbook of Cultural Legal Studies*. London: Routledge.
Crawley, K., and Peters, T. (2018) 'Introduction: Representational Legality.' In T. D. Peters and K. Crawley (Eds.), *Envisioning Legality: Law, Culture and Representation*. London: Routledge.
Cree, V. E., Clapton, G., and Smith, M. (Eds.) (2016) *Revisiting Moral Panics*. Bristol: Bristol University Press.
Crenshaw, K. (1991) 'Mapping the Margins: Intersectionality, Identity Politics, and Violence Against Women of Color.' *Stanford Law Review*, 43, pp. 1241–1299.
Crenshaw, K. (2018) 'Demarginalizing the Intersection of Race and Sex: A Black Feminist Critique of Antidiscrimination Doctrine, Feminist Theory, and Antiracist Politics.' *University of Chicago Legal Forum*, 1, pp. 139–167.
Cvetkovich, A. (2003) *An Archive of Feelings: Trauma, Sexuality, and Lesbian Public Cultures*. Durham, NC: Duke University Press.
D'Abreu, L. C. F., and Krahe, B. (2014) 'Predicting Sexual Aggression in Male College Students in Brazil.' *Psychology of Men & Masculinities*, 15(2), p. 152.
Darling, O. (2021) '"Systemic, Transhistoric, Institutionalised, and Legitimised Antipathy": Epistemic and Sexual Violence in a Girl Is a Half-Formed Thing and Milkman.' *Contemporary Women's Writing*, 15(3), pp. 307–325.
D'Avolio, M., Cavalcanti, R., and Dadusc, D. (2023) *Anti-Carceral Feminism: Abolitionist Conversations on Gender-Based Violence: Navigating Resistance as Everyday Praxis*. London: Bloomsbury Academic, pp. 223–242.
Deer, S. (2015) *The Beginning and End of Rape: Confronting Sexual Violence in Native America*. Minneapolis: University of Minnesota Press.
de la Garza, S. A. (2019) 'No More Magic Mirrors: Confronting Reflections of Privileged Feminisms in #MeToo.' *Women and Language*, 42(1), pp. 175–181.
Deleuze, G., and Guattari, F. (1987) *A Thousand Plateaus: Capitalism and Schizophrenia*. Minneapolis: University of Minnesota Press.
Derrida, J. (1980) 'The Law of Genre.' *Critical Inquiry*, 7, p. 55.
Derrida, J. (1992) 'Force of Law: The "Mystical Foundation of Authority."' In *Deconstruction and the Possibility of Justice*, 1st ed. London: Routledge, pp. 3–67.
Derrida, J. (2006) *Geneses, Genealogies, Genres and Genius: The Secrets of the Archive*. Edinburgh: Edinburgh University Press.
Dimock, W. C. (2006) *Through Other Continents: American Literature Across Deep Time*. Princeton: Princeton University Press.
Donoghue, E. (2010) *Room*. London: Picador.

Dougherty, C., and Calafell, B. M. (2019) 'Before and Beyond #MeToo and #TimesUp: Rape as a Colonial and Racist Project.' *Women and Language*, 42(1), pp. 213–218.
Edelman, L. (2004) *No Future: Queer Theory and the Death Drive*. Durham, NC: Duke University Press.
Estrich, S. (2014) *Real Rape: How the Legal System Victimises Women Who Say No*. Cambridge, MA: Harvard University Press.
Ewick, P., and Silbey, S. S. (1998) *The Common Place of Law: Stories from Everyday Life*. Chicago: University of Chicago Press.
Faulkner, J. (2011) *The Importance of Being Innocent: Why We Worry About Children*. Cambridge: Cambridge University Press.
Faulkner, J. (2014) *Young and Free: [Post]colonial Ontologies of Childhood, Memory, and History in Australia*. Melbourne: Lexington Books.
Faulkner, J. (2023) *Representing Aboriginal Childhood: The Politics of Memory and Forgetting in Australia*. London: Routledge.
Fisher, W. A., et al. (2013) 'Pornography, Sex Crime, and Paraphilia.' *Current Psychiatry Reports*, 15(6), pp. 362–362.
Flood, M. (2018) *Engaging Men and Boys in Violence Prevention*. London: Palgrave Macmillan.
Flood, M. (2020) 'Sexual Violence Prevention with Men and Boys as a Social Justice Issue.' In L. M. Orchowski and A. Berkowitz (Eds.), *Engaging Boys and Men in Sexual Assault Prevention: Theory, Research and Practice*. London: Elsevier.
Flynn, G. (2007) *Sharp Objects*. New York: Broadway Books.
Flynn, G. (2013) *Gone Girl*. New York: W & N.
Franke, K. M. (2006) 'Gendered Subjects of Transitional Justice.' *Columbia Law Review*, 95(5), pp. 1288–1293.
Freeman, E. (2000) 'Packing History, Count(er)ing Generations.' *New Literary History*, 31(4), pp. 727–744.
French, T. (2007) *In the Woods*. London: Viking.
Frow, J. (2006) *Genre*. London: Routledge.
Frow, J., Hardie, M., and Smith, V. (2020) 'The Bildungsroman: Form and Transformations.' *Textual Practice*, 34(12), pp. 1905–1910.
Garcia, S. E. (2017) 'The Woman Who Created #MeToo Long Before Hashtags.' *New York Times (Online)*.
Gallagher, S. V. (2002) *Truth and Reconciliation: The Confessional Mode in South African Literature*. Portsmouth: Heinemann.
Geertz, C. (1983) *Local Knowledge: Further Essays in Interpretive Anthropology*. New York: ACLS Humanities Publishing.
Giddens, T. (2018) *On Comics and Legal Aesthetics: Multimodality and the Haunted Mask of Knowing*. London: Routledge.
Gilmore, L. (1994) *Autobiographics: A Feminist Theory of Women's Self-Representation*. Ithaca: Cornell University Press.
Gilmore, L. (2001) *The Limits of Autobiography: Trauma and Testimony*. Ithaca: Cornell University Press.
Gilmore, L. (2003) 'Jurisdictions: I, Rigoberta Menchú, The Kiss, and Scandalous Self-Representation in the Age of Memoir and Trauma.' *Signs: Journal of Women in Culture and Society*, 28(3), pp. 695–718.
Gilmore, L. (2017) *Tainted Witness: Why We Doubt What Women Say About Their Lives*. New York: Columbia University Press.
Gilmore, L. (2023) *The #MeToo Effect: What Happens When We Believe Women*, 1st ed. New York: Columbia University Press.
Gilmore, L., and Marshall, E. (2019) *Witnessing Girlhood: Toward an Intersectional Tradition of Life Writing*, 1st ed. New York: Fordham University Press.

Giraudoux, J. (1987) *Électra*. Paris: Editions Grasset.
Goodrich, P., and Zartaloudis, T. (Eds.) (2023) *The Cabinet of Imaginary Laws*. Abingdon: Routledge.
Gray, J. M. (2016) *The Politics of Rape: Sexual Atrocity, Propaganda Wars, and the Restoration Stage*. London: Routledge.
Halberstam, J. (1998) *Female Masculinity*, 1st ed. Durham: Duke University Press.
Halberstam, J. (2005) *In a Queer Time and Place: Transgender Bodies, Subcultural Lives*. New York: New York University Press.
Halley, J., Kotiswaran, P., Rebouché, R., and Shamir, H. (2018) *Governance Feminism: An Introduction*. Minneapolis: University of Minnesota Press.
Harkins, G. (2003) 'Seduction by Law: Sexual Property and Testimonial Possession in Thereafter Johnnie.' *Discourse*, 25(1/2), pp. 138–165.
Harkins, G. (2007) 'Surviving the Family Romance? Southern Realism and the Labor of Incest.' *Southern Literary Journal*, 40(1), pp. 114–139.
Harkins, G. (2009) *Everybody's Family Romance Reading Incest in Neoliberal America*, 1st ed. Minneapolis: University of Minnesota Press.
Harkins, G. (2020) *Virtual Pedophilia: Sex Offender Profiling andUS Security Culture*, 1st ed. Durham, NC: Duke University Press.
Hartman, S. V. (1997) *Scenes of Subjection: Terror, Slavery, and Self-Making in Nineteenth-Century America*. Oxford: Oxford University Press.
Hawkins, P. (2015) *The Girl on the Train*. London: Black Swan Books.
Henry, C., and Talbot, H. (2019) 'The Complexities of Young New Zealanders' Use and Perceptions of Pornography: A Quantitative Survey in Context.' *Porn Studies*, 6(4), pp. 391–410.
Henry, N., and Powell, A. (2017) *Sexual Violence in a Digital Age*. London: Palgrave Macmillan.
Hershinow, S. I. (2019) *Born Yesterday: Inexperience and the Early Realist Novel*. Baltimore: Johns Hopkins University Press.
Hesford, W. (2011) *Spectacular Rhetorics: Human Rights Visions, Recognitions, Feminisms*. Durham: Duke University Press.
Hickey-Moody, A., and Malins, P. (Eds.) (2008) *Deleuzian Encounters: Studies in Contemporary Social Issues*. New York: Palgrave.
Hutton, C. (2019, July 21) 'Why Anna Burns' Milkman Is Such a Phenomenon.' *OUP Blog*. Available at: blog.oup.com/2019/07/why-anna-burns-milkman-is-such-a-phenomenon/ (Accessed: 14 March 2020).
James, A., and Prout, A. (2015) *Constructing and Reconstructing Childhood: Contemporary Issues in the Sociological Study of Childhood*. London: Routledge.
Kahn, P. W. (2008) *Sacred Violence: Torture, Terror, and Sovereignty*. Minneapolis: University of Michigan Press.
Kennedy, R. (2011) 'An Australian Archive of Feelings.' *Australian Feminist Studies*, 26(69), pp. 257–279.
Kim, M. E. (2020) 'Anti-Carceral Feminism: The Contradictions of Progress and the Possibilities of Counter-Hegemonic Struggle.' *Affilia*, 35(3), pp. 309–326.
Kramer, R., and Remster, B. (2022) 'The Slow Violence of Contemporary Policing.' *Annual Review of Criminology*, 5(1), pp. 43–66.
LaCapra, D. (1999) 'Trauma, Absence, Loss.' *Critical Enquiry*, 25(4), pp. 696–727.
Lamm, K. (2015) 'Texting Girls: Images, Sounds, and Words in Neoliberal Cultures of Femininity.' *Women & Performance*, 25(2), pp. 111–127.
Larsson, S. (2005) *The Girl with the Dragon Tattoo*. London: Knopf.
Lehner, S. (2014) 'The Irreversible and the Irrevocable: Encircling Trauma in Contemporary Northern Irish Literature.' In O. Frawley (Ed.), *Memory Ireland Volume 3:The Famine and the Troubles*. Syracuse, NY: Syracuse University Press, pp. 272–292.

Leonard, J. (Ed.) (1995) *Legal Studies as Cultural Studies: A Reader in (Post)Modern Critical Theory*. Albany: State University of New York Press.
Locke, J. (1948) 'An Essay Concerning Human Understanding, 1690.' In W. Dennis (Ed.), *Readings in the History of Psychology*. London: Appleton-Century-Crofts, pp. 55–68.
Loney-Howes, R., Longbottom, M., and Fileborn, B. (2024) 'Gender-Based Violence and Carceral Feminism in Australia: Towards Decarceral Approaches.' *Feminist Legal Studies*, pp. 1–23.
Mack, A. N., and McCann, B. J. (2018) 'Critiquing State and Gendered Violence in the Age of #MeToo.' *Quarterly Journal of Speech*, 104(3), pp. 329–344.
Mack, A. N., and Na'Puti, T. R. (2019) '"Our Bodies Are Not Terra Nullius": Building a Decolonial Feminist Resistance to Gendered Violence.' *Women's Studies in Communication: The #MeToo Moment: A Rhetorical Zeitgeist*, 42(3), pp. 347–370.
MacNeil, W. P. (2007) *Lex Populi: The Jurisprudence of Popular Culture*. San Paolo: Stanford University Press.
MacNeil, W. P. (2012) *Novel Judgements: Legal Theory as Fiction*. London: Routledge.
Malamuth, N. M., Hald, G. M., and Koss, M. (2012) 'Pornography, Individual Differences in Risk and Men's Acceptance of Violence Against Women in a Representative Sample.' *Sex Roles*, 66(7–8), pp. 427–439.
Malone, P. (2022) 'Measures of Obliviousness and Disarming Obliqueness in Anna Burns' Milkman.' *Textual Practice*, 36(7), pp. 1143–1174.
Manderson, D. (2012) *Kangaroo Courts and the Rule of Law: The Legacy of Modernism*. London: Routledge.
Manderson, D. (2018) *Law and the Visual: Representations, Technologies, Critique*. Toronto: University of Toronto Press.
Marais, M. (2011) 'J.M. Coetzee's Disgrace and the Task of the Imagination.' *Journal of Modern Literature*, 34(4), pp. 1–22.
Marshall, E., and Gilmore, L. (2015) 'Girlhood in the Gutter: Feminist Graphic Knowledge and the Visualization of Sexual Precarity.' *WSQ: Women's Studies Quarterly*, 43(1), pp. 95–114.
Marston, C., and Lewis, R. (2014) 'Anal Heterosex among Young People and Implications for Health Promotion: A Qualitative Study in the UK.' *BMJ Open*, 4(8), pp. e004996–e004996.
Martellozzo, E., Monaghan, A., Adler, J. R., Davidson, J., Leyva, R., and Horvath, M. A. (2016) *'I Wasn't Sure It Was Normal to Watch It . . .' A Quantitative and Qualitative Examination of the Impact of Online Pornography on the Values, Attitudes, Beliefs and Behaviours of Children and Young People*. London: National Society for the Prevention of Cruelty to Children (NSPCC) and the Children's Commissioner for England.
McBride, E. (2013) *A Girl Is a Half-Formed Thing*. London: Faber & Faber.
Mccalman, J., Bridge, F., Whiteside, M., Bainbridge, R., Tsey, K., and Jongen, C. (2014) 'Responding to Indigenous Australian Sexual Assault: A Systematic Review of the Literature.' *SAGEOpen*, 4(1).
McClintock, A. (1995) *Imperial Leather: Race, Gender, and Sexuality in the Colonial Contest*. New York: Routledge.
McGlynn, C. (2010) 'Feminist Activism and Rape Law Reform in England and Wales: A Sisyphean Struggle?' In *Rethinking Rape Law*. London: Routledge-Cavendish, pp. 155–169.
McRobbie, A. (2008) *The Aftermath of Feminism: Gender, Culture, and Social Change*. London: Sage.
Meister, R. (2011) *After Evil: A Politics of Human Rights*. New York: Columbia University Press.

Mezey, N. (2003) 'Law as Culture.' In A. Sarat and J. Simon (Eds.), *Cultural Analysis, Cultural Studies, and the Law: Moving Beyond Legal Realism*. Durham, NC: Duke University Press.

Miller, B. (2017) *The Handmaid's Tale*. Los Angeles, CA: MGM Television.

Nel, P., and Paul, L. (Eds.) (2011) *Keywords for Children's Literature*. New York: New York University Press.

Nelson, F. (2017) 'The Girl: Dead.' *Girlhood Studies*, 10(3), pp. 39–53.

Nixon, R. (2011) *Slow Violence and the Environmentalism of the Poor*. Cambridge, MA: Harvard University Press.

O'Keefe, T. (2017) 'Policing Unruly Women: The State and Sexual Violence During the Northern Irish Troubles.' *Women's Studies International Forum*, 62, pp. 69–77.

Olson, G. (2022) *From Law and Literature to Legality and Affect*. Oxford: Oxford University Press.

Onwuachi-Willig, A. (2018) 'What about #UsToo? The Invisibility of Race in the #MeToo Movement.' *Yale Law Journal Forum*, 128, pp. 105–120.

Peter, J., and Valkenburg, P. M. (2007) 'Adolescents' Exposure to a Sexualised Media Environment and Their Notions of Women as Sex Objects.' *Sex Roles*, 56(5–6), p. 381.

Peter, J., and Valkenburg, P. M. (2009) 'Adolescents' Exposure to Sexually Explicit Internet Material and Notions of Women as Sex Objects: Assessing Causality and Under-Lying Processes.' *Journal of Communication*, 59(3), pp. 407–433.

Peter, J., and Valkenburg, P. M. (2016) 'Adolescents and Pornography: A Review of 20 Years of Research.' *The Journal of Sex Research*, 53(4–5), pp. 509–531.

Purcell, N. J. (2012) *Violence and the Pornographic Imaginary: The Politics of Sex, Gender, and Aggression in Hardcore Pornography*. London: Routledge.

Richardson, S. (1740) *Pamela, or Virtue Rewarded*. London: Samuel Richardson.

Richardson, S. (1748) *Clarissa,or the History of a Young Lady*. London: Samuel Richardson.Richie, B. E. (2012) *Arrested Justice: Black Women, Violence, and America's Prison Nation*. New York: New York University Press.

Rothman, E. F., and Adhia, A. (2016) 'Adolescent Pornography Use and Dating Violence Among a Sample of Primarily Black and Hispanic, Urban-Residing, Underage Youth.' *The Journal of Behavioral Science*, 6(1).

Ruprecht Fadem, M. E. (2015) *The Literature of Northern Ireland: Spectral Borderlands*. New York: Palgrave.

Russell, Y. (2013) 'Thinking Sexual Difference Through the Law of Rape.' *Law and Critique*, 24(3), pp. 255–275.

Russell, Y. (2016) 'Woman's Voice/Law's Logos: The Rape Trial and the Limits of Liberal Reform.' *The Australian Feminist Law Journal*, 42(2), pp. 273–296.

Russell, Y., and Conaghan, J. (2023) *Sexual History Evidence and the Rape Trial: A Multidisciplinary Critique*. Bristol: Bristol University Press.

Sarat, A. (2001) *Law, Violence and the Possibility of Justice*. Princeton: Princeton University Press.

Sedgwick, E. K. (2003) *Touching Feeling: Affect, Pedagogy, Performativity*. Durham, NC: Duke University Press.

Serisier, T. (2018) *Speaking Out: Feminism, Rape and Narrative Politics*. London: Palgrave Macmillan.

Serisier, T. (2023) 'Beyond Speaking Out: MeToo and the Limits of Narrative Politics.' In *New Directions in Sexual Violence Scholarship*, 1st ed., vol. 1. London: Routledge, pp. 209–225.

Sharp, C., and Leiboff, M. (Eds.) (2020) *Cultural Legal Studies: Law's Popular Cultures and the Metamorphosis of Law*. Abingdon: Routledge.

Sheldon, R. (2016) *The Child to Come: Life after the Human Catastrophe*. Minneapolis: University of Minnesota Press.
Silka, L. (2022) *Shining Girls*. Apple TV+.
Simić, O. (2018) *Silenced Victims of Wartime Sexual Violence*. London: Routledge.
Smart, C. (1989) *Feminism and the Power of Law*. London: Routledge.
Spillers, H. (2003) *Black, White, and in Color: Essays on American Literature and Culture*. Chicago: University of Chicago Press.
Stephens, S. (1995) *Children and the Politics of Culture*. Princeton: Princeton University Press.
Stockton, K. B. (2009) *The Queer Child, or Growing Sideways in the Twentieth Century*. Durham, NC: Duke University Press.
Tambe, A. (2018) 'Reckoning with the Silences of #MeToo.' *Feminist Studies*, 44(1), pp. 197–203.
Tarzia, L., and Tyler, M. (2021) 'Recognizing Connections Between Intimate Partner Sexual Violence and Pornography.' *Violence against Women*, 27(14), pp. 2687–2708.
Taylor, C. (2019) *Foucault, Feminism, and Sex Crimes: An Anti-Carceral Analysis*. Notre Dame: Notre Dame Philosophical Reviews.
Temkin, J., Gray, J. M., and Barrett, J. (2018) 'Different Functions of Rape Myth Use in Court: Findings from a Trial Observation Study.' *Feminist Criminology*, 13(2), pp. 291–320.
Terwiel, A. (2020) 'What Is Carceral Feminism?' *Political Theory*, 48(4), pp. 421–442.
Tiqqun. (2012) *Preliminary Materials for a Theory of the Young-Girl*. Translated by Ariana Reines. Los Angeles: Semiotext(e).
Tombs, S. (2018) 'The UK's Corporate Killing Law: Un/fit for Purpose?' *Criminology & Criminal Justice*, 18(4), pp. 488–507.
Tombs, S. (2020) 'Home as a Site of State-Corporate Violence: Grenfell Tower, Aetiologies and Aftermaths.' *The Howard Journal of Crime and Justice*, 59, p. 120.
Torres, M. (2018) 'State Violence.' In A. Treviño (Ed.), *The Cambridge Handbook of Social Problems*. Cambridge: Cambridge University Press, pp. 381–391.
van Marle, K., and Motha, S. J. (Eds.) (2013) *Genres of Critique: Law, Aesthetics and Liminality*. Sun Press.
van Rijswijk, H. (2019) 'Feminist Genres of Violence and Law's Aggressive Realism.' In *Routledge Handbook of Law and Theory*, 1st ed. London: Routledge, pp. 329–346.
Ward, G. (2015) 'The Slow Violence of State Organized Race Crime.' *Theoretical Criminology*, 19(3), pp. 299–314.
Warren-Crow, H. (2014) *Girlhood and the Plastic Image*. Hanover, NH: Dartmouth College Press.
Weiner, M. (2007–2015). *Mad Men*. Created by Matthew Weiner. Produced by Lionsgate Television. London: AMC.
Whannell, L. (2020) *The Invisible Man*. Los Angeles: Blumhouse Productions.
Wiegman, R. (2019) *Differences: A Journal of Feminist Cultural Studies*. Special issue: *Sexual Politics, Sexual Panics*, 30 (1).
Wiesner. (2021) 'The Feminist War on Crime: The Unexpected Role of Women's Liberation in Mass Incarceration by Aya Gruber (Review).' *Feminist Formations*, 33(1), pp. 279–282.
Williams, R. (1976) *Keywords: A Vocabulary of Culture and Society*. London: Fontana.

Woolf, V. (1984) *The Common Reader*. San Diego, CA: Harcourt.
Wright, A. (2013) *The Swan Book*. Sydney: Giramondo Publishing.
Wright, P. J., Tokunaga, R. S., and Kraus, A. (2015) 'A Meta-Analysis of Pornography Consumption and Actual Acts of Sexual Aggression in General Population Studies.' *Journal of Communication*, pp. 1–23.
Ybarra, M. L., Mitchell, K. J., Hamburger, M., Diener-West, M., and Leaf, P. J. (2011) 'X-Rated Material and Perpetration of Sexually Aggressive Behaviour Among Children and Adolescents: Is There a Link?' *Aggressive Behavior*, 37(1), pp. 1–18.
Young, A. (2010) *The Scene of Violence: Cinema, Crime, Affect*. London: Routledge.

Chapter 2

(Undoing) The *Bildungsroman* of Consent

Introduction: The Continuing Dominance of Consent

The concept of consent is produced at the intersection of legal and cultural discourses. The law continues to adhere to 'consent' as its linchpin in evaluating sexual violence, despite evidence that this conceptual framework is problematic. The trope of consent, and the related framework of contract, are ingrained in cultural representations of sexual violence. So much so that, as I explore in this chapter, they structure a form of *bildungsroman* for young women. In this chapter, I argue that the figure of the girl is central to understanding contemporary cultural and legal discourses of consent. The relationship between the figure of the girl and the concept of consent is deeply rooted in both historical and contemporary contexts, reflecting complex socio-legal dynamics and cultural narratives. This chapter critically examines the ways in which the girl is constructed as a subject within the frameworks of violation and consent. However, because of its significance, the figure of the girl also offers a powerful site for reimagining frameworks of responsibility for sexual violence, and this chapter explores how radical creators are writing against the grain of existing discourses.

Historically, the *bildungsroman* genre for girls has focused on their sexuality, with young women's moral and existential development arising through scenes of desire, sexual violence and 'seduction,' frequently through the axis of consent. The figure of the girl has been intertwined with, even overdetermined by, themes of innocence, vulnerability, and victimhood since the origins of the English novel. In Samuel Richardson's *Pamela* (1740) and *Clarissa* (1748), young female protagonists face attempts at seduction and rape, which are integral to their psychological, ethical, and existential development. These early novels both diagnosed a social reality and set a precedent for the trope of sexual violence as a catalyst for the girl's growth, a theme that persists through to contemporary legal and cultural narratives.

In this chapter, I briefly consider the cultural genealogy of consent and then critically examine contemporary didactic approaches based on consent, with its cross-cultural, policy, and quasi-legal domains. In recent years, a

DOI: 10.4324/9780429263675-2

didactic approach to consent has gained prominence in Australia and similar jurisdictions; it is therefore important to understand the limitations and implications of this approach. The didactic framework is evidenced by recent legal reforms that clarify definitions of consent and educational programs that aim to teach young people about consent. The didactic discourse is reflected in Jess Hill's recent acclaimed documentary *Asking for It: Creating Consent Culture* (2023) and in Chanel Contos's bestselling book *Consent Laid Bare: Sex, Entitlement and the Complications of Desire* (MacMillan, 2023). I examine these approaches and texts, focusing on how girls and young women who have spoken out about sexual violence have been placed at the centre of the didactic-consent approach in Australia. I argue that, while their testimony and advocacy have been framed within the didactic-consent framework, their advocacy and documented experiences are much more nuanced than what the didactic approach would suggest; these texts in fact speak to the greater significance of power imbalances and structural injustices. However, it seems that law and culture are caught up with this didactic approach, which seems to be imbricated with an ingrained trope where the adolescent girl's being is necessarily based on her sexuality, and her *bildungsroman*—her didactic journey—is seen as the dominant way forward.

The continuing high rate of sexual violence against girls underscores the reality that the cultural and legal emphasis on consent is an abstract ideal produced by (and disguising) underlying power dynamics and systemic inequalities. This is particularly true for marginalised groups, such as First Nations girls and women, who face higher rates of sexual violence in the context of ongoing colonialism (Behrendt, 2000, p. 355). Since the figure of the girl is central to understanding contemporary cultural and legal discourses surrounding consent, we can find considerable resistance to the consent narrative in emergent cultural forms that centre the figure of the girl. Kate Elizabeth Russell's 2020 novel *My Dark Vanessa* and Michaela Coel's comedy-drama limited television series *I May Destroy You* (HBO, 2020) both exemplify this critical interrogation of consent narratives. These contemporary texts thematise consent and then interrogate it, showing how it fails to protect people from sexual violence and how, in many cases, the discourse of consent in fact facilitates abuse by disguising power imbalances. Ultimately, however, these works emphasise the importance of knowledge and awareness in negotiations of sexuality but also reveal the limitations of focusing solely on the individual agency that the consent framework mandates.

I then turn to seemingly unlikely genres which, in bleak ways, diagnose the uselessness and harm of consent narratives, each film also conveying an extreme affect of hopelessness. This bleakness should ultimately lead to hope, however—let's raze the law of consent to the ground, and let's raze the cultural narratives to the ground, too, so that we can lay fresh frameworks based on a structural, decolonising approach to sexual violence. The first text that offers this bleak diagnosis is *David Robert Mitchell's* It Follows (2014), which I argue uses the full potential of the horror genre to eviscerate the notion of individual agency as effective in combating sexual violence. With the main character being relentlessly pursued by a demon after an ambiguous act of sex, *It Follows* foregrounds the horror of continuing violation to highlight the limitations of consent as a protective framework.

The second bleak diagnosis of the uselessness and harm of consent narratives is provided by Lars von Trier's 2003 film *Dogville*, which I argue serves as an aesthetic and affective critique of the subordination produced through liberal law and democracy. My reading focuses on the figure of Grace, a young woman who seeks refuge in a small town but is instead subjected to escalating violence and degradation by the townspeople. I examine how the film critiques the concepts of the social contract and consent, showing how these notions not only fail to protect the vulnerable, but are perversely used to justify and perpetuate violence and subjugation while disguising this violence through the rhetoric of consent. The townspeople's treatment of Grace is justified through the language of contractual obligation and mutual benefit, masking the exploitation and violence she endures. *Dogville* illustrates how the subjugation of a structurally vulnerable subject is constitutive—Grace's subjugation becomes central to the town's sense of community and order, revealing the material realities behind abstract concepts of justice and contract. By demonstrating that not only consent, but any framework based on the ideology of individual agency is ineffective in combating sexual violence; it becomes clear that collective action in fighting back is the baseline starting point.

The Legal Framing of Consent

Although feminist legal scholars have lost faith in the possibility of resurrecting sexual assault law through improved uses of the framework of 'consent,' the consent framework continues to dominate both legal and cultural responses to increasingly dire rates of sexual violence. This dominance of the consent framework is clear in recent changes to Australian sexual assault laws which incorporate ideas of 'affirmative consent.' For example, The Crimes Legislation Amendment (Sexual Consent Reforms) Act 2021 (NSW) implemented consent reforms that aim to clarify consent provisions in the Crimes Act 1900 (NSW), including that consent is a free and voluntary agreement that should not be presumed. The provision now includes a requirement that places a positive onus on the accused to consider consent:

> A belief in consent is not reasonable if the accused person did not, within a reasonable time before or at the time of the sexual activity, say or do anything to find out whether the other person was consenting.
>
> (Pt 3, Div 10, Sub-div 1A (ss 61HF–61HK))

Despite such formal changes across Australian law, Julia Quilter argues that in practice, the legal system has not significantly moved away from the old common law expectation for victims to demonstrate resistance as evidence of non-consent (Quilter, 2020). Elisabeth McDonald argues that merely adopting a consent model that requires affirmative or clear communication does not adequately address the pervasive cultural prejudices that impact legal proceedings. McDonald suggests that deeply ingrained gender stereotypes and cultural misconceptions about sexual assault overshadow the legal definitions of consent, influencing the outcomes of criminal trials (McDonald, 2020). Harvard Law School professor and attorney Janet Halley has argued that affirmative consent is a 'conservative' approach (Halley, 2016, p. 258), one that 'install[s] traditional social norms of male responsibility and female helplessness' (Halley, 2016, p. 259), thus strengthening the trope of the girl as necessarily a figure of violation. Further, Halley points out that in a legal framework hinging on affirmative consent, a person can still verbally consent to a sexual act that they do not want (Halley, 2016, p. 277). Despite this scepticism, there has been an upsurge in consent discourse, particularly focused on the girl or young woman, which has crossed political, policy, and legal reform discourses.

Consent as a Cultural-Legal Construction

On 7 May 2017, during the ABC *Four Corners* programme titled '*I Am That Girl*,' a young woman named Saxon Mullins gave up her anonymity and described how, as an 18-year-old in 2013, she was sexually assaulted by 24-year-old Luke Lazarus. Lazarus was the son of one of the owners of the nightclub and had approached Mullins and started dancing with her on the dance floor. He told her he was a part owner of the club and asked Mullins if she wanted to go with him to the club's VIP area. Mullins agreed but instead of taking her to a VIP area, Lazarus took her outside the club to a back lane where Mullins says he anally raped her. In the first trial, *R v Lazarus* [2015], Lazarus was found guilty by a jury of one count of sexual intercourse without consent, contrary to s 61I of the *Crimes Act 1900* and was sentenced to five years in jail, with a three-year non-parole period. But his legal team appealed against the conviction, and the court held that Judge Huggett had erred in her directions to the jury over whether Lazarus knew that Mullins was not consenting; the Court of Criminal Appeal was satisfied that the trial judge misdirected the jury and ordered that there be a new trial (*Lazarus v R* [2016] NSWCCA 52 per Hoeben CJ at CL, Adams J and Fullerton J). Due to the extent of media coverage, Lazarus was granted a retrial with a judge alone. At the end of this second trial, Judge Tupman concluded that Lazarus had 'reasonable grounds' for believing that Mullins was consenting to intercourse and acquitted Lazarus (*R v Lazarus* (Unreported, District Court of New South Wales, Judge Tupman, 4 May 2017 at 37, 41). Upon a second appeal, the NSW Court of Appeal in *R v Lazarus* [2017] NSWCCA 279 found that Judge Tupman had failed to direct herself in relation to making a finding about the steps taken by the accused to establish whether the complainant was consenting, but the court refused to grant a new, third trial, saying it was not in the interests of justice—it would be 'oppressive' because it had been five years since the incident, Lazarus had already been through two trials and had served 11 months in prison *R v Lazarus* [2017] NSWCCA 279 at [168] (Bellew J)).

These legal cases revolved around the issue of consent. Mullins consistently maintained that she did not consent to the sexual act that occurred. In contrast, Lazarus argued that he believed that Mullins had consented. 'He must have realised there was a possibility she was not consenting to that act,' Judge Sarah Huggett concluded in the first trial, 'but went ahead with that act, not caring one way or another as to whether she was consenting' (*R v Lazarus* [2015] cited in *I Am That Girl*, 2018). In contrast, in the second trial, Judge Tupman preferred Lazarus's account to Mullins's and found that Mullins had not explicitly told him to stop; Judge Tupman made this conclusion in part because in Mullins's first police statement she used the equivocal phrase: 'I think . . . I told him to stop' (Unreported, District Court of New South Wales, Judge Tupman, 4 May 2017 at 37–41). Referring to Judge Tupman's judgment, Mullins says that 'She called me an unreliable witness to my own rape' (*I Am That Girl*, 2018). Mullins also narrates the questions explicitly and implicitly asked of her as the judge constructed the question of consent and therefore sexual violence: 'Why did I start dancing with him? Why did I leave my friend? If I "really didn't want it," then I would've physically stopped him' (*I Am That Girl*, 2018). Looking back after ten years, Mullins says that there were 'questions about why I did everything I did. . . . And no questions about why he did everything he did—why there was no one-second question to ask if I wanted to have sex' (*I Am That Girl*, 2018). Further, in appraising the question of consent, '[the judge] really took to heart a statement from one of the defence's witnesses about what she described as "contemporary morality"' (*I Am That Girl*, 2018). Here, Mullins is referring to Judge Tupman's use of the phrase 'contemporary morality' to explain how young people viewed anal sex; in making this evaluation, Judge Tupman referred to the evidence of a defence witness—a young woman who was friends with Lazarus—who said she had had anal sex on first dates (Unreported, District Court of New South Wales, Judge Tupman, 4 May 2017 at 37–41). Judge Tupman found that this provided 'some objective insight into contemporary morality' (Unreported, District Court of New South Wales, Judge Tupman, 4 May 2017 at 38). It was a combination of this 'contemporary morality'—presumably, Judge Tupman adjudicating the ordinariness or otherwise of anal sex on a first 'date'—combined with her perception of Mullins's lack of physical and verbal resistance that led Judge Tupman to conclude that Lazarus had formed the belief that Mullins had consented to sex on reasonable grounds (Unreported, District Court of New South Wales, Judge Tupman, 4 May 2017 at 41–42). However, the judge's assumptions on these points are not supported by research, instead relying on myths about how people respond to trauma (they frequently do not 'resist' as freezing is a trauma response). Here, Judge Tupman gave more credence to what she terms 'social norms' than to the context of Lazarus's acts (for example, his deception in taking Mullins to a back alley rather than to a 'VIP room,' and the coercion involved in disorienting Mullins). Further, it seems that by 'social norms,' Judge Tupman is implicitly referring to specific kinds of sex acts (for example, anal sex) yet does not assert that there is any connection between particular sex acts and sexual violence but rather implicitly relies on a 'common sense' finding on this point. Further, Judge Tupman weights these factors over the testimony of Mullins regarding her specific experience. In advocating how consent should be evaluated, Lazarus recounts events using a similar logic to Judge Tupman's, although in reverse, moving from the specific incident to the wider consequences of weighting norms over the context and testimony connected to specific circumstances. In an interview with 2GB's Ben Fordham, Lazarus said, '[Mullins's] physical body language told me she wanted to be there. I witnessed in front of me a woman participating in sex' (cited in Cooper, 2018, n.p.). The interview proceeded as follows, Lazarus moving far beyond Mullins's testimony concerning the specific events of that night to the more significant (in his opinion) role of norms:

Luke Lazarus:	'So if I'm a man assessing the situation . . . I'd ask you how is a man to know a woman is not consenting when she's participating?'
Fordham:	'She never said the word no?'
Lazarus:	'No, Definitely not . . . and that's been found in the trial. It's never even been her claim that she used the word 'no''

(cited in Cooper, 2018, n.p.)

Lazarus also said in the interview:

- 'It has never been in the complainant's evidence that I was aggressive or forceful.'
- 'My response has always been very clear.'
- 'Her physical actions . . . showed that she was consenting.'
- 'My opinion that that was true was found to be reasonable one. A very experienced judge found that it was reasonable for me to believe that she was consenting.'

(cited in Cooper, 2018, n.p.)

Lazarus's views were reinforced by the trial judge. 'She did not take any physical action to move away from the intercourse or attempted intercourse,' Judge Tupman said in her judgment (Unreported, District Court of New

South Wales, Judge Tupman, 4 May 2017 at 41–42). Mullins explains this lack of physical resistance as an effect of trauma. She describes how Lazarus led her from the dance floor to the alley behind the club:

> [Lazarus] opened the door and I was kind of a bit confused. But he was like 'No no this is the way.' We started to kiss. I realised this wasn't the VIP room and that I didn't want to be here doing this. I stopped kissing him and said 'I have to get back to my friend. . . .' He said, 'turn around and put your fucking hands on the wall.' My brain caught up really quickly . . . that I was in this dark alleyway with nobody else just this person that I really didn't know at all. I didn't even know which door we'd come out of.
>
> (*Asking for It* Ep 2., 2023)

Mullins states:

> I went to move away and he kind of pulled me back and pulled my stockings and my underwear down. So, I pulled them back up and I said, 'No I really have to go now.' . . . He said, 'Put your fucking hands on the wall.' And . . . so I did.
>
> (*I Am That Girl*, 2018)

Lazarus mostly agrees with this account, but he denies swearing and says that while he did pull Mullins's stockings and underwear down, she didn't protest. Mullins told the jury that Lazarus became 'frustrated' and 'aggressive' after she informed him she wanted to go back inside a nightclub to her friend and she just froze:

> Being trapped with someone you don't know . . . you don't know where you are, you don't know how to leave . . . and someone is . . . what I thought was threatening me. I thought the safest thing for me to do is to do what he says. . . . There wasn't any request. It was a demand. From someone I had never met before. In a dark alleyway. Alone. And I was scared. . . . I just thought, 'Just do what he says and then you can go.' . . . I didn't know him. And you know, the few things he said to me before we went outside were just nice, calm, normal things and then all of a sudden, after I tried to leave it was, 'Put your fucking hands on the wall,' it wasn't, 'No, please, stay with me.'
>
> (*I Am That Girl*, 2018)

Afterwards, Lazarus asked Mullins to put her name in his phone. In court, he would say it was to add to a list of women's names he called 'the trophy list' (*I Am That Girl*, 2018). The next day, Lazarus sent text messages to a friend: 'I honestly have zero recollection of calling you, was a sick night. Took a chick's virginity, lol,' he wrote. 'Bahahaha. Nice popping [those] cherries.

Tight?' the friend replied. 'So tight . . . It's a pretty gross story. Tell ya later,' Lazarus wrote (*I Am That Girl*, 2018).

Mullins's account of what happened that night, and of her subsequent poor treatment by the legal system, highlights the difficulties of proving non-consent in a legal system that not only prioritises the defendant's perception of consent over the victim's experience of trauma and coercion but privileges an unspoken cultural (mis)understanding of consent. Despite Mullins's consistent assertion that she did not consent, Lazarus's belief in her consent was deemed reasonable by the court, illustrating the pervasive influence of rape myths in legal adjudications. The Lazarus cases led to significant media attention and public debate in Australia that focused on the legal definition of consent. Following the *Four Corners* programme 'I Am That Girl' (2018), the NSW Attorney-General announced that the NSW Law Reform Commission would review and report on consent in relation to sexual assault offences. The Commission produced a final report that recommended changes to the law,[1] which were subsequently implemented.[2]

The Lazarus cases hinged on consent, so in that sense, it makes sense that public outrage about the injustice to Mullins led to changes that improved the law on the basis of consent. Saxon Mullins's story has moved between legal and cultural domains, supporting the current dominant response of redressing sexual violence with a focus on consent while sidelining other significant issues. This response is generally seen to address the cultural or social problem of 'rape culture,' with the belief that the way to counter harm and stop sexual violation is to educate the population in general and young people in particular on what consent *is*. Yet research on the efficacy of consent education in reducing sexual violence has yielded mixed results; for instance, Melanie Beres's study highlights that while consent education has transformative potential, there is scepticism about its ability to change perpetrating behaviour (Beres, 2020). Further, the didactic approach detracts from the fundamental reasons that sexual violence permeates our society; it sidelines issues of power, leading with the assumption that, collectively and individually, people commit acts of sexual violence (and implicitly, that victim/survivors are unwitting targets of violence) due to lack of understanding, rather than because people will exercise power over one another. Reading over Saxon Mullins's account in the previous section, it isn't clear at all

1 New South Wales Law Reform Commission, *Consent in Relation to Sexual Offences. Final Report*. September 2020 https://lawreform.nsw.gov.au/documents/Publications/Reports/Report%20148.pdf.

2 For example, The Crimes Legislation Amendment (Sexual Consent Reforms) Act 2021 implemented consent reforms that aim to clarify consent provisions in the Crimes Act (1900), including that consent is a free and voluntary agreement that should not be presumed—discussed previously.

why consent would be the focus—rather, a number of other behaviours and factors 'flash up' for attention. Reading Mullins's account, the most striking factors include Lazarus's acts of deception, which meant that Mullins was disoriented in a back lane, intoxicated, when she expected to be inside in a 'VIP room' near other people; Lazarus's false imprisonment of Mullins after she declared her wish to return indoors; and Lazarus's coercive statements and forceful actions (including, arguably, battery and common assault). Lazarus deceived Mullins by inviting her to a 'VIP room' and then instead taking her to a back alley behind the club. Intoxicated and disoriented, she was very much in a vulnerable position—she was still a teenager; she was six years younger than Lazarus, who was the son of an owner of the club; she was physically smaller; and she wasn't familiar with the club she was in, or even the city she had travelled to. Trauma research reveals that fawning and freezing are typical responses for victims, possibly producing what Lazarus, in this case, subjectively interpreted as 'consent' (and a judge agreed with him) despite Lazarus's assessment being objectively unreasonable, even reckless. Why, then, is consent the hinge that determines legal and cultural understandings of sexual violence when that hinge involves such a narrow examination of dialogue and conduct in contrast to the more significant factors of power and duress—the material realities of age, gender and class, and the range of contextual circumstances in the time period around the act of assault?

The Cultural Framework of Consent and the *Bildungsroman* of the Girl

When the coming-of-age genre centres on a girl protagonist, the narrative frequently focuses on the experience of trauma, more specifically on sexual violence, as the key to a young woman's psychological, ethical, and existential development. The power of this trope is evidenced by the fact that the early English novel began with the *bildungsroman* of young women being threatened with rape or 'seduction.' Samuel Richardson's *Pamela; or Virtue Rewarded*, published in 1740, unfolds through a series of letters written by a young servant, 15-year-old Pamela Andrews, to her parents. After the death of her mistress, Pamela is targeted by her master, Mr. B., who attempts to 'seduce' her and later tries to rape her. Pamela consistently resists Mr. B., maintaining her virtue and religious faith. Over time, Mr. B.'s intentions transform from an intention to commit violence to an intention to 'love,' and he proposes marriage. Pamela, initially cautious, eventually accepts his offer of marriage, and the novel concludes with her social rise and moral vindication, both seen as being rewards for her sustained virtue, tested through the ruse of 'seduction.' Richardson's subsequent novel, *Clarissa, or the History of a Young Lady* (Richardson, 1748), one of the longest novels in the English language, takes up these same themes and dilemmas.

Clarissa tells the story of Clarissa Harlowe, a young woman manipulated by both her family and her 'suitor,' Robert Lovelace, who all attempt to convince her to trade her virginity for a higher social status. Clarissa steadfastly refuses this 'seduction,' but eventually Lovelace abducts Clarissa, and then brutally rapes her, leading to her social ruin and death. *Clarissa* is structured by the binary of consent/resistance. Sexual violence is not so much an event in the novel as a continuing structure, the context within which Clarissa's ethical and material realities are produced. Sexual violence is bound up with the framework of consent: Clarissa's personhood and moral growth have their origins in trauma, and the narrative of character development occurs via threats and scenes of sexual violence. Not only is sexual violence a major trope in the *bildungsroman* for girls but it is constitutive of the main characters' humanity. We see these effects in historical novels, including *Evelina* (Burney, 1778), *Tess of the D'urbervilles* (Hardy, 1891), and *Lolita* (Nabokov, 1955). This fetishisation is also strong in contemporary genre and literary fiction—*The Girl with the Dragon Tattoo* (2008), *Fifty Shades of Grey* (2011), *The Virgin Suicides (1993)*—in genres ranging from thriller and soft porn to tragedy. Fiona Nelson argues that there is a 'dead girl genre of Young Adult (YA) literature'—books where 'dead' is represented as a viable sexual subject position for teenage girls, who are immersed in a culture that precludes their full agency (Nelson, 2017, p. 39).

This trope is thematised in Kate Reed Perry's novel *True Story* (Penguin Books, 2021). Alice, a high school student who learns she was sexually assaulted while unconscious, attempts to write about her experience for a contemporary *bildungsroman* genre, her college admissions essay. Alice writes draft after draft, each annotated by her teacher's comments ('Can this essay go deeper?'), and as readers, we witness her being taught the proper way to write about sexual violence at the same time that she is being taught to write herself into young adulthood. The novel tells Alice's story through a number of genres—trauma memoir, horror, confessional, thriller, and epistolary tale, the 'truth' seeming to elude all forms. But overall, it is a *bildungsroman*, a story of a young woman finding her identity and doing so by working through the truth of a trauma that is her origin story, represented as her core.

Creators also write against this tradition, rewriting the figure of the girl and playing with the genre of *bildungsroman*. For example, Frow, Hardie, and Smith argue that the colonies assume greater significance in re-worked versions of the *bildungsroman*, where the colonies serve as sites of critique, speaking back to Empire, rather than merely as sites for the material advancement of young men, further complicating the genre's narrative expectations (Frow et al., 2020, p. 1905). These counter-*bildungsromans* are explored later in this chapter and also in Chapter 4 in my reading of the novels of Alexis Wright.

The Didactic Turn and the Limits of Consent Education

The didactic approach to addressing sexual violence, which focuses on educating individuals about consent, has gained prominence in Australia. This strategy involves two main components: first, legal reforms aimed at providing clearer guidelines and definitions of consent, such as specifying that silence or lack of physical resistance does not constitute consent. Second, educational programs designed to teach young people about consent are increasingly seen as a way to counter rape culture and reduce sexual violence, focusing on what are perceived to be the root causes, which include cultural attitudes and norms related to masculinity, sexuality, and gender (Powell and Henry, 2014, p. 3). A report by the National Association of Services Against Sexual Violence highlights that these programs, especially as implemented within schools, are the most common approach to prevention in the country (Carmody, 2009, p. 14). The Women NSW strategy further supports this approach, aiming to enhance knowledge, awareness, and understanding of the causes of domestic and family violence and influencing attitudes to encourage behavioural change (Women NSW, 2016, p. 3). The importance of education in these efforts is underscored by dedicated funding for educational activities under 'Respectful Relationships' initiatives (Walden and Wall, 2014, p. 11).

Jess Hill's three-part documentary *Asking for it: Creating Consent Culture* reads:

> Jess Hill explores the contemporary sexual revolution seeking to bring about an era of 'enthusiastic consent' at a time when millions of Australians are living with an epidemic of sexual violence.
>
> (SBS, 2023)

The documentary is framed through the framework consent, and understanding/education is seen as a way through 'rape culture' with the organising question of 'How can we create a consent culture?'[3] Reflecting on Saxon Mullins's story and those of other survivors and advocates, Hill interrogates how Australia, as a nation, can replace our rape culture with a culture of consent. Australia is clearly in need of change, as the three-part documentary argues: 1/3 Australian women have experienced sexual violence, the highest of any Western country, while 1/5 Australians say that women who claim they are sexually assaulted are lying or exaggerating (SBS, 2023, ep. 2).

3 Meek traces the origins of 'consent culture' to the 2011 blog of Kitty Stryker, who later edited the 2017 compilation *Ask: Building Consent Culture*; by 2014, the term 'consent culture' had become so popular that it was included in the Urban Dictionary (Meek, 2021, p. 104).

Jess Hill, the presenter and consultant producer on the series, argues the following:

> As #MeToo has shown, 'sexual freedom' can be expressed at great cost to those who've had sex they didn't want. The consent revolution is the next evolutionary step towards a truly liberated sexuality where everyone involved can expect to feel pleasure. I hope this series really gets people thinking about their own life experiences, and pumps new energy into the national movement to end rape culture.
>
> (SBS, 2023, ep. 1)

Asking For It draws on the testimony from a number of survivors. Saxon Mullins says in the documentary:

> a 'huge, huge part' of further moving the dial on our attitude toward and understanding of consent . . . is having relationships and sexuality education from day dot—young, young kids learning about their bodies and all of those tiny conversations that actually lead into really big ideas, and really big fundamental understandings from within.
>
> (SBS, 2023, ep. 1)

However, Mullins acknowledges that a didactic approach is not sufficient, emphasising the role of power relations, especially institutional power:

> The other part—which seems to me to be easy, but apparently is not—is not letting this kind of behaviour slide. . . . But our politicians, people in our justice system, police officers: we are allowing people who are the arbiters of our justice to perpetrate the violence of which we're trying to seek justice. . . . How can we work within a system like that? . . . Someone who is in a position of power, and they're not being called out for their bad behaviour—it continues that cycle of, 'Well, I would never do it, but I'm also not going to say anything about it. . . . You're not helping. You're perpetuating—that person thinks that their behaviour is OK.
>
> (SBS, 2023, ep. 1)

Mullins considers the significance of issues of power—of compliance, duress, social and cultural pressure, bullying, peer pressure, and the power dynamics of gender and age—alongside advocating for quality consent education, embedded across our national curriculum, from kindergarten onwards. Although the series frames consent as a 'cultural' issue, the interviews with Mullins and other survivors show that they see these issues as issues of power rather than of culture or knowledge.

In 2021, Chanel Contos, a young Australian woman who was then studying in the UK, posted on Instagram asking people to share their stories of sexual assault during their schooling years; the post went viral, and almost 7,000 people, mostly girls and young women, sent in testimonies describing experiences of sexual assault. Virtually none of these instances had been reported to police, and almost all the assaults were perpetrated by people (mostly boys and young men) they knew. In her subsequent book, *Consent Laid Bare* (MacMillan, 2021), Contos argues that when it comes to sex, we are still working with an outdated social contract that privileges men's pleasure at the expense of women's suffering. Contos asks whether consent is possible in a world where female sexuality is overwhelmed by the forces of porn, patriarchy, and male entitlement and hopes to give girls and women the encouragement to seek sex that is truly enjoyable. The book frames the answer to the problem of sexual violence as being didactic, *Consent Laid Bare* equipping girls and women with the information they need to properly consent, while asking boys and men to become advocates for sex that is centred around intimacy rather than fuelled by aggression. Chanel Contos is also the founder of Teach Us Consent, an initiative pushing for mandatory consent education in Australia, and for this was honoured with the Australian Human Rights Commission Young People's Medal in 2021 and the title of NSW Young Woman of the Year in 2023. Chanel's work has been recognised with the distinguished Diana Award, and in 2022, she was named one of BBC's 100 inspiring and influential women globally and was recently chosen by Julia Gillard to lead the Youth Advisory Committee for the Global Institute for Women's Leadership.

Consent Laid Bare tells the story of Contos herself as a teenager, a *bildungsroman* where the turning point is the moment in which she was taught the meaning of consent. With this new knowledge, Contos retrospectively understands past acts against herself and her schoolmates as sexual assault, establishing both sexual violence and consent as the hinges of existential development for their adolescence. She tells the story as follows:

> I'm 15 years old and my school has booked a speaker for the Year 10 students. I am excited because it means I get to miss science and spend the day with two friends I don't normally see in class. . . . We are told sexual assault means sexual intercourse with another person without that person's consent. We are taught that this includes genital penetration with any part of the body of another person or a foreign object, including digitally, and placing a penis into the mouth of another person, or cunnilingus—without consent. The most surprising thing this man says to us is that if someone is intoxicated, consent is void. Hearing these definitions is how my friends and I re-label acts of unpleasant/painful/awkward/embarrassing/drunk sexual experiences to date as criminal acts. . . . As we continue to listen to the speaker, we mouth the names of various boys, wide-eyed with shock but also with an overwhelming sense of validation. Behaviours

> that we have regarded as completely normal, like arse-grabbing or groping, are suddenly being labelled as 'indecent assault.' Surely not.
>
> (Contos, 2023, p. 25)

In this framework, consent and knowledge are the agents of political change: they allow Contos and her friends to 're-label acts of unpleasant/painful/awkward/embarrassing/drunk sexual experiences' and 'partying behaviour' as 'criminal acts' (Contos, 2023, p. 25). These are important points of individual empowerment, but I do think that foregrounding the role of consent—and individual agency—detracts from the serious structural problems that facilitate sexual violence. Contos describes this moment as the beginning of her journey advocating for consent education. She wonders how her life would have been different if the consent talk had been given when she was 13 instead of 15:

> When I found out that the guy who sexually assaulted me had also sexually assaulted another girl, my first thought was: 'If I had known what consent was, I could have reported him and stopped him from doing the same thing to her.'
>
> (Contos, 2023, p. 28)

I think this is especially problematic when the didactic approach is seen as a solution for managing perpetrators or potential perpetrators of sexual violence, as though the narrative of a girl understanding the nature of violence can be used as a structure to understand perpetration of that violence—that both perpetrators and victim/survivors inhabit the same *bildungsroman* framed by consent. Contos continues:

> Now I think: 'If he had known what consent was, maybe he would have never done it to me, or anyone else.' . . . In order to process the magnitude of boys who have committed sexual assault, I've adopted the view that the vast majority of these instances were perpetrated without the perpetrator understanding the weight of their actions because they lacked any education in consent. Again, the type of sexual assault that I am talking about here is one where the confusion comes from the absence of understanding the nature of consent.
>
> (Contos, 2023, p. 29)

Although Contos's book is framed as an argument for consent education, there are many times when Contos acknowledges deeper structural issues of power:

> We end up teaching men 'how not to rape' when we should actually be striving for a world where healthy intimacy is the standard, and rape would be

> a bizarre thing to do if you were operating within a social contract based on equality. This is especially difficult in a world that's structured to cater to male satisfaction and is saddled with taboos around female sexuality.
>
> (Contos, 2023, p. 53)

Contos thereby divides sexual violence into different categories—sexual assault based on a lack of understanding and sexual assault based on structural issues. This is problematic, because the seeming opaqueness of consent, and of sexual violence, is part of the continuum of gender violence. Women are conditioned to fear sexual violence from strangers, rapists who are 'angry' or 'sadistic,' as Contos writes in her first chapter (Contos, 2023). But Contos is focused, she says, on what she describes as the 'entitled opportunist rapist,' the type of boy she grew up with, the type otherwise likely to be described as a 'good guy,' even as he is actively rewarded by society for seeking his own gratification (Contos, 2023, p. 23). These dynamics, she says, were magnified in the milieu of elite Sydney private schools in which she grew up, a world of parties and luxury holidays and rugby games at the intersection of wealth and whiteness and class. This world shapes the country's corridors of power—from the law and politics to the media. And yet, Contos argues, this opportunist is likely to be swayed by education. The entitled opportunist, Contos writes, is 'unlikely to reoffend if they are held accountable for their actions or taught explicitly what consent is' (Contos, 2023, p. 23). Understanding the nature of sexual violence is important, but didacticism cannot be the main framework of response; these schoolboys are operating within the wider system of patriarchy, and in the examples Contos examines, patriarchy is compounded by the privilege of wealth and institutional power. If didacticism is foregrounded, then these power dynamics are heavily disguised and maintained. Whether they understand consent or not, boys and young men usually aren't held accountable for their actions, so if education about consent is prioritised, this education becomes one of choice or preference rather than compulsion, whereas girls cannot opt out of these power structures only by knowing of them. Contos researched and wrote her masters thesis on the connection between colonialism and the history of elite boys' schools in Australia and has a deep understanding of how sexual violence is structural and how/why Australia's foundational and continuing colonial violence has produced contemporary Australia, which has one of the highest rates of sexual violence in the OECD (SBS, 2023, ep. 3). For young thinkers and activists, then, 'consent' is standing in for a number of key structural concepts, but mainstream cultural, political, and quasi-legal arenas are only picking up on the 'consent' narrative, insisting that these more complex ideas be organised through the dominant, narrow idea of consent.

The didactic approach has historical origins in the 1970s and 1980s when radical feminists used the term 'rape culture' to highlight the structural nature of sexual violence. But the current paradigm has transformed this approach into a cultural overlay that distracts from the core issues of patriarchy, colonialism, and late capitalism. This shift has led to a concerning disarticulation of sexual violence from its political roots, moving it into the realm of personal and interpersonal dynamics. By focusing predominantly on 'culture,' we risk neglecting the structural and material conditions that underpin sexual violence and diminishing the role of institutions in prevention efforts. If we interpret 'culture' as encompassing narratives, norms, and beliefs, the cultural paradigm suggests that we should prevent sexual violence by challenging and reframing gender norms, representations, and attitudes. Intervention at this level is important, but we also need to push against what Anna Hush terms 'the dominant injunction to "change the culture"' (Hush, 2023, p. 10), since we need to transform not only the culture of sexual violence but the material conditions that co-produce this culture. This includes the political requirement to challenge continuing colonialism, as well as conditions ranging from neo-liberal 'risk management' approaches to harm to the gendered and racialised reality of late capitalism. Writing specifically about policies that presume a 'universally experienced "campus rape culture,"' Grace Kyungwon Hong (2018) argues that a didactic, culture-focused perspective is 'inadequate because it fattens out the very different hierarchies of power that are animated by and contribute to sexual violence,' including racism, queerphobia, and racism. This means that the rape culture narrative reinscribes the universal (and false) view that everyone is equally at risk of rape.

The emphasis on 'culture' and didacticism have had perverse effects: instead of drawing attention to the structural issues behind sexual violence, where the rapist is seen as someone who is acting out the traditional patriarchal norm, the rapist is seen as an exception to this norm, as an individual who has not been adequately taught how to form healthy, respectful relationships that emphasise clear communication about consent (Messner, 2016, p. 60). Messner, Greenberg, and Peretz have named this 'the good man/bystander approach' to rape prevention, dominant since the 2000s (Messner et al., 2015, pp. 121–123), and exemplified by the 'My Strength Is Not for Hurting' education campaign in US schools (Murphy, 2009). Messner explains that this education program teaches young men to use their masculinity ethically, such as by understanding respectful intimacy and respecting their sexual partners as equals. It also includes a 'bystander' component that encourages men to intervene to prevent acts of sexual violence by other men, thus intervening in the rape culture within male groups and organisations (Messner, 2016, p. 62). While the focus on a 'better' masculinity is clearly better than the approach of 'boys will be boys,' there are problems with framing sexual violence as an individual ethical issue rather than as a wider political and structural issue, as the individualist approach deflects the structural and institutional contexts of violence. This deflects from the structure of patriarchy itself—in this framework, 'good' masculinity is the saviour of women, rather than the critical lens being focused on masculinity/patriarchy itself. For Messner, '(t)oday's antiviolence pedagogy deploys dominant forms of masculinity, rather than arguing for masculinity's eradication or radical transformation' (Messner, 2016, p. 62). As Tanya Serisier argues, this approach is also classed and racialised: the didactic approach to the prevention of sexual violence positions middle-class white men as those who possess 'respectable' knowledge about consent, and those without such knowledge as ignorant and wanting (Serisier, 2021, p. 15). Salter argues that the didactic approach corresponds with neoliberal characterisations of social problems using frameworks of individual failure and 'bad' cultures (Salter, 2016a, p. 466; see also Salter, 2012, 2016b, 2016c). Further, the focus on 'bad' cultures can slide into a focus on 'other cultures,' a tendency that is heightened in our fascist times of anti-immigrant sentiment, Islamophobia and anti-Black racism (Phipps, 2020, pp. 12–34). Examples of this in the Australian conservative media include frequent click-bait arguments about 'sexual assault by young migrants from cultures with deeply ingrained hostility towards Western women' (Oriel, 2019).

The idea of 'rape culture' is also integral to some of the feminist literature around how law frames sexual violence through scholarship that asserts that the law has reached a 'best practice plateau,' and justice for victims is now being held back primarily by the aberrant 'attitudes' of criminal justice actors charged with implementing that law (Russell, 2017, p. 274). But it is the law itself that is the problem, Russel argues, not an inchoate 'culture' that attends it: instead of looking at culture, we should look at structural issues, including courtroom processes, and law's complicity in its own failures, since 'it relies, for its own survival and coherence, on the erasure of woman as a subject' (Russell, 2017, p. 275).

While consent education is an important component in the fight against sexual violence, it must be part of a broader strategy that addresses deep-rooted power dynamics and structural inequalities. The instrumentalisation of girls and young women within the consent discourse must be avoided by paying attention to their observations about how structural inequalities and power imbalances have also determined their experiences of sexual violence. We also need to more deeply investigate the nature of 'rape culture' and how it relates to the consent framework.

Taking on Rape Culture in the Cultural Domain

Since the 1970s and 1980s, the figure of the girl has undergone significant reclamation in popular culture, challenging the narratives that previously normalised and perpetuated rape culture. Recent films and novels have begun to critically interrogate these representations, reclaiming the narrative to highlight issues of consent, power dynamics, and the systemic structures that perpetuate sexual violence. These contemporary narratives reflect a shift towards acknowledging and addressing structural issues, providing a more nuanced and critical perspective on the experiences of girls and women, and moving beyond the framework of consent.

Popular culture has been called out for normalising and even producing rape culture. This pervasiveness naturalises rape as not only a social reality but as a mainstream fantasy (Projansky, 2001, p. 3). Reflecting on the 1980s John Hughes films that made her a star in *The New Yorker* (6 April 2018), actor Molly Ringwald recalled how, in *The Breakfast Club* (1985), Bender and Claire (whom she played) become a couple after Bender 'sexually harasses Claire throughout the film' (Ringwald, 2018, n.p.), including a scene where Bender crawls under her school desk to look up her skirt. Similarly, in *Sixteen Candles* (1984), the 'geek' sexually harasses Samantha (Ringwald) again and again, until she relents and gives him her underwear as evidence of a sexual conquest that never occurred. The teen films of the 1970s and 1980s 'often epitomised rape culture' (Meek, 2021a, p. 101)—with notable mainstream films including *Porky's* (1981), *Revenge of the Nerds* (1984), and *Weird Science* (1985), which show teen boys forcing or tricking girls into sex, spying on naked girls, selling photos of naked girls, and having sex with intoxicated girls. Brett Kavanaugh, defending himself against sexual assault allegations, cited teen movies from the 1980s to minimise his violence as one of the 'goofy or stupid things' he did in high school (Paschal, 2018, n.p.). As Sarah Projansky argues, 'depictions of rape are a pervasive part of this culture, embedded in all of its complex media forms, entrenched in the landscape of visual imagery' (Projansky, 2001, p. 2).

Recent films, TV series, and novels interrogate the boundaries and implications of the role of consent in contemporary discourses about sexual violence. Texts such as *Baby Reindeer* (dir. Tofilska and Bornebusch, 2024); *Consent* (dir. Amrani, 2023); *Cat Person* (dir. Fogei, 2023); Carly-Williams, 2024); Angel, K., *Tomorrow Sex Will Be Good Again* (2021); Orenstein, P., *Boys and Sex* (2020) probe the adequacy of the term, its application, and the hidden power dynamics that the framework of consent may obscure, querying under what conditions true autonomy can be exercised. As two key texts that are typical examples of this trend, Kate Elizabeth Russell's novel *My Dark Vanessa* (2020) and the 2020 HBO TV series *I May Destroy You* examine the relationship between knowledge and power in the concept of 'consent' and question whether consent is the best framework to make sense of sexual violence rather than questions of power—duress, coercion at an individual level, and patriarchy, capitalism, and colonialism at a structural level.

My Dark Vanessa tells the story of the 'relationship' Vanessa Wye, a 15-year-old boarding school student, and Jacob Strane, her 42-year-old Harvard-educated English Lit teacher. Moving between the timelines of 2001, when Vanessa is 15, and 2017, when Vanessa is an adult during the rise of #MeToo, Russell examines the way the adult Vanessa recharacterises the dynamic she had with her teacher. Vanessa's interpretation of that 'relationship' changes from one of 'first love' to one of abuse. What is particularly striking is the shift for the reader in how they view Vanessa: in one timeline, the reader experiences Vanessa from her teenaged point of view, as a young woman enthralled by her own 'powers' of sexuality; in the second timeline, the reader experiences the adult Vanessa's view of teenaged self as a child who is manipulated and abused by the adult Strane. The legal narrative shifts from a story of teenage Vanessa having a romance with her teacher, where she consents to sex, to the reframing of these acts by adult Vanessa as criminal acts, and the reframing of their early relationship as not one of flirtation but of grooming. After their 'relationship' ends, they stay in contact, with Vanessa continuing to be psychologically trapped by Strane's fantasy well into adulthood. Russell also exposes the fetishisation of the young girl not only by the perpetrator but by our culture more widely. The novel plays with the mainstream trope of the teenage girl who is viewed not as a child but as a young seductress whose coming-of-age necessarily revolves around her sexuality. The novel interrogates how culturally we continue to hold young girls partially responsible for the criminal acts of men and how this culpability is internalised by victims. Russell plays with some of the leading cultural texts that centre this trope: for example, Strane grooms Vanessa through a shared love of literature, and Strane gifts her a copy of Nabokov's *Lolita*. The novel argues that Strane's criminal acts of grooming occur partly through didactic acts, and the novel itself is didactic, showing how Vanessa comes to understand the true nature of Strane's act—and hopefully, the reader in turn absorbs this session. But it is also important to see this reframing within its political context, #MeToo providing an audience for this work.

In the 2020 HBO TV series *I May Destroy You*, Michaela Coel presents the story of a working-class English black woman named Arabella who is drugged and then sexually assaulted at a bar by an unknown man. The series, inspired by Coel's own experiences with sexual assault, explores the nuanced terrain of ambiguous sexual encounters, which Coel has termed 'blurry thefts of consent,' and the profound impact of these events (*Dazed Digital*, 21 September 2021). *I May Destroy You* explores the challenging healing process of a character grappling with the reality of multiple types of assaults inflicted on herself and her close friends in the course of everyday life. While she attempts the process of healing from a stranger rape through the support of her friends, Bella again finds herself in the position of victim as she is violated by a seemingly consensual sexual act in the episode 'That Was Fun.' While having sex with Zain, a fellow writer helping Bella finish her book, Zain removes the condom without Bella's consent and then later pleads ignorance at her lack of approval. While she is shocked when she finds out what happened, she accepts his explanation of 'I thought you knew' as miscommunication in the moment. Later, Bella becomes aware of the violation as two women on a podcast she is listening to describe the act of removing the condom without consent as 'stealthing,' using Zain's words verbatim as a common excuse used to deceive sexual partners. Two police investigators inform Bella that Zain's actions are considered rape, even if the sex started with consent. 'The problem is when people don't know what is a crime, and what isn't a crime they don't report it. And then people get away with it,' the investigator tells Bella, this didactic moment inspiring Bella to take matters into her own hands (*I May Destroy You* 2021). Armed with the knowledge that Zain's actions are a crime, Bella decides to 'out' him in front of his mother, his publishers, and an audience gathered to hear each of them read from their respective upcoming books. Bella calmly and coolly tells the audience of her assault: 'Zain Sareen is a rapist. . . . He is a rapist, not rape-adjacent, or a bit rapey. He's a rapist under UK law' (*I May Destroy You* 2021). Here, knowledge is thematised as the key to culpability: it is only when Bella understands the nature of the act that she can pursue justice, both through the criminal system and by extra-legal means. And yet it is only when power relations are in Bella's favour that there are consequences for Zain's assault. The police inform Bella that Zain's actions were criminal, but this is not only a transfer of knowledge—in doing so, the institutional power of the police (and state law) also supports Bella. Similarly, when Bella 'outs' Zain, it is in the context of a supportive community of allies, friends, and family: her reframing of the act is important, but also important are the social and power relations involved.

Kate Elizabeth Russell's *My Dark Vanessa* and Michaela Coel's *I May Destroy You* challenge the notion that consent alone can address the complexities of sexual violence. Through the figure of the girl, these stories demand a more comprehensive standard that addresses both individual experiences and the broader social and political contexts in which they occur. By doing so, they emphasise that autonomy and justice require challenging not just interpersonal dynamics but the political structures. However, the fact that consent is still thematised, even to be complicated or rejected, shows its power in mainstream culture—it's as though sexual violence cannot be represented without it.

The Political Economy of Consent

Consent is a conceptual linchpin in our understanding and adjudication of sexual violence, framing both legal and cultural narratives. More widely, consent is important in our economic, social, and political lives, from our everyday experience of 'consenting' to dense legal terms with multinational corporations to the tacit understanding that we have opted-in to the social contract. 'It would be hard to overestimate the importance of the roles of consent and contract in modern conceptions of legitimate social, economic, and political relations,' Moira Gatens writes (Gatens, 2008, p. 31). Consent has travelled across disciplines and domains as a trope and a key term, influencing public debate in both private and public law (Drakopoulou, 2007).

Consent, and its gendered nature, is therefore operating at different levels of politics, law, and economics—from our political origin stories to its role in the production of the gendered legal subject. Any analysis of legal consent requires an understanding of the gendered nature of consent in our social contract origin stories, although, as Nan Seuffert points out, legal feminists have paid less attention to this nexus for the legal subject in contrast to feminist political theorists' focus on the political subject (Seuffert, 2020, p. 156). Consent anchors and justifies our modern state through the narrative of a 'legitimising consensuality' seen to underlie our social contract (Mills, 2007, p. 82). Contract theory underpins liberal legal law and the democratic origins of modern states where the social contract, as theorised by John Locke, is comprised by individuals who submit to authority by consent (John Locke, *The Second Treatise of Government*, Liberal Arts Press, first published 1690, 1952 ed). This consent is said to be tacitly given by any person who enjoys the benefits of government, including through the possession of property or use of facilities such as a public road (Locke, 1690, p. 119). Carole Pateman famously argued that this kind of consent is not meaningful and is essentially submission, even enforced submission (Pateman, 1980, pp. 150–151). Nevertheless, consent is said to legitimise the modern state. In *The Sexual Contract*, Carole Pateman argued that liberal social contract theory is inherently patriarchal (Pateman, 1980) and that these stark origins cannot be overcome by re-iterations and re-workings: instead of facilitating cooperation on equal terms, the function of contracts is to legitimate patriarchal (and other) forms of domination under the pretence of equality. For Pateman, contract is a central problem for subordination, 'a central modern mechanism for the reproduction of sexual and racial hierarchies' (Mills, 1997, p. 7). In their book *Contract and Domination*, Carole Pateman and Charles W. Mills engage in a comprehensive dialogue on the relevance and potential future of contract theory. Their work is a means to explain the ways that the model of the consenting subject favours the powerful white cis man and a means by which women and non-white subjects are subordinated (Pateman and Mills, 2007). While Pateman critiques liberalism for its role in perpetuating inequality, Mills offers a contrasting viewpoint, suggesting that contract theory can be repurposed for radical political endeavours, especially by viewing contract through a diagnostic lens. Mills introduces the notion of a 'domination contract' as an alternative to traditional liberal social contract theory. This concept aims to use the contractual framework as a diagnostic device, a way of understanding racial, sexual, and economic injustices, as well as a way to de-naturalise gender and race categories (Pateman and Mills, 2007, pp. 79–105).

The contract is an abstraction of material relations of power, proceeding *as though* each party were equal, but behind this abstraction is the reality of racial, classed, and gendered power. Accordingly, Wendy Brown argues that consent is a mechanism that produces authority and subordination at the same time that this authority (and subordination) is legitimated (1995, p. 163). Given this context, it is difficult to see how consent can be reformed in the direction of social justice—either legally or culturally. Modern fictions of consent in fact reproduce and disguise structural inequalities, notably the colonisation of Indigenous people (Tully, 2011, p. 242). Maria Giannacopolous emphasises the intricate relationship between the concept of consent and the establishment of apparent 'legitimacy' in the founding narratives of settler colonial states (Giannacopoulos, 2020). Giannacopolous analyses how these narratives, by relying on the notion of consent, ironically show the illegitimacy of states such as Australia, where sovereignty was never in fact surrendered by First Nations peoples. Giannacopoulos calls this link between lack of consent in the founding of the state and the state's ongoing refusal to engage with its violent origins, *nomocide*, or the genocide of law: 'the killing function performed by law in reproducing colonial conditions in contemporary Australia' (Giannacopoulos, 2020, p. 250). Giannacopolous's position parallels Pateman's critique of hypothetical voluntarism, suggesting that such after-the-fact consent cannot rectify the foundational issues of consent and legitimacy in settler colonial contexts. Further, formal consent denies the reality of colonial violence that constrains the agency of First Nations women, evidenced by the higher rates of sexual violence against First Nations women in the past and in the present; under colonialism, the consent of First Nations women is 'perpetually assumed,' a habit that 'writes out the violence, coercion and duress of white men' (Behrendt, 2000, p. 355). Tess Ryan argues that sexual violence against First Nations communities cannot be fully understood without considering the broader context of colonisation and the structural power discrepancies it introduced, thus making 'consent' redundant (Ryan, 2023, p. 103).

The Aesthetics of Subordination Through Consent

Aesthetics and affect play pivotal roles in perpetuating the trope of consent as the cornerstone of the social contract, which in turn animate both legal and cultural uses of consent. This section examines films that focus on the figure of the girl, utilising extreme genres such as horror to explore themes of consent and subordination. Through these narratives, we see how the aesthetic and emotional dimensions of consent are manipulated to uphold systems of power and control. David Robert Mitchell's film *It Follows* thematises anxiety and horror around the concept of consent. The film, which has not been widely recognised as a commentary on consent, portrays sexual violence as an unstoppable force that operates according to its own rules and logic. *It Follows* critiques the limitations of consent as a protective framework, highlighting the broader power dynamics at play and the inadequacy of consent alone in addressing the complexities of sexual violence. Lars von Trier's *Dogville* serves as an aesthetic and affective critique of liberal law and democracy, centred on the figure of the degraded girl/woman. The film, the first in von Trier's USA: Land of Opportunity trilogy, portrays the inhabitants of a small town who subject a fugitive, Grace Margaret Mulligan, to escalating violence and degradation, all while justifying their actions as lawful and just. Both *Dogville* and *It Follows* illustrate the interplay between aesthetics, affect, and the concept of consent, revealing how cultural narratives can obscure the material conditions of subordination and exploitation. These films challenge viewers to question the validity of consent as a cornerstone of justice and to consider the deeper structural forces that perpetuate violence and inequality. By focusing on the figure of the girl, these narratives emphasise the need to move beyond abstract notions of consent and engage with the material realities of power, control, and subjugation in contemporary society.

It Follows: Unwanted Sex as a Force-field

It Follows (dir. David Robert Mitchell, 2014) is a horror film that has not been widely considered a film about sexual violence and consent but very clearly thematises anxiety, even horror, about these concepts. The film begins on an archetypal suburban American street. It's dusk, and quiet, apart from birdsong. The camera pans to an average house and, in the continuing silence, a teenaged girl, Annie, runs out the front door. Annie runs along the street in underclothes and high heels—she has probably been getting ready for bed when something happened. Annie suddenly stops in the street and stares at something that the audience can't see. Her neighbour, then her father, each call out to her, but she ignores them, transfixed by something that nobody else can see, but which nevertheless terrifies her. She runs back inside her home to get her car keys, then comes outside again and drives away. In the next shot, Annie is sitting on the edge of a body of water in the light of her car's headlights, fearful but despondent, as she leaves a final message for her parents. The last shot of Annie is her dismembered and grotesquely re-arranged body on the shoreline—her legs are torn and twisted. Whatever Annie was fearing has caught up with her.

The next scene shifts back to suburbia, and back to apparent happy normality, focusing on a different teenage girl, Jay (Maika Monroe). We first see Jay floating, relaxed, in an above-ground swimming pool, listening to the sound of children playing nearby. Jay then goes inside her house to get ready for a date with an apparently nice guy called Hugh (Jake Weary). They go on a date to the movies, where Hugh is scared by something that Jay can't see. They then have sex in Hugh's car, and Hugh cloroforms Jay. Once she is unconscious, Hugh ties Jay to a wheelchair in an abandoned building and explains to her the nature of the demon that is now pursuing her, thereby explaining to the viewer the rules of the monster that are an essential part of the horror genre. Hugh explains that because Jay has had sex with him, she will be followed, at a zombie's walking-pace, by a demon that only she and other cursed people can see and which will pursue her relentlessly until it kills her. Then the demon will come after Hugh, and back through the chain of people who have had sex with each other. The only way Jay can put some distance between herself and the demon is to have sex with someone else—whether consensual or not is not specified—and so pass the curse on to them. Hugh says,

> This thing . . . it's going to follow you. Somebody gave it to me, and I passed it to you. . . . It could look like someone you know, or it could be a stranger in a crowd. Whatever it helps to get close to you. It could look like anyone.
>
> (Mitchell, 2014, n.p.)

He encourages her to sleep with someone else and 'pass it along' as soon as she can:

> You can get rid of it, okay? Just sleep with someone as soon as you can. Just pass it along. If it kills you, it'll come after me. . . . Never go into a place that doesn't have more than one exit. It's very slow but it's not dumb.
>
> (Mitchell, 2014, n.p.)

As evidence of Hugh's speech, the demon emerges from the darkness at the edge of the building in the form of a naked woman, walking directly towards Jay. Hugh takes Jay home and places her on the nature strip, dressed only in her bra and underpants. Her sister Kelly (Lili Sepe) and friends Yara (Olivia Luccardi) and Paul (Keir Gilchrist) rush up to her and call the police, assuming that she has been sexually assaulted. The police ask, 'It was consensual?' 'Yeah,' Jay replies—meaning the sex, but not the chloroform or false imprisonment, and not the curse she has been assigned (Mitchell, 2014, n.p.). The demon relentlessly follows Jay, walking slowly but persistently towards her, and only she and others who have been cursed can see it. As Jay tries to cope with the terror and the growing sense of dread, she enlists the help of her friends, including her sister Kelly, her friend Paul, and their neighbour Greg (Daniel Zovatto). Together, they attempt various strategies to evade and understand the entity, including trying to track its origin and figuring out if there is a way to destroy it.

The great advantage of the genre of horror is that it can provide new visual, linguistic, affective, and aural frameworks to represent and explain sexual violence. Horror is particularly effective at giving language to the more extreme elements of human experience, exploring death and suffering in excessive and often nasty ways and foregrounding that which society normalises and makes invisible. Horror does this through innovative tropes, including haunting and monstrosity, and through figures such as the vampire, the demon, and the zombie.[4] In *Zombie Capitalism*, the political scientist McNally justifies a turn to horror as an antidote to our obliviousness, since 'capitalism—and the work that is integral to it—are so naturalised that we do not see the harms, or we accept them as natural, part of the routine and everyday' (McNally, 2011, p. 9). We draw upon horror to render the familiar strange. Elsewhere, Penny Crofts and I have developed the idea of *routine horror*, which encapsulates the horror of the everyday (Crofts and van Rijswijk, 2024). This idea builds upon Hannah Arendt's idea of the banality of evil, which she developed in response to the horrific events of the Holocaust and Eichmann's trial (Arendt, 1994). Arendt's use of the term *banality* can be interpreted in a number of ways, including an intention to break from traditional representations of evil as exceptional. For Arendt, Eichmann was a bureaucrat, who followed rules and simply wanted to be good at his job, and yet this seemingly anodyne thoughtlessness resulted in the brutal deaths of millions of people.[5] Here, we propose the concept of *routine horror* to develop Arendt's idea of banal evil further—going beyond an exploration of limit-events such as the Holocaust to explore how horror shapes the everyday laws and politics of our lives (Crofts and van Rijswijk, 2024). Routine horror provides an account of the slow violence that is structural and, more specifically, bound up in our institutions. For Rob Nixon, slow violence is 'a violence occur[ing] gradually and out of sight, a violence of delayed destruction . . . dispersed across time and space, an attritional violence that is typically not viewed as violence at all' (Nixon, 2011, p. 2). *It Follows* represents the routine horror of sexual violence: it represents sexual violence as a relentless, slow force, generating trauma that radiates beyond each victim-survivor. Almost nobody can escape this contagion of experiencing and producing harm. Throughout this horrific violence, the monotonous world of suburban normality continues. Scared for her life, Jay nevertheless continues with school, friends, the mall, and movies, her terror revealed to be part of the routine, violent normality of suburban life. There are no safe places—all are potential or actual sites of violence, and nobody else is able to see the demons who stalk the suburbs. The film's analogy to the high rates of sexual violence in our society, especially against teenage girls, is clear. Joshua Grimm argues that Jay's experience 'is that of a sexual assault victim' (Grimm, 2018, p. 62). Clearly, Jay has not given consent: while Jay was happy to have sex (she suggested to Hugh that they return to the car), consent was not given with full knowledge: she would likely not have consented to sex if she had known that Hugh was transferring a demon

4 There has recently been an explosion in innovative scholarship using the horror lens to provide new frameworks for culpability and suffering. See e.g., (Linnemann, 2022; Crofts, 2024, 2022a, 2022b; Crofts and van Rijswijk, 2024).

5 Arendt's representation of Eichmann as a bureaucrat motivated by promotion rather than any malice towards Jews has been challenged (Stangneth, 2016).

to her. Grimm says, 'In a film where the word "yes" is spoken just five times, while the word "no" is spoken 42 times, consent is a constant discussion' (Grimm, 2018, p. 63). Jay is initially met with incredulity when she explains her experience to her friends—nobody can see the entity besides her. The police take her statement but don't even track Hugh down, despite the fact that he has chloroformed and tied Jay up, and Jay has given the police his address. Further, the film is saturated by the imagery of sexual violence, representing its pervasiveness, which nobody besides Jay can see. The first time Jay sees the entity in her home, it takes the form of an assault victim: a young woman bruised and bloodied, her shirt torn and her hands tied behind her back. The entity takes the form of her friend Greg's mother, who then violently sexually assaults Greg until he is dead. For Grimm, 'Jay is battling a brutal sexual injustice only she can see' (Grimm, 2018, p. 64). This is obviously sex under a domain of force—consent is meaningless for both parties, in different ways. The perpetrator is in a moral and legal grey zone, at best, and the victim has no awareness of what's going on.

The film blends horror and psychological suspense, with a pervasive sense of paranoia and inevitability. The slow, inevitable approach of the entity creates a constant state of tension and fear, as Jay and her friends realise that the demon will never stop following its target. The ending of *It Follows* is intentionally left open to interpretation, contributing to the film's unsettling effect. After a series of failed attempts to evade the entity, Jay and her friends devise a plan to lure it into a swimming pool at a local high school. They hope to electrocute it using electrical appliances, but the plan goes awry. The entity, which has taken the form of Jay's father, attacks her in the pool. Eventually, Paul shoots the entity in the head, causing it to sink into the water. However, it remains unclear whether the entity is truly dead.

In the final scenes, Jay and Paul have sex. The film concludes with Jay and Paul walking hand-in-hand down a suburban street, with a figure walking behind them in the distance. The camera lingers on this figure, leaving viewers to wonder whether it is the entity or simply someone passing by—the entity may still be following them, implying that the curse might be inescapable. *It Follows* posits sexual violence as an operating force field: it has rules, it has power dynamics, it has a logic that can be navigated but not, at present, be defeated. The affect it produces is a sense of hopelessness, even horror, at individual and collective efforts to thwart sexual violence. Since this violence and trauma cannot be resolved, people have to pass it along to others in order to survive. The demon's relentless pursuit of Jay symbolises the pervasive and inescapable nature of sexual violence, emphasising that the issue extends beyond individual agency to include societal and structural forces. The film portrays sexual violence as an unstoppable force, with consent raised as a question but demonstrated to be essentially irrelevant. It demonstrates that not only consent, but any framework based on the ideology of individual agency is ineffective in combating sexual violence; rather, collective action in fighting back and treating trauma are the baseline starting points. By setting the horror within the backdrop of suburban normality—where people go to work, wash their cars, and attend classes in a routine manner, unable to see the horror as it unfolds in the foreground—the film underscores how sexual violence is embedded in everyday life, so quotidian and normalised that it has become invisible. Even though it is demonically powerful, it is invisible to everyone apart from the victim/survivor and the perpetrator/the one who passes it along.

Dogville: The Social Contract as Tool of Subordination

Dogville is an aesthetic and affective critique of liberal law and liberal democracy, with this critique turning on the figure of the degraded girl/woman. *Dogville* is the first film in von Trier's USA: Land of Opportunity trilogy, which includes *Manderlay* (2005) and the deferred *Wasington.* The film portrays the inhabitants of a small town who subject a fugitive, Grace Margaret Mulligan, to escalating violence and degradation, all while justifying their actions as lawful and just. Grace is depicted more as a girl than a woman, the film emphasising her vulnerability and lack of autonomy as she attempts to escape the control of her mob-boss father. The film critiques both the concept of the social contract and the idea of consent, showing how these notions can be used to justify and perpetuate violence and subjugation. The viewers are not only invited to judge the actions of Dogville's residents and Grace's responses but also to reflect on the broader implications of consent and justice within a liberal democratic framework. By revealing the material realities underlying abstract concepts of justice and contract, *Dogville* challenges us to reconsider the relationship between consent and subordination in contemporary society.

Dogville effectively represents subjugation, allowing for a radical critique of consent. The film thematises and diagnoses the aestheticisation of subordination and material violation as intrinsic to liberal political and legal practice. By staging community-building, *Dogville* exposes the hidden dynamics of the social contract, making them painfully visible to viewers. The gendered and racialised nature of contracts and law in liberal democracies is disturbingly highlighted through the sexual and physical violence inflicted on Grace's body. Rancière argues that the film centres on suffering caused by evil rather than on a 'system of domination that could be understood and destroyed' (Rancière, 2006, p. 5). However, I contend that *Dogville* critiques the norm rather than the exception. My analysis reveals how the film critiques the legal, social, and cultural concept of consent, emphasising its disproportionate influence in legal and extra-legal judgments about sexual violence. Consent not only fails to aid in making these judgments but also disguises the actual operating logics and material power relations at play, creating an illusion of justice.

Dogville demonstrates the ways that women, non-white people, and any 'outsider' to the dominant group are subjected to violence that is justified by abstract representational practices under political and legal liberalism. *Dogville* demonstrates, step-by-step, the production of cultural and legal abstractions—of justice, judgment, contract, and debt—and the specific violence these abstractions both produce and disguise. In *Dogville*, the meaning of 'consensual contract' comes to exceed even the literal idea of exchange, becoming instead an authorising metaphor for exploitative, even sadistic sexual violence. In other words, the inhabitants of Dogville 'speak the quiet part out loud,' dispensing even with the pretence that either Grace's individual autonomy or any underlying social contract determines their conduct. The film instead reveals the material truth: that discourses of consent, autonomy, and equality can produce subordination, humiliation, and violation *and* at the same time produce a legitimising authority for the collective that inflicts this violence. Grace's subjection in fact becomes central to Dogville's political life—they are created, as a community, through her subjugation. This resonates as a story of an individual, but the character of Grace also embodies an abstract representation of structural violence, encapsulating the intersecting dimensions of gender, race, and class. This portrayal underscores the ways in which individual harm, and representation of this harm, figure into the wider social contract.

Dogville is set in 1933, in Depression-era America: the mines have closed, there is no money, and people live in fear. The inhabitants of Dogville claim they 'don't ask nothin' from nobody,' but proceed to exploit Grace, a fugitive seeking to escape her mafia-affiliated father. Upon her arrival in the town, Grace encounters Thomas Edison Jr., a philosopher and writer who convinces the town to shelter her. Under Tom's influence, Grace begins to offer her labour to the community, marking the start of a contractual relationship defined by increasing exploitation. He tells Grace that 'Dogville has offered [her] two weeks,' so she should 'offer them' something in return. This bargain begins the language of contractual obligation. Despite the townspeople's insistence on the fairness and mutual benefit of these arrangements, Grace's situation actually deteriorates into forced labour and violence, a transition meticulously documented through the town's collective discussions. Over a series of exchanges, Grace agrees to work harder for less pay, is increasingly exploited, and is ultimately subjected to rape and enslavement. The authority to inflict pain on Grace is thematised as arising from the will of the people. What becomes striking is the contrast between the neutral, objective language of contract, provided by the townspeople, and the particular, violent ways in which Grace is affected by their arrangement, which is essentially a relationship of subordination. Nevertheless, the language of fairness and exchange is used to mediate the acts of violence and exploitation perpetrated against Grace. To begin with, in order to downplay the significance of what Grace is required to do, the labour that Grace provides during these two weeks is characterised as superfluous, excessive, and unnecessary: the townspeople state that they 'have to think of work' for her to do. When they assert they do not need anything done, Grace offers to do 'something [they] don't need done.' Finding that she is in fact endlessly working, and that there is always difficult work to do, Grace observes that there is an '[a]wful lot to do here in Dogville, considering nobody needs anything done.' She works hard at the jobs that the townspeople least want to do: teaching the children, tilling a garden that is barren, and caring for a disabled woman. The townspeople's *representation* of Grace's work, however, continues to deny these material realities. When the police arrive in Dogville and accuse Grace of a crime the townspeople know she could not have committed, they nevertheless use the excuse of Grace's purported criminality to exercise full sadistic violence against her. Grace tries to escape by paying Ben, who trucks goods between Dogville and the outside world, to courier her. Ben agrees to a contract of carriage but then betrays her, as does Tom. By the end of the film, Grace is tied to a long and heavy chain, for the 'protection' of the community. Most of the men of the town go to her each night to rape her, in full view of the community; the children of Dogville sadistically ring the bell each time this happens. Dogville then betrays Grace to her father and the mafia, calling the number on the Wanted poster and revealing Grace's whereabouts.

Dogville demonstrates that a logic of power based on the 'will of the people,' said to instantiate morality and justice, is in fact arbitrary and violent. *Dogville* thereby thematises a narrative frequently used to justify subjugation of those who are said to lie outside community's boundaries. In a film about genocide and slavery, contract is thematised as the key to social and political interaction, thereby exploring the relationship between suffering, contract, and authority. The townspeople's justification of their violence towards Grace as contractually fair underscores the manipulative use of contractual language to mask exploitation and brutality. *Dogville* serves as a diagnostic tool, illustrating how the notion of fair exchange is exploited to create an authoritative collective or 'sovereignty' that falsely claims to represent the 'will of the people,' despite evident oppression. Grace's ordeal, involving forced labour, mockery, and sexual violence, is a collective act of subjugation, witnessed and tacitly approved by the entire community. The film's stark set design, with buildings simply outlined in chalk, amplifies the collective visibility of Grace's abuse, implicating the whole town in her exploitation. In Dogville, then, it is not freedom, equality, or the rule of law that founds and sustains the democratic order: rather, Dogville's social contract is bound together through its violent subordination of an outsider. Material and specific violence underpins and sustains the democratic way of life that Dogvillians defend through their town meetings and voting procedures, such as the collective decision to not only harbour Grace, but also to enslave and exchange her for money.

The film prompts viewers to contemplate the nature of the just response to Dogville's actions, especially when Grace, upon her liberation by her father and his mafia associates, is positioned to enact judgment. Initially reluctant to exert her newfound authority, Grace rationalises the townspeople's behaviour as their best efforts under dire circumstances. However, upon reflecting on their moral standing, she concludes that their actions cannot be excused merely as human weakness. This realisation compels Grace to reclaim her power, grounded in what she states to be a moral imperative to rectify wrongs. The ensuing retribution is swift and encompasses the entire town, rooted not only in personal vindication but also in a broader sense of justice for humanity. This extends to the execution of all townspeople, including children, ensuring collective responsibility for Grace's suffering. The visibility of the crimes against Grace underscores the town's complicity, amplifying the sense of justice felt by viewers as she retaliates. Grace's actions suggest a departure from traditional notions of justice, leveraging mafia power rather than democratic consensus or legal frameworks. This approach underscores a critique of societal laws as manifestations of raw power, with Grace embodying a shift from victim to avenger.

Dogville delves into the nuanced theme of exceptionalism, presenting an ambiguous exploration of the interplay between violence and legal norms. The townspeople justify their exploitation of Grace, who appears as both an outsider and a seeker of asylum, under the guise of adhering to the rule of law. They rationalise their actions through the lens of exceptional circumstances—poverty and historical hardship—coupled with the principle of exchange/contract. This rationalisation process is a recurring motif throughout the film, serving to legitimise the townspeople's acts of violence, including slavery and rape, as deemed necessary under their self-defined legal and moral frameworks. As the film progresses to its climactic moment of revenge, the audience is confronted with their own complicity, straddling the line between identification with Grace and a critical assessment of the violence she perpetrates. This dual perspective reveals a broader commentary on the viewer's passive complicity in the events unfolding on screen, challenging the notion of the jurist as a detached observer. Ultimately, *Dogville* compels viewers to reckon with their own complicit role in the narrative, highlighting the ambivalent pleasure derived from witnessing the film's harrowing conclusion. We are likely to maintain our identification with her, however, and feel some relief at her vengeful violence, while at the same time judging the excess of Grace's violence. The film exposes our own complicity as honorary liberal thinkers with Dogville and with Grace, as well as our own sadistic satisfaction with the destructive conclusion. Here, the jurist is a voyeur, someone who takes ambivalent pleasure in pain.

The film invokes subjection in order to prove its point about the use of particular logics in modernity—the ways in which subjectivity is articulated with subjection, and the ways in which subjection becomes instrumentalised within the liberal political economy. Although it doesn't have law as its focus, it does set up the terms of engagement that underpin law, particularly the role of the contract. It also clearly articulates the relation between an individual contract that leads to Grace's subjugation with the wider social contract of the town. *Dogville* not only illustrates the deadlocks of liberal reasoning, but the aesthetics of it, and the way it feels to be a complicit player within it—not only the moral position of this point of view, but the pleasure and pain of it. Aesthetics and affect are not epiphenomenal to questions of legality (Olson, 2022); when we go beyond the analysis of the social contract as a logic or concept, and explore it instead as an aesthetic, we see how contract animates violence in democracy beyond reason, no longer marking exchange but instead figuring violent exploitation. Ultimately, *Dogville* rejects the possibility that liberalism's promises (of neutral engagement, equality, and justice) can be achieved by participating in the conditions of abstraction—that is, intervention cannot succeed where it is based on debates about the quality of abstract values of fairness or equality. In liberal traditions, reason is naturalised as the key mode of constituting and critiquing legal and political forms. *Dogville* points to what opens up, in terms of both critique and possibility, when aesthetics or affect become the focus of enquiry. Despite the logical deadlock of the film's denouement, there is the possibility of moving between aesthetic and empathic positions—for example, by putting aside logic and investigating empathy, disgust, pleasure, and horror. Instead of inhabiting the abstract position of the viewer, or lawyer-philosopher, we could take up the particular positions of Grace or the villagers, even the dog. Inhabiting these different positions perhaps opens up new critical modes—for example, rethinking the nature of contract from Grace's position. The underlying logic is contractual, and it completely ignores the material realities of power. Everyone witnesses the sexual violence against Grace, and while everybody can say that she 'consents' in the most formal and technical sense, her violent subjection is also apparent. Further, the feint of consent is bound up with the aesthetic of subjugation—they are not at odds at all but complement each other. Grace's subjection pulls Dogville together and makes it what it is: the town is created through her suffering.

The hope offered by the seemingly hopeless films *It Follows* and *Dogville* is that they point to what we have ignored and not seen; in their bleak diagnoses, they indicate the much more radical frameworks we need to embrace to remedy the pervasiveness of sexual violence. We need to move beyond the liberal social contract and its abstractions; we need to move beyond colonialism, patriarchy, and capitalism and their structural subjugations. We need to move beyond the framework of individual agency towards collective action.

Conclusion: Where Is the *Bildungsroman* of the Sexual Perpetrator?

In this chapter, I have explored how the figure, voice, and experiences of girls have been instrumentalised for legal change based on the concept of consent, despite the inherent problems with this framework. The legal system's reliance on better consent laws falls into the trap of a linear, teleological narrative, promising that rape law will inevitably and incrementally improve over time. This framework is matched by the societal belief that a better cultural response to rape will also develop incrementally. However, such promises are misleading and ultimately insufficient. The recent emphasis on the girl as an apparent agent for cultural change through the consent framework should not be seen as a sign of progress but rather as a symptom of structural resistance to substantive change.

Society, including the legal system, often shows little genuine concern for addressing sexual violence. Young men aged 15–19 years are the demographic most likely to perpetrate sexual violence, and young women of that age group are the most likely to be victims of sexual violence (Australian Institute of Health and Welfare, 2020). Further, one quarter of young men aged 18–30 have used physical violence against an intimate partner, and one-fifth have used sexual violence against an intimate partner; both behaviours are more likely among the young men who more strongly endorse more traditional stereotypes of masculinity (Flood, 2024). While stories of violation have long been central to the young girl's *bildungsroman*, the narrative of boys as perpetrators is generally absent from their coming-of-age stories. Recent foregrounding of the consent-didactic approach suggests that we can merely map the consent experience of girls' *bildungsroman* onto the experience of boys, even though they occupy different structural positions. If we are going to take a didactic approach, it would be better to focus on structural power systems (patriarchy, colonialism, capitalism) and instruction on how *not* to become a sexual violence perpetrator, stalker, or coercive controller. Instead of an appeal to boys and men to understand, we could communicate a public safety message of zero tolerance, as has been done with legal reform based on harm reduction including the so-called 'coward punch' laws (Schreiber, 2016) and for drink-driving offences.

We still fail to fully recognise the systemic violence inflicted upon women and children as an everyday occurrence. These failures are evident not only in the legal system but also in mainstream social and cultural life. To truly address sexual violence, which is occurring on an epidemic scale, we must adopt a materialist, political approach that dismantles colonialism, capitalism, and patriarchy. Only by recognising and addressing the systemic violence inflicted upon women and children as a matter of everyday life can we hope to create meaningful change. This requires not only reforming laws and cultural practices but also fundamentally challenging the underlying power structures that perpetuate inequality and exploitation.

Bibliography

ABC Television (2018, May 7) 'I Am That Girl.' *4Corners*. Available at: www.abc.net.au/news/2018-05-07/kings-cross-rape-case-that-put-consent-on-trial/9695858 (Accessed: 19 October 2023).

Adalian, J. (2018, June 11) 'Inside the Binge Factory.' *Vulture*. Available at: www.vulture.com/2018/06/how-netflix-swallowed-tv-industry.html (Accessed: 12 February 2024).

Amrani, N. (2023) *Consent*. London, UK: BBC Channel 4.

Angel, K. (2023) *Tomorrow Sex Will Be Good Again*. New York: Verso.

Arendt, H. (1994) *Eichmann in Jerusalem: A Report on the Banality of Evil*. London: Penguin.

Australian Institute of Health and Welfare (2020) *Sexual Assault in Australia. Cat. no. FDV 5*. Canberra: AIHW.

Behrendt, L. (2000) 'Consent in a (Neo)Colonial Society: Aboriginal Women as Sexual and Legal "Other".' *Australian Feminist Studies*, 15(33), pp. 353–355.

Beres, M. (2020) 'Perspectives of Rape-Prevention Educators on the Role of Consent in Sexual Violence Prevention.' *Sex Education: Sexuality, Society and Learning*, 20(2), pp. 227–238.

Brown, W. (1995) *States of Injury: Power and Freedom in Late Modernity*. Princeton: Princeton University Press.

Brown, W. (2015) *Undoing the Demos: Neoliberalism's Stealth Revolution*. New York: Zone Books.

Burney, F. (1778) *Evelina, or the History of a Young Lady's Entrance into the World*. London: Thomas Lowndes.

Carly-Williams, C. (2024) *Queenie*. London, UK: BBC Channel 4.

Carmody, M. (2009) *Sex & Ethics: The Sexual Ethics Education Program for Young People*, 1st ed. South Yarra, Vic: Palgrave Macmillan.

Chambliss, W. J. (Ed.) (2011) *Crime and Criminal Behavior*. Thousand Oaks, CA: SAGE Publications Inc.

Contos, C. (2023) *Consent Laid Bare*. Sydney: Macmillan.

Cooper, L. (2018, May 17) 'Luke Lazarus Breaks Silence Over 2013 Kings Cross Rape After Being Acquitted.' *9 News*. Available at: www.9news.com.au/national/kings-cross-rape-case-luke-lazarus-acquitted-breaks-silence-saxon-mullins-story/b62cd7ce-ba73-4d36-910a-d45133454123 (Accessed: 2 March 2024).

Cowdrey, K. (2018, October 16) '"Milkman" by Anna Burns Wins Man Booker Prize.' *The Bookseller*. Available at: www.thebookseller.com/news/anna-burns-named-first-northern-irish-writer-win-man-booker-876051 (Accessed: 9 August 2021).

Crofts, P. (2022a) 'The Corporate Monster Metaphor.' *Law, Text, Culture*, 26, pp. 73–96.

Crofts, P. (2022b) 'The Horror of Corporate Harms.' *Australian Journal of Corporate Law*, 38(1), pp. 23–45.

Crofts, P. (2024) *Evil Corporations*. Ed. Penny Crofts, 1st ed., vol. 1. London: Routledge.

Crofts, P., and van Rijswijk, H. (2024) *The Horror of Corporate Harms*. London: Routledge (forthcoming).

Dawson, B. (2021, September 20) 'Michaela Coel Dedicates Her Emmy Win to Sexual Assault Survivors.' Available at: www.dazeddigital.com/film-tv/article/54221/1/

michaela-coel-dedicates-emmy-win-to-sexual-assault-survivors-i-may-destroy-you (Accessed: 9 August 2021).
Drakopoulou, M. (2007) 'Feminism and Consent: A Genealogical Inquiry.' In R. Hunter and S. Cowan (Eds.), *Choice and Consent: Feminist Engagements with Law and Subjectivity*. London: Routledge-Cavendish, pp. 9–30.
Eugenides, J. (1993) *The Virgin Suicides*. New York: Farrar, Straus and Giroux.
Fischel, J. J. (2019) *Screw Consent: A Better Politics of Sexual Justice*. Oakland: University of California Press.
Flood, M. (2024) *The Man Box 2024: Re-Examining What It Means to Be a Man in Australia*. Melbourne: Jesuit Social Services.
Flowers, R. B. (2006) *Sex Crimes: Perpetrators, Predators, Prostitutes, and Victims*, 2nd ed. Springfield, IL: Charles C. Thomas.
Fogei, S. (Dir.) (2023) *Cat Person*. London, UK: Studio Canal.
Frow, J., Hardie, M., and Smith, V. (2020) 'The Bildungsroman: Form and Transformations.' *Textual Practice*, 34(12), pp. 1905–1910.
Gatens, M. (2008) 'Paradoxes of Liberal Politics: Contracts Rights and Consent.' In D. I. O'Neill, M. L. Shanley, and I. M. Young (Eds.), *Illusion of Consent: Engaging with Carole Pateman*. Philadelphia: Pennsylvania State University Press, pp. 31–47.
Giannacopoulos, M. (2020) 'White Law/Black Deaths: Nomocide and the Foundational Absence of Consent in Australian Law.' *Australian Feminist Law Journal*, 46(2), pp. 249–268.
Grimm, J. (2018) 'The Horror of Consent: David Robert Mitchell's It Follows.' *Journal of Horror Studies*, 2(1), pp. 60–64.
Halley, J. (2016) 'The Move to Affirmative Consent.' *Signs: Journal of Women in Culture and Society*, 42(1), pp. 257–280.
Hardy, T. (1891) *Tess of the D'Urbervilles*. London: James R. Osgood, McIlvaine and Co.
Henry, N., and Powell, A. (2014) *Preventing Sexual Violence: Interdisciplinary Approaches to Overcoming a Rape Culture*. New York: Palgrave Macmillan.
Hill, J. (2023) *Asking for It: Creating Consent Culture Series 1—Ep 1–3*. Sydney: SBS.
Hong, G. K. (2018) 'Speculative Surplus: Asian American Racialization and the Neoliberal Shift.' *Social Text*, 36(2), pp. 107–122.
Hush, A. (2023) 'Thinking Beyond "Cultural Change": Towards a Materialist Theory of Sexual Violence Prevention.' In *New Directions in Sexual Violence Scholarship*, 1st ed., vol. 1. Routledge, pp. 9–26. https://doi.org/10.4324/9781003379331-3
I May Destroy You (2020) *HBO and BBC One*. Produced by Michaela Coel, Simon Meyers, and Simon Maloney. London, England and Ostia, Italy.
James, E. L. (2011) *Fifty Shades of Grey*. New York: Vintage Books.
Lamm, K. (2015) 'Texting Girls: Images, Sounds, and Words in Neoliberal Cultures of Femininity.' *Women & Performance*, 25(2), pp. 111–127.
Larsson, S. (2008) *The Girl with the Dragon Tattoo*. Translated from Swedish by R. Keeland. London: MacLehose Press.
Linnemann, T. (2022) *The Horror of Police*. Minneapolis: University of Minnesota Press.
Locke, J. (1952) *The Second Treatise of Government*. New York: Liberal Arts Press.
Lübecker, N. (2011) *The Politics of the Imagination: Aesthetics and Cultural Exchange Between France and Denmark*. Copenhagen: Museum Tusculanum Press.
MacKinnon, C. A. (1989) *Toward a Feminist Theory of a State*. Cambridge, MA: Harvard University Press.
Malone, P. (2022) 'Measures of Obliviousness and Disarming Obliqueness in Anna Burns' Milkman.' *Textual Practice*, 36(7), pp. 1143–1174.

McDonald, E. (2020) 'Communicating Absence of Consent Is Not Enough: The Results of an Examination of Contemporary Rape Trials.' *Australian Feminist Law Journal*, 46(2), pp. 205–224.
McNally, D. (2011) *Monsters of the Market: Zombies, Vampires and Global Capitalism*. London: Brill.
Meek, J. (2021a) *Teenage Rape Culture in 1980s Cinema: Porky's, Revenge of the Nerds, andWeird Science*. New York: Springer.
Meek, M. (2021b) 'Exposing Flaws of Affirmative Consent through Contemporary American Teen Films.' *Girlhood Studies*, 14(1), pp. 101–116.
Messner, M. (2016) 'Getting Consent "Right": Sexual Assault Law Reform in New South Wales.' *Australian Feminist Law Journal*, 42(1), pp. 58–70.
Messner, M., Greenberg, M. A., and Peretz, T. (2015) *Some Men: Feminist Allies and the Movement to End Violence Against Women*. New York: Oxford University Press.
Miller, F., and Wertheimer, A. (2009) *The Ethics of Consent: Theory and Practice*. New York: Oxford University Press.
Mills, C. W. (1997) *The Racial Contract Built Upon the Sexual Contract, Extending Pateman's Critique to Racial Exclusion*. Ithaca, NY: Cornell University Press.
Mills, C. W. (2007) 'The Domination Contract.' In C. Pateman and C. Mills (Eds.), *Contract and Domination*. Cambridge: Polity Press, pp. 79–105.
Mitchell, D. R. (2014) *It Follows* [Film]. Directed by David Robert Mitchell. Los Angeles: Northern Lights Films.
Murphy, J. (2009) 'My Strength Is Not for Hurting: Men's Anti-Rape Websites and Their Construction of Masculinity and Male Sexuality.' *Journal of Media and Cultural Studies*, 23(2), pp. 137–151.
Nabokov, V. (1955) *Lolita*. Paris: Olympia Press.
Nelson, F. (2017) 'The Girl: Dead.' *Young Adult Literature Quarterly*, 5(1), pp. 38–45.
Nixon, N. (2011) *Slow Violence and the Environmentalism of the Poor*. Boston: Harvard University Press.
O'Keeffe, A. (2014, May 18) 'A Girl Is a Half-Formed Thing Review—Eimear McBride's Daring and Dazzling Novel.' *The Observer*. Available at: www.theguardian.com/books/2014/may/18/girl-is-a-half-formed-thing-review-daring-dazzling-eimear-mcbride (Accessed: 9 August 2021).
Olson, G. (2022) *From Law and Literature to Legality and Affect*. Oxford: Oxford University Press.
Orenstein, P. (2020) *Boys and Sex*. New York: Profile Books.
Oriel, J. (2019) 'We Still Need to Decide Who Comes Here and How.' *The Australian*, July 22, 2018, p. 12.
Paschal, O. (2018, September 27) 'Read Brett Kavanaugh's Defiant Statement to the Senate Judiciary Committee.' *The Atlantic*. Available at: www.theatlantic.com/politics/archive/2018/09/brett-kavanaugh-delivers-fiery-opening-statement/571570/ (Accessed: 11 November 2023).
Pateman, C. and Mills, C. (2007) *Contract and Domination*. Cambridge: Polity Press.
Pateman, C. (1980) 'Women and Consent.' *Political Theory*, 8(2), pp. 149–168.
Phipps, A. (2020) *Me, Not You: The Trouble with Mainstream Feminism*. Manchester: Manchester University Press.
Projansky, S. (2001) *Watching Rape: Film and Television in Postfeminist Culture*. New York: New York University Press.
Quilter, J. (2020) 'Getting Consent "Right": Sexual Assault Law Reform in New South Wales.' *Australian Feminist Law Journal*, 46(2), pp. 225–246.

Rancière, J. (2006) 'The Ethical Turn of Aesthetics and Politics.' *Critical Horizons*, 7(1), pp. 5–20.

Reed Perry, K. (2021) *True Story*. New York: Penguin Books.

Richardson, S. (1740) *Pamela, or Virtue Rewarded*. London: Samuel Richardson.

Richardson, S. (1748) *Clarissa,or the History of a Young Lady*. London: Samuel Richardson.

Ringwald, M. (2018, April 6) 'Reflections on John Hughes Films.' *The New Yorker*.

Russell, K. E. (2020) *My Dark Vanessa*. New York: HarperCollins.

Russell, Y. (2017) 'Woman's Voice/Law's Logos: The Rape Trial and the Limits of Liberal Reform.' *Australian Feminist Law Journal*, 42(2), pp. 273–296.

Ryan, T. (2023) 'No Consent and No Disclosure.' In *Black Australian Women and Sexual Violence*. https://doi.org/10.4324/9781003379331-8.

Salter, M. (2012) *Organised Sexual Abuse*. http://doi.org/10.4324/9780203082188 (Accessed: 21 May 2024).

Salter, M. (2016a) '"Real Men Don't Hit Women": Constructing Masculinity in the Prevention of Violence Against Women.' *Australian and New Zealand Journal of Criminology*, 49, pp. 463–479. http://doi.org/10.1177/0004865815587031 (Accessed: 21 May 2024).

Salter, M. (2016b) 'Real Men Do Hit Women.' *Meanjin*, 75, pp. 97–104. Available at: www.webofscience.com/api/gateway?GWVersion=2&SrcApp=PARTNER_APP&SrcAuth=LinksAMR&KeyUT=WOS:000371845300028&DestLinkType=FullRecord&DestApp=ALL_WOS&UsrCustomerID=891bb5ab6ba270e68a29b250adbe88d1 (Accessed: 21 May 2024).

Salter, M. (2016c) 'Men's Rights or Men's Needs? Anti-Feminism in Australian Men's Health Promotion.' *Canadian Journal of Women and the Law*, 28, pp. 69–90. http://doi.org/10.3138/cjwl.28.1.69 (Accessed: 21 May 2024).

Schreiber, J., et al. (2016) 'Kings to Cowards: One-Punch Assaults.' *The Journal of Law, Medicine & Ethics*, 44(2), pp. 332–341.

Serisier, T. (2021) *Speaking Out: Feminism, Rape and Narrative Politics*. New York: Palgrave Macmillan.

Seuffert, N. (2020) 'The Law and Politics of Consent: Legal and Political Subjectivity.' *Australian Feminist Law Journal*, 46(2), pp. 153–168.

Stangneth, B. (2016) *Eichmann before Jerusalem: The Unexamined Life of a Mass Murderer*. London: Vintage.

Tofilska, W., and Bornebusch, J. (2024) *Baby Reindeer* [TV series]. London, UK: Clerkenwell Films.

Tully, J. (2011) 'Consent, Hegemony, and Dissent in Treaty Negotiations.' In J. Webber and C. M. Macleod (Eds.), *Between Consenting Peoples: Political Community and the Meaning of Consent*. Vancouver: UBC Press, pp. 233–256.

von Trier, L. (2003) *Dogville* [Film]. Denmark: Zentropa Entertainments.

Walden, V., and Wall, L. (2014) *Respectful Relationships Education: Violence Prevention and Respectful Relationships Education in Victorian Secondary Schools*. Melbourne: Department of Education and Early Childhood Development.

Women NSW (2016) *NSW Domestic and Family Violence Blueprint for Reform 2016–2021: Safer Lives for Women, Men and Children*. Sydney: NSW Government.

Wood, J. (2014, September 22) 'Useless Prayers.' *The New Yorker*. Available at: www.newyorker.com/magazine/2014/09/29/useless-prayers (Accessed: 9 August 2021).

Legal Cases

Lazarus v R [2016] NSWCCA 52 per Hoeben CJ at CL, Adams J and Fullerton J
R v Lazarus [2017] NSWCCA 279
R v Lazarus [2015]
R v Lazarus (Unreported, District Court of New South Wales, Judge Tupman, 4 May 2017

Legislation

Crimes Act 1900 (NSW)
Crimes Legislation Amendment (Sexual Consent Reforms) Act 2021 (NSW)

Chapter 3

Feminist Imaginaries of Justice

Forgiveness, Revenge, Tragedy, Contract?

Introduction: The Figure of the Girl in Feminist Revenge Narratives

This chapter builds upon the previous chapter's interrogation of consent by examining the relationship between representations of violation and frameworks of justice as focalised through the overdetermined figure of the girl. This chapter critically examines the work of contemporary filmmakers who, rather than perpetuating the notion of the girl as inherently subordinated, use the trope of violation as a point of departure from which to shape radical theories of justice. In my reading of these texts, I explore how violation is mobilised, animated, and instrumentalised to form new frameworks of responsibility and accountability. In particular, I focus on the possibilities and limitations of responding to sexual violence with acts of revenge. The recent #MeToo movement, which included elements of revenge, exemplified extra-legal justice through the public exposure of perpetrators who had not been held accountable by the law. Although revenge is often viewed as an unwholesome or shameful impulse, this chapter takes revenge seriously and examines its potential as a legitimate framework for justice.

In recent years, a new wave of feminist revenge films has emerged. These films reject simplistic notions of revenge, instead offering more complex and nuanced approaches. The films selected here focus on the figure of the girl, thematising her voice and agency, transforming her from a passive victim into an active agent of justice. Emerald Fennell's *Promising Young Woman* (2020a) subverts the traditional revenge narrative by focusing on systemic and institutional complicity in sexual violence; revenge is both embraced and rejected, offering a complex critique of how justice is sought and administered outside (and alongside) legal frameworks. I examine how the film navigates vengeance as justice, focusing on how, through the protagonist, Cassie, the film interrogates the limitations and complexities of acts of retribution, highlighting the tension between the desire for vengeance and the pursuit of systemic change. I explore how Fennell moves beyond simplistic notions of retribution towards a more nuanced and darkly sublimated view of the

DOI: 10.4324/9780429263675-3

possibilities (and impossibilities) of justice. Jennifer Kent's *The Nightingale* (2018) explores colonial and gendered violence, emphasising the importance of solidarity over individual acts of agency. Miriam Toews's novel *Women Talking* (Bloomsbury Publishing, 2019) and its film adaptation in 2022 by Sarah Polley present a collective response to sexual violence, highlighting the potential for non-violent resistance. Finally, Karyn Kusama's *Jennifer's Body* (2009) reimagines the violated girl as a powerful, vengeful demon, using horror-comedy to theorise what could happen, in terms of justice, if a girl's violation led to her 'super-agency.' These texts, spanning genres from thriller and horror to drama and historical fiction, each start with scenes of the girl's suffering. They explore how individual and collective responses to harm can reimagine the social contract and propose radical new forms of addressing pain and violation.

The New Rape-Revenge Genre

The rape-revenge genre asserts that revenge is a legitimate, albeit extra-legal, act. It is a significant subgenre within horror, thriller, western, and crime stories. A large part of the genre involves the viewer's witnessing of an initial injustice (usually violence), followed by the viewer's purported pleasure derived from acts of revenge; the novels and films in the *Girl with a Dragon Tattoo* series are exemplary in this genre (Larsson, 2015). Recently, there has been a trend of experimenting with this form, using the revenge narrative as a starting point and then combining genres to create something new. The approach of these feminist creators takes the problem of the overdetermination and fetishisation of the suffering girl as a starting point, suggesting that the way out of suffering is to inflict suffering in return. This act of vengeance serves to ease personal suffering and also acts as a warning to others. Nietzsche's interpretation of pain as central to the contract is relevant here, as revenge tragedy can be seen as a reworking of both the sexual and social contract.

Film scholar Alexandra Heller-Nicholas explains that the 'basic' rape-revenge film is 'one whereby a rape that is central to the narrative is punished by an act of vengeance, either by the victim themselves or by an agent (a lawyer, policeman, or, most commonly, a loved one or family member' (Heller-Nicholas, 2011, p. 3). Rape-revenge films follow a two-part structure, with turning points that rely on the transformative power of violence—the original rape and then the vengeful violence in response to that assault (Henry, 2014, p. 4). A well-known example of this structure is the infamous rape-revenge film *I Spit on Your Grave* (Zarchi, 1978). In the first half of the film, the main character, Jennifer Hills, is gang-raped. The rape scene takes 34 minutes in total, adopting the point of view of the rapists and lingering on Jennifer's violation and suffering. In the second half, Jennifer methodically kills each of the men who gang-raped her, one by one, in gratuitously detailed ways. As with other early rape-revenge films of the 1960s and 1970s, *I Spit on Your Grave* was considered an example of low culture, a problematic film that was marketed for the problematic demographic of young and uneducated men. Roger Ebert, reviewing the film, stated as follows:

> It is a movie so sick, reprehensible and contemptible that I can hardly believe it's playing in respectable theaters. . . . This movie is an expression of the most diseased and perverted darker human natures. . . . There is no reason to see this movie except to be entertained by the sight of sadism and suffering.
>
> (Ebert, 2018, n.p.)

Of course, the problematic aspects of this genre have not been relegated to the past but have carried into the twenty-first century. In *Kill Bill Vols 1 and 2* (dir Quentin, 2003, 2004), a former assassin, known simply as The Bride (Uma Thurman), wakes from a coma four years after her jealous ex-lover Bill (David Carradine) attempts to murder her on her wedding day. Upon waking, she seeks revenge on every person who took part in harming her. Both movies linger on suffering, especially the suffering of The Bride: each movie begins with the sound of Thurman shuddering in fear and pain, and the first images are of her battered, trembling, and bloodied face while Bill, off-screen, asks her whether she finds him sadistic. The film hits what Henry identifies as the key markers of the basic rape-revenge genre: a young, usually white woman, is transformed from a violated victim into a fetishised femme fatale (Henry, 2014). But Henry also argues that the subgenre now needs redefining, after significant new feminist forms of the form, which she terms 'revisionist rape-revenge films,' have emerged in the past 15 years, especially following #MeToo. This subgenre reverses the appropriating and sexualising male gaze of the earlier forms (Henry, 2014, p. 6). In the films examined in the next section, the directors take care to remove sexual assault scenes as a spectacle of suffering, replacing these scenes with depictions of the effects of sexual violence. They also position the agency of victim-survivors in innovative ways that offer new frameworks for justice.

Promising Young Woman: The Possibilities of Revenge

The trailers and tagline of *Promising Young Woman* suggest a basic rape revenge story: 'Take her home and take your chances.' The film opens with the threat of quotidian rape: a scene of men in a club, who notice a young woman, Cassandra/Cassie (Carey Mulligan), drunk and alone in a corner. The men watch Cassandra with menace, one stating that she is 'asking for it.' One of the men, Jez, walks over to 'help' her and orders an Uber to take Cassandra home. Instead, Jez takes Cassandra to his place, gives her more alcohol, and brings her to bed. After he begins to kiss her, Cassandra sits up and, clearly sober, demands, 'What are you doing?' The positions of power are then flipped: instead of being an incapacitated and would-be sexual assault victim, Cassandra reveals herself to be the fully cognisant agent, capable, presumably, of revenge in the form of reporting him to the law. But in the next shot, we see Cassie walking home in the early hours—her scenes of revenge apparently go no further than confronting and perhaps frightening her would-be perpetrators, hopefully changing their future behaviour. We learn that Cassie does this regularly but that her life has otherwise atrophied: she lives with her parents and works in a coffee shop, after dropping out of medical school.

The film begins ten years after its origin story, when Nina Fisher, a 'promising young woman,' is violently raped. Nina is now dead from suicide. Nina was Cassie's best friend, and Cassie left university after Nina's assault/suicide; Cassie is now miserable. This is when Ryan (Bo Burnham)—Cassie's former university classmate, now a successful paediatrician—re-enters her life, through the romantic trope of happening to come by her coffee shop. As their romance progresses, Cassie begins to formulate more calculated revenge plans against those who harmed Nina. Initially, Cassie focuses her revenge not on individual perpetrators but on the institutions, enablers, and bystanders who are responsible for Nina's death: members of the professions and social alliances that normalised, enabled, and even produced Nina's rape. Cassie and Nina's former friend, Madison (Alison Brie), continues to maintain her view that if someone is intoxicated and behaves a certain way, they 'deserve' to be raped. So Cassie gets Madison intoxicated and makes her believe that she has had non-consensual sex with a stranger. Cassie then targets Dean Walker (Connie Britton), who ensured there were no institutional consequences to the perpetrator, Al Monroe, for raping Nina, because the dean did not want to 'ruin a young man's life' over a 'he said, she said situation.' Accordingly, Cassie sets up a ruse to make the dean think that her own daughter is at risk of gang rape. Cassie then targets the lawyer who successfully represented the rapist (Alfred Molina), and who used Nina's social media posts to victim-blame her for her own sexual assault. The villains here are professionals and institutions, not the grubby rednecks from *I Spit on Your Grave*—the film complicates the trope of basic rape-revenge films where rapists are habitually depicted as repulsive, their portrayal building on racist and classist stereotypes. Further, Cassie's spaces—her parents' house and the café—along with her fashion choices and nail polish produce what Fennell calls a kind of 'feminine uncanny,' which gives spaces that are traditionally coded as feminine (the home, service industries) a false sense of safety until they reveal their inherent hostility (Bastién, 2022, n.p.).

Cassie discovers that the perpetrator, Al Munroe (Chris Lowell), is preparing to get married and so switches her focus to a revenge plan against him. She travels to his bachelor party disguised as a stripper, and after showing up to the cabin, she drugs the participants, separates Al from his friends, ties him up, and reveals her identity to him. She is about to carve Nina's name onto his belly with a scalpel when Al gets free and suffocates Cassie with a pillow. This is a moment of shock for the viewer, who has been trained by basic rape-revenge films to expect a spectacle of vengeful and cathartic violence. Instead, the viewer is given a protracted, realistic scene of murder. Unlike the rest of the film, which is highly stylised and draws on a number of different genres, the murder of Cassie is given to us in the register of realism, made stark by its contrast with the rest of the film. The shocking and realistic depiction of Cassie's death at the hands of her friend's rapist withholds the rape-revenge narrative's typical fantastical wish-fulfilment through what Karen Crawley describes as a 'collapse' into realism (Karen Crawley, 2023, n.p.).[1] In the feminist revisionist tradition, *Promising Young Woman* refuses to linger on scenes of sexual violence. Earlier in the film, when Cassie watches the video showing Nina's rape, the camera only shows Cassie's reaction, with a close-up of her face, thus excluding any possibility of sexual fantasies and only allowing for empathy from the viewers. In the scene where Cassie is murdered by Al, however, Cassie's realistic agony is shown for more than three minutes. Cassie's face is not visible because of the pillow pushed against her head, but we hear her whimpering; the only movement that grabs the eye is the writhing of her hand and feet, which eventually go limp. The focus of the shots shifts from Cassie to Al Munroe, who, in his ultra-masculine bachelor party cabin, is weeping with fear, one hand still tied to the bed, as he waits for Cassie to die. Time passes and Joe (Max Greenfield), Al's best friend, discovers Cassie and Al, and jokes, 'You killed the stripper at your bachelor party? What is it, the '90s?' Joe tells Al, 'You did nothing wrong. This is not your fault,' and then offers to help him get rid of Cassie's body. Viewers are then given a long shot of the men burning Cassie's body. This feels like the end of the film, and instead of the vindictive ending that the narrative arc promised, the viewer is presented instead with a tragedy. While the audience is still reeling from this change in tone, Al's wedding scene begins, and Al and Anastasia say their marriage vows, when Ryan, once Cassie's boyfriend, receives a pre-scheduled text message from Cassie: 'You didn't think this was the end, did you?' This is proceeded by the arrival of a group of police vehicles, alarms blaring. As the police arrest Al, Cassie's messages keep arriving: 'Now it is. Enjoy the wedding! Love, Cassie&Nina:-).' This ending is, of course, utterly dissatisfying if one expects the 'moment of triumph' of the basic rape-revenge film (Bastién, 2022, n.p.). Zsófia O. Réti considers it to be a 'twisted take' on the wedding trope of

1 Crawley, K. 'Promising Young Woman: Ambivalence and Disappointment in Feminist Attachments to Law.' Paper presented at the 'Righteous Feminist Violence: The Cinematic Jurisprudence of Revenge' panel of the Law, Literature and Humanities of Australasia Conference, *Deux in Machina*, QUT, December 2023. See the review here: www.lawlithum.org/women-on-the-edge-of-justice-by-elizabeth-rajapakshe/

the romantic comedy genre (Réti, 2023, p. 202), and further argues that the most radical element of the film is its reframing of the rape-revenge story within the genre of romantic comedy, thus challenging and rewriting the toxic tropes that play into perpetuating rape culture, including the trope of the 'good guy' who seems likable and harmless, but who is in fact a perpetrator; the premise of relationships beginning or developing through mutual deception; and the disguise of duress beneath romantic language and gestures (Reti, 2023, p. 203). We see the familiar tropes—Cassie is asked out by a former peer from medical school who happens to order from her coffee; soon they are dancing in a grocery shop to a sweet musical montage. When Ryan sees Cassie in a bar, seemingly drunk and held up by a random man, their encounter is followed by yet another rom-com trope: an apology (although no explanation) and then a scene where they 'make up.' Cassie realises after watching the video of Nina's rape that Ryan was there, laughing with the rest of the people at the party. When she finds it out, he tearfully apologises. Cassie, however, contrary to rom-com heroines, does not fall into his arms and has no intention to forgive him. The film is significant in showing revenge to be a fantasy and although cathartic and emotionally satisfying, it's not an answer. Fennell says of the scene between Cassie and Al:

> It's important that the audience wants her to pick up that scalpel. All of us do. By that stage, we're ready. We're primed for it. We might be frightened of her. It was important to me that the first moment that violence comes into it—this lie we're all sold, that if you're a woman in a revenge movie that you can just grab a machete—and what happens is, she loses. It felt, to me, incredibly untrue to give her the upper hand.
>
> (Fennell, 2020a)

A productive tension is created by Fennell's film promising, and then refusing, the catharsis of successful revenge. The refusal to provide revenge is at once a more realistic portrayal of how violence works, as Fennell points out, and it also provides the space for a more complex theorisation of justice arising out of the understandable desire for revenge.

Reframing *Promising Young Woman*: Revenge Refused

The title *Promising Young Woman* is a reversal of a dominant trope in responses to sexual violence that operates across both legal and social domains: that society, and the law, need to consider the future of young men in considering the consequences of sexual violence. Under this trope, the young woman's future is not weighted as important as the young man's. The film's argument, which we know to be true, is that there is a tacit equation operating in both law and in society more widely, where the cost of judging a boy/man for sexual violence is measured in how that might affect their future. These costs are generally held to be greater than the costs of letting this violence go, with a lower cost being assigned to the complainant girl/woman (exemplified by Cassie's life of CPTSD and the economic, social, and psychological harms that flow from Al's sexual violence). An example of the operation of this logic in mainstream culture is Brock Turner's 2016 case, where Brock was habitually referred to by the media as the 'Stanford swimmer' even after he was proven guilty and sentenced as a sex offender. Emerald Fennell, the director of the film, has explained her intention to invert the conventions of the revenge genre (Fennell, 2021a)—for example, by not depicting the sexual assault itself but rather interrogating the aftermath through Cassie's grief-stricken reaction upon witnessing her best friend's ordeal and also by exploring the complicity of Nina's former friends (and current boyfriend) alongside the professions and institutions that refused both Nina and Cassie their futures. The ending of the film defies the rape-revenge convention, however, by replacing the victory of the rape victim (or their agent) through their infliction of joyous violence against the perpetrator with a legal solution. Barbara Creed finds the narrative arc of the film to be an effective and satisfying resolution that she defines as revolt rather than as revenge. Creed argues that Cassie's death is tragic but 'not depressing'—her death is an 'act of martyrdom' that is 'unexpectedly uplifting' (Creed, 2022, p. 57). Since Cassie questions everything, revenge is transformed into 'a full-scale revolt' against 'the ancient universal practice of rape to keep women fearful and obedient' (Creed, 2022, p. 57). According to Barbara Creed, the difference between revenge and revolt lies in their underlying goals and the scope of their impact: revenge is typically personal and involves retaliating against an individual or a specific group responsible for harm, often through similar acts of violence whereas revolt is 'against the universal and entrenched practices of rape culture, which is a crucial power structure of the patriarchal symbolic order' (Creed, 2022, p. 51). Creed categorises the following films as rape-revolt films rather than rape-revenge films (Creed, 2022, p. 51): *Revenge* (Coralie Fargeat, 2017), *The Nightingale* (Kent, 2018), and *Promising Young Woman* (Emerald Fennell, 2020a), as well as television series including *The Handmaid's Tale* (2017–2021), *Big Little Lies* (2017–2019), and *I May Destroy You* (2020). In contrast to revenge, revolt is broader and more systemic, aiming to challenge and dismantle the patriarchal symbolic order and the systemic power structures that sustain male violence and rape culture (Creed, 2022, p. 51). For Creed, Cassie is effective in holding 'everyone responsible,' in punishing each of the culpable actors, both those who committed harmful acts and those who were complicit, and that her collective acts form a warning to would-be rapists as in her death she 'becomes the monstrous-feminine of prophecy and retribution' (Creed, 2022, p. 57).

My experience of watching the film, in contrast to Creed's, was that it was *incredibly* depressing. I agree with Creed that *The Nightingale*, discussed next, is a revolt-revenge film, but I think *Promising Young Woman* does different, more diagnostic work. *Promising Young Woman* points to the structural and cultural issues that prevent justice but does not point to a way forward—for reasons discussed later, this impasse is productive. I want to suspend that observation for a little to explore Karen Crawley's argument that *Promising Young Woman* is symptomatic of feminism's 'affective and indeed melancholic attachment to the forms of law.'[2] Crawley argues that the appearance of the police in the final scenes rejects the rape-revenge genre's usual rejection of (failed) legal solutions. The basic rape-revenge film is premised on this failure of state laws and offers us instead a fantasy of extra-judicial violence, but in *Promising Young Woman*, the ultimate revenge is paradoxically achieved through punishment by the state (signified by the triumphant-seeming arrival of the police cars) and is a justice that can only be achieved through Cassie's martyrdom (Crawley, 2023, n.p.). Drawing on Lauren Berlant (2021), Crawley argues that the film appeals to and illustrates the 'cruel optimism' of feminist attachments to legal reform as a means of redressing or even abolishing sexual violence. Continued investment in an institution that not only fails us but harms us is an example of when 'something you desire is actually an obstacle to your flourishing' (Berlant, 2021, p. 1; Crawley, 2023, n.p.).

I wonder, though, whether the film is not so much a rape-vengeance story but a grim elegy for the promising young woman. In the end, Cassie's martyrdom might not effect much change at all. Cassie's 'promise' has already died at the film's opening, not only because she has left medical school to work at a coffee shop, but because she has lost all sense of meaning and possibility. We can't say that Cassie has agency in this—that she has chosen to lose all meaning and possibility—rather, this is the inevitable position she and Nina hold after violence and trauma. The film demonstrates the impossibility of achieving justice through various means. It illustrates not only the inability to hold individuals accountable through the judicial system—the perpetrator, the boyfriend, the complicit medical students, the lawyer, the Dean—but also the impossibility of reforming institutions. Furthermore, the film explores the limitations of seeking extra-judicial justice through vengeance. As Crawley points out, the appearance of law enforcement at the end evidences a *melancholic* attachment to the law that is doomed to fail (Crawley, 2023, n.p.). The perpetrator of Nina's rape, and of Cassie's death, Al, is arrested by police to a triumphant soundtrack, but why would we trust that state law will actually carry through with justice? Do we not have in mind the abundance of evidence that shows that law continues to fail girls and women in its poor adjudication of sexual violence?

2 Crawley, K. 'Promising Young Woman: Ambivalence and Disappointment in Feminist Attachments to Law.' See note 1.

Promising Young Woman is elegiac both for the promising young woman and for the possibility of achieving justice for sexual violence. It argues that one cannot rely on state law, and neither can one rely on extra-judicial revenge. Every site is permeated by structural injustice, and there is no way out. Cassie can act as a vigilante (in confronting random men who try to sexually assault her when she is 'drunk' and in her violence against Al), she can be a didactic agent (in her actions towards Madison, towards the Dean, and towards the lawyer), she can be a masochistic avenger (as in the ending), but to what ends? The film seems to say that society is rigged, law is rigged, and many of the stories we tell about sexual violence are also rigged.

Thomas Pfau argues that the elegiac is '*the* defining characteristic of aesthetic production in Modernity,' a mode of symbolic and discursive production that increasingly pervaded art, literature and theory from the mid-eighteenth century onwards (Pfau, 2010, p. 548, emphasis in original). Pfau locates the power behind this elegiac sensibility in its mourning of ideality, rather than of empirical existence: he argues that the modern elegiac impulse arises through disenchantment, especially with Enlightenment logics and rationalities (Pfau, 2010, p. 549). The significance of the elegiac is also due to modern temporality, common also to law, which, with its teleological approach, institutes clear 'programmatic breaks' with the past, bringing about what Walter Benjamin described as a 'homogenous [and] empty' time that is 'inherently mournful' (Pfau, 2010, p. 549). The elegy is about time and movement: it provides a formal space of encounter and engagement that moves the mourner through loss, provides a working through of contending social forces and collective grief, and towards consolation and hope. The literary critic Peter Sacks suggests that social critique and social change are part of this process, a dialectic between the mourning of loss and the collective synthesis of the inheritance of the dead—a way to connect the past with the future (Sacks, 1985, pp. 35–36). The elegy submits mourning's formidable psychic turbulence to the rigorous formal mechanics of elegiac temporality. This order attests to the dangers that threaten the mourner's progress: on one side, melancholia—the refusal to relinquish what has been lost, to submit to reality, to attach one's desire to a substitute object; on the other, the rage that may explode the bounds of genre, move from symbolic expression to true murder or suicide, into a failed mourning that is revenge tragedy. The classical elegy works within a loss-consolation paradigm, providing a structure through which to engage with harm, and to move with loss through time, towards resolution; this final hope is epitomised in the final line of John Milton's 'Lycidas': 'Tomorrow to fresh woods and pastures new' (Sacks, 1985, pp. 4–10). The elegy's history moves from the Greeks through Shakespeare to Shelley, and into modern and post-modern forms, when elegy came to mean something more ruminative, cerebral, and darkly sublimating. We can think of law as having a classical elegiac structure: law figures harm as being located primarily in the person, as having occurred in the past, and as being capable of resolution.

The classical elegy was reworked into an anti-elegy by modernists as they sought new frameworks and metaphors to respond to the violence of modernity, especially the rupturing event of the Great War, which made existing representational forms seem redundant.[3] From Walter Benjamin's angel of history, to Freud's theories of shock and psychoanalysis, and on to the transitional justice processes after World War II, legal and literary writers throughout the twentieth century sought new forms to understand and adjudicate modern violence.[4] If the classical elegy structured an art for resolving, re-constituting and 'saving' loss, then the modernist anti-elegy structures, in the words of Elizabeth Bishop, an 'art of losing' (cited in Ramazani, 1994, p. 4). In contrast to the loss-consolation paradigm of traditional elegies, the anti-elegy is characterised by a resistance to resolution: in Jahan Ramazami's words, it entails 'not so much solace as fractured speech, not so much answers as memorable puzzlings' (1994, p. ix). Structurally, the final closure of hope or consolation is refused, and instead of loss being transcended or redeemed, the reader continues to be immersed in loss, inhabiting a state of 'resistant mourning' (Rae, 2007, p. 14). These deconstructive practices themselves can be thought of as elegiac in mode, 'locating the very possibility of reading and writing in an impossible desire for presence, completion, and coherence' (Lilley, 1997, p. 247).

Promising Young Woman does not offer resolution or a means to move forward and falls into the form of anti-elegy rather than elegy. The film's refusal to offer a resolution, and its aesthetic of continuing rupture, are essential parts of its argument. The anti-elegy holds a space for both an aesthetic of rupture and an aesthetic of connection. Repetition, refrain, repeated questions, rhythms of movement, all discipline pain without resolving it. The anti-elegy provides a structure to go beyond a model of harm as personal, or even as psychosocial. We have seen the attempts to move through harm using a range of frameworks, and the failures and limitations of the meta-narratives of reconciliation, redemption, transitional justice, apology, forgiveness, and of human rights, to effectively change relations between people and bring about the proper conditions of social justice. I suggest here that instead of thinking of rape as its legal conception—and the associated roles of

3 On the roles of legal and literary modernism in responding to the harms of modernity, see Reichman, Ravit. "New Forms for our New Sensations': Woolf and the Lesson of Torts.' *Novel: A Forum on Fiction* 36.3 (2003): 398–422.

4 See e.g., Ravit Reichman, *The Affective Life of Law: Legal Modernism and the Literary Imagination* (Stanford University Press, 2009); Shoshana Felman, The Juridical Unconscious: Trials and Traumas in the Twentieth Century, (Harvard University Press, 2002); Honni van Rijswijk, 'Neighbourly Injuries: Proximity in Tort Law and Virginia Woolf's Theory of Suffering,' (2012) *Feminist Legal Studies* vol 20, pp 39–60.

perpetrator, victims, bystander—we consider using the modernist reworked form of the elegy (the anti-elegy) to represent sexual violence as continuing psychosocial rupture, thereby encountering the collective social/political change that is encouraged through this mode. The anti-elegy form provides a metaphor of harm and responsibility that reorganises time and destabilises law's claims to authority over the adjudication of harms. This reading takes the framework of harm beyond the personal, to include material, cultural and institutional sites that produce sexual violence—histories and contexts that are separated and obscured in law. Viewing *Promising Young Woman* through the genre of anti-elegy structures the work as a critical text that interrogates the ways in which practices of representation produce material realities, as well as concepts including law, violence, and justice.

The anti-elegy rejects the trauma framework as a means of making sense of, and moving through, trauma. It stays with rupture. We might intuit that if any harm is still open, then all harms are open, as they are all interconnected. The argument of the film as elegy is that there is nothing else we can do within existing legal and social/cultural frameworks. The 'resolution' signifies a point of despair for our existing laws and social places—the *depression* of witnessing Cassie's death—but with the promise that, this sorrow being unresolved, this rupture being unremedied, we are compelled to find new forms of meaning and justice. In the traditional elegy, mourning is resolved but in the anti-elegy, mourning is refused in favour of something more complex: despair but also anger and hope. The murder that we witness at the film's close thus repositions the audience parallel to the same emotional headspace that motivated Cassie's earlier vengeful actions; we feel the loss of someone we had become close to, we are shocked by the injustice of it all. But I think Fennell directly implicates the audience as complicit spectators to a crime not just as empathetic onlookers for the vicarious experience of sexual violence and death but also recipients of the call to justice. Our anger, confusion, and sense of unfairness is a call to action to demand more not only of law but of social and cultural forms.

Reading *Promising Young Woman* as an anti-elegy is a productive approach as it encourages the viewer to critically engage with the limitations of not only legal frameworks but with existing social justice frameworks. The film's refusal to offer a conventional resolution or cathartic revenge underscores the systemic nature of gendered violence and the inadequacies of existing mechanisms to address it. By framing the narrative through the lens of anti-elegy, we are compelled to stay with the ongoing, unresolved suffering that sexual violence creates in the lives of survivors and the ongoing failure of the legal system to redress this. This perspective pushes us to recognise that true justice cannot be achieved within the current structures of law and society. Instead, it demands a radical transformation of our material conditions. Cassie's journey, marked by both acts of retribution and ultimate martyrdom, serves as a powerful critique of the societal and institutional failures that perpetuate injustice and also a powerful critique of the viewer: if you are hoping that the police and legal system will fix these harms, you are wrong. The anti-elegiac mode, with its focus on unresolved pain, invites viewers to move beyond the pursuit of legal remedies and to envision new forms of justice that address the root causes of violence and inequality. In this way, *Promising Young Woman* calls for a fundamental reimagining of how we approach justice by staying with rupture, urging us to dismantle and rebuild the very foundations of our social and legal systems.

Women Talking: From Revenge to Structural Reimagining

Women Talking takes *Promising Young Woman*'s invitation to consider what happens after rupture. The novel and subsequent film are explicitly focused on the aftermath of violence, taking this temporal moment seriously as a time to theorise justice, and placing the power to determine justice in the hands of the victims and survivors. Through secret meetings, the women of the community engage in a critical examination of their faith's teachings on nonviolence, reinterpreting these principles from a feminist perspective. While the initial impulse might be toward revenge, the women ultimately reject this path in favour of a more profound reworking of their underlying social and sexual contracts. Toews's narrative, inspired by real events in a Bolivian Mennonite colony, is a blend of fact and fiction that uses feminist imagination to respond to the horrors endured by the women. Through their deliberations, the women embody a form of non-violent resistance that grounds the collective reorganisation of their political and social lives. The film and novel illustrate that individual agency is produced through material conditions and that true justice requires a fundamental reorganisation of these conditions. By centring their discussions on forgiveness, accountability, and future possibilities, the women of *Women Talking* forge a new path that rejects violence and subordination. This transformative vision contrasts sharply with the dystopian reimagining of the social contract in Lars von Trier's *Dogville*, highlighting the potential for peaceful and democratic political engagement to create a just and equitable community. The film does, however, raise important questions about the feasibility and implications of their chosen path, particularly for marginalised and colonised populations, and leaves the audience to ponder the broader applicability of their solutions.

The Novel

Miriam Toews's novel *Women Talking* unfolds within an isolated Mennonite community shaken by the revelation that numerous women and girls have been the victims of covert, serial rapes during the night by some of the community's men and boys. This shocking discovery challenges the community's claimed adherence to pacifism, exposing the deep-seated patriarchal violence within. The novel is explicitly concerned with the question of justice following sexual violence and places the power to adjudicate justice in the hands of the victims/survivors of an isolated religious community, which in turn leads them to redefine their political community. Toews, a Canadian author with Mennonite heritage, based the novel on true events. In her 'Note on the Novel,' Toews explains that *Women Talking* is 'a reaction through fiction' to the violent and repeated rapes that took place between 2005 and 2009 in Manitoba Colony, 'a remote Mennonite colony in Bolivia' where over 200 women and girls were drugged and assaulted by men from their own community (Toews, 2018, p. vii). Toews describes the novel's form as a blend of fact and fiction, a manifestation of 'feminist imagination,' in part as a response to what the community has endured: each time that the women and girls woke up bleeding, hurt, confused, they were told that they had experienced an act of Satan or of ghosts, or else the result of a 'wild female imagination' (Toews, 2018, p. ix). The film also plays on this reference: after an initial teaser, the film displays a text that reads: 'What follows is an act of female imagination.' In secret meetings, the women and girls of the community deliberate on their next steps, engaging in a critical examination of their faith's teachings on nonviolence and reinterpreting these principles through a feminist perspective. The novel concludes with an acknowledgement dedicated to women and girls living under patriarchal, authoritarian regimes worldwide, whether Mennonite or not, Toews suggesting that this specific, historical re-evaluation is a model for confronting gendered violence more universally.

Victoria Glista argues that the novel's exploration of nonviolence is inspired by feminist political theory, notably that of Judith Butler who advocates for paradoxical forms of 'rageful love, militant pacifism . . . [and] radical persistence' (Butler, 2016, p. 292 cited in Glista, 2023, p. 96). The text offers a model of non-violent resistance or 'aggressive nonviolence' characterised by horizontal power relations and a collective reorganisation of bodily norms (Glista, 2023, p. 96). Through their negotiations, the women of the colony embody a nonviolence that is both a rejection of oppression and a proactive engagement in creating an alternative form of political life. Kehler characterises the novel as a feminist theological narrative that reimagines peace from a grassroots, feminist standpoint; Kehler suggests that Toews challenges the notion of peace as a passive state to be possessed rather than an active engagement with the demanding responsibilities it entails (Kehler, 2020, pp. 409–410).

The Film

In Sarah Polley's Academy Award-winning film adaptation of Toews's novel, the word Mennonite deliberately goes unsaid, making the specific universal. This opens up the interpretation of the film as a universal allegory for ways of dealing with sexual violence. The film begins with the voice-over of a young girl, Autje, addressing someone in the future: 'This story ends before you were born.' Polley's decision to substitute the original male narrative voice of the novel (August's) with Autje's voice-over and direct address to Ona's child, a child born of sexual violence, is coherent with her idea that '[t]here's some sense of the future speaking back to the past, instead of being mired in it' (Mead, 2022, n.p.). The first image, however, is located in the present and is of a young woman waking to find her thighs bloodied and bruised by violence. 'Mother!' she calls. 'Again.' The voiceover continues: 'When we woke up, feeling hands that were no longer there, the elders told us that it was the work of ghosts, or Satan. Or that we were lying to get attention, or that it was an act of wild, female imagination. It went on for years. To all of us.'

The film is set almost entirely within the confines of a hayloft, where the women of the colony gather to deliberate on their collective response to the violence committed against them. Salome Friesen, whose four-year-old daughter Miep (Emily Mitchell) has contracted a sexually transmitted disease as a result of the violence, attacks the rapists with a scythe, and the men are driven to the police headquarters, not to be given over to justice but 'for their own protection,' as the narrator recalls. The men demand that, in the meantime, the women either forgive them or be banished from the colony. The film only gradually reveals the full horror of the assaults. At first, we get only a broad idea of the violence, but as the story progresses, we learn that the attacks affected everyone from infants to elderly women, led to suicides, and resulted in pregnancies and STDs. Toews aimed in her novel to convey the brutality of these attacks through brief but vivid fragments rather than representing full scenes of sexual violence. Following Toews' method, director Sarah Polley uses quick flashbacks in her film to show the aftermath of the assaults, helping viewers understand the gravity of the harm but avoiding the spectacle of sexual violence in and of itself.

The women are illiterate and uneducated, so Ona requests that August, the schoolteacher of the colony, take minutes of the discussion and compile notes that can serve as a historical artifact, an archive of both their judicial process and their political evolution. The women in the film share both unified and differing opinions. August captures their debate, effectively putting the absent perpetrators on trial through their discussion. The fear of venturing into an unknown world, leaving the colony's safety, and risking their eternal salvation causes some women to advocate for staying. At the start of their conversation, Scarface Janz tells the others that leaving is not an option, claiming, 'we have everything we want in the colony' (Polley, 2022). Salome reacts with scorn and strong disagreement. In response to her dissent, Scarface bluntly advises her to 'Want less' (Polley, 2022). Early in the film, Ona Friesen describes herself and her peers as 'women without a voice.' If, in general terms, sexual assault victims are at risk of becoming 'tainted witnesses' when they take their account to the public sphere (Gilmore, 2017, p. 44), the characters in *Women Talking* are, when the plot starts, completely negated as narrators of their own experience. Once the conditions for speaking out are modified, though, and they are able speak out safely, Mejal Loewen, who suffers from undiagnosed PTSD, declares, 'They made us disbelieve ourselves. And that was worse than . . .' (Polley, 2022). Lowen's voice trails off, indicating the violence with silence. The women's agency, and their ability to find their voices, are made possible by a change in conditions: the departure of the men, the seclusion of the hayloft, and the availability of time to create justice and a new political world. The film and novel demonstrate that individual agency is not based on will but produced (or denied) through material conditions.

Forgiveness or Revenge?

In her analysis, Rebecca Mead concludes that '[a]bove all, Polley was captivated by the possibility of forgiveness' (Mead, 2022, n.p.), and forgiveness is the topic that the women revisit most often. Early on, when Scarface defends the option of forgiving the men, Salome takes a firm stand: 'I cannot forgive them. I will never forgive them!' (Polley, 2022). Although she progressively changes her mind about staying—initially she wants to remain in the colony and fight, teaching girls to stand up for themselves—she does not move an inch from her initial position on forgiveness, and she reacts more angrily at every new thread of talk about it. Salome reaches the conclusion that 'I will become a murderer if I stay' (Polley, 2022). This statement is important because the scene is a turning point for all the women, who reason that they must leave in order to prevent more violence. Agata concludes, 'Perhaps forgiveness can in some instances be confused with permission' (Polley, 2022). This perspective resonates with broader feminist discussions on accountability and the limitations of forgiveness within systems of oppression. As Ann Russo argues, 'One of the formidable barriers to owning up to how we are implicated in systems of oppression is the binary framework of guilt/innocence that pervades the dominant culture' in our society (Russo, 2019, p. 22). While contemplating the defensive discourse of 'not-all-men,' Ona, the young woman who is pregnant with the child of a rapist, asks, 'It is possible that not all men in the prison are guilty of the attacks. But are they guilty of not stopping the attacks? Are they guilty of knowing about the attacks and doing nothing?' (Polley, 2022). The protagonists of *Women Talking* emerge as a 'collective witness,' an expression that Gilmore coins to indicate how survivors are able to benefit from the credibility that arises from shared experience, including patterns of abuse, trauma-related disruptions, and structural disadvantage (Gilmore, 2023, p. 99). Rather than isolating and dismissing survivors one at a time, their collective witness replaces routine epistemic violence with testimonial justice, and the form through which this is enacted is survivor storytelling (Gilmore, 2023, p. 103). Agata explains, 'Leaving and fleeing are different words, with different meanings. They each say something about us' (Polley, 2022). Eventually, they settle upon leaving, which they consider more apt to reflect their agency in the face of the attacks.

When Polley closes the film with a shot of Ona's newborn, Autje's voice-over reassures the baby (and, by extension, the viewers): 'your story will be different from ours' (Polley, 2022). Polley says that the film '[is] a fable about a lot of cultures—about all of us' (Mead, 2022, n.p.). The women's two-day dialogue is a self-aware discussion of the consequences of the culprits' actions for the colony as a whole. Autje narrates, 'Where I come from, where your mother comes from, we didn't talk about our bodies. So when something like this happened, there was no language for it. And without language for it, there was a gaping silence and in that gaping silence was the real horror' (Polley, 2022). For Glista, materiality is essential to the political philosophy that emerges in *Women Talking*, which is an 'embodiment of feminist politics or what Bonnie Honig calls the "corporealis[ation] of different habits" that are transformational and world-building' (Glista, 2023, p. 96). Contrary to interpretations that might prioritise the novel's emphasis on dialogue and the spoken word as its central motif, given its title and thematic focus on discourse, Kehler contends that the physical body plays a pivotal role as a catalyst for transformation within the narrative as an 'engine of change' (Kehler, 2020, p. 97). She suggests that the body plays a crucial role in the story, not as a secondary element, but as a fundamental and essential mode of initiating or expanding the change discussed by the women (Kehler, 2020, p. 99). Significantly, Toew and Polley reject the trope of the wound that is perceived to communicate in and of itself, beyond language. Instead, the physicality of the women's wounded bodies leads them to collective discourse. Their discourse is embodied, but not in a passive way. This narrative pushes back against women and girls being essentialised as traumatised victims who require others to speak for them. The women's and girl's formation of a new politics and legality is marked through their physical space: the hayloft, set above the rest of the male-dominated community, transforms into not only a symbolic but a material refuge, allowing them not just to discuss but also to reconcile their past, present, and future. By centring the story in the hayloft, director Sarah Polley highlights the need for a secure and isolated space where the women can openly communicate, away from the controlling influence and scrutiny of men, challenging the power dynamics that have traditionally kept them silent.

The occasion of sexual violence opens up the terms of political economy more widely: how will the women determine the terms of judgment? Who has a voice in this determination? How will this violence, and their response, shape the terms of their future community? How can they shape this community in a non-violent way? The women discuss the ethical and political consequences of the main forms of justice: forgiveness (as directed by the men), revenge (stay and fight and stand their ground), and self-exile. In a specific way, their discourse occupies the space between the sexual contract and the social contract: they get at the hinge between (sexual) harm and government. The film considers whether violence can be judged, even overcome, without further acts of violence. It presents options such as exile, radical political re-making, and creating a place without men.

As the women adjudicate sexual violence, they simultaneously remake their political world. They set the terms for a new way of relating to each other, prioritising the ethical values of their religion. This approach contrasts sharply with the inhabitants of Dogville, considered in Chapter 2 of this book, whose body politic evolves through the subordination of a stranger. The women in *Women Talking* explicitly refuse violence and subordination as techniques of relation and governance. Both *Women Talking* and *Dogville* explore the reinvention of the social contract arising from sexual violence. They reveal not only an analogy between the sexual contract and the social contract but also how the social contract can hinge on sexualised domination and subjugation. In *Dogville*, the community reimagines their social contract in a bleak, dystopian way, based on (sexual) subordination. In contrast, *Women Talking* envisions the social contract in a transformative, utopian way, moving from a status quo of sexual subordination to a position of freedom through peaceful and democratic political engagement and decision-making.

Similar to *Dogville* in its thematisation of bodies as a source of law and politics, *Women Talking* nevertheless differs in its outcome, rejecting the Nietzschean fatalism of *Dogville*. The film raises important questions about whether their solution is specific to their material circumstances or can be extrapolated as a wider solution. *Women Talking* responds with non-violent consensus leading to walking away from the men, but this raises further questions that are not answered. Is the logic suicidal? Where will the women walk to, how will they support themselves, and how will they survive? Will they face further violence further along the road? Where and how will they settle somewhere new—are there free spaces available, or are these spaces only 'free' by displacing others? How universal is their solution? How feasible is self-exile for colonised people, for instance? How viable is walking for Black and poor women? Earlier in the story, the women question whether the non-perpetrating men of the colony are culpable as bystanders for failing to prevent the assaults or for being aware of them and taking no action. The women also consider whether the boys among them present a danger and whether they should bring the boys with them. But what happens when the boys reach adulthood? Does the community hope that they will be different from the men and boys of the past colony because the community has been re-made? Or will they necessarily become perpetrators? These questions are left open, but it's possible that a genocidal logic is operating and that boys or men will necessarily be excluded.

The Nightingale: Revenge Through Alliance

The Nightingale (dir Kent, 2018) demonstrates an understanding of how the histories of colonialism inform contemporary scenes of sexual violence, as figured through the girl. Set in 1825 Tasmania during one of the most brutal periods of colonisation, the story follows Clare Carroll, a young Irish convict seeking retribution for the brutal violence inflicted upon her and her family by a British officer, Lieutenant Hawkin, and his subordinates. Clare works as a servant for Lieutenant Hawkins—her sentence has finished years ago, but he continues to hold her captive. When a senior officer visits Hawkins, Clare is forced to sing and serve drinks for the men. Afterwards, she visits Hawkins to inquire about a letter of recommendation that would free her, her husband, Aidan, and their infant daughter. In response, Hawkins propositions Clare and then rapes her. That night, a fight erupts between Aidan and Hawkins; his second-in-command, Sergeant Ruse; and Ensign Jago. The visiting officer deems Hawkins unfit for promotion, and Hawkins orders Ruse and Jago to travel through the thick bush to Launceston, Tasmania, to negotiate with the officer. Before departing, Hawkins, Ruse, and Jago gang-rape Clare, kill Aidan, and murder her baby.

The following morning, Clare reports the violence to an official, who does nothing. Determined to seek justice herself, she enlists the help of a First Nations tracker named Billy to pursue Hawkins and the others, lying to Billy about the purpose of their journey. As they travel, Clare's initial hostility towards Billy dissipates as she realises how much they have in common. Billy reveals his real name, Mangana, *Palawa* for 'blackbird,' and shares his wish to reunite with his surviving relatives up north. Meanwhile, Hawkins and his group recruit three convicts and another First Nations guide, Charlie, for their journey. Sergeant Ruse kidnaps a First Nations woman named Lowanna and sexually assaults her. A group of First Nations warriors attempt to rescue the captives, but this attempt results in the death of one convict and the injury of Jago. Hawkins kills Lowanna and escapes with Ruse and the remaining convicts, leaving Jago behind. As revenge for the soldiers' inhumanity, Charlie diverts the journey to a dead end, leading to his own death by Ruse. Mangana finds the bodies of Charlie and Lowanna and vows vengeance on Hawkins and Ruse.

When Clare encounters Ensign Jago, the officer who killed her baby, she attacks and kills him in a frenzied, brutal manner, leaving herself traumatised. Clare and Mangana then approach the soldiers but are forced to split up after Clare freezes at the sight of Hawkins. Mangana is captured and forced to guide the soldiers, but he escapes when Eddie hesitates to kill him. Hawkins then kills Eddie. Clare reunites with Mangana, and they encounter a chain gang of First Nations men. One prisoner informs Mangana he is the last of his people before the captors kill the gang. In Launceston, Clare confronts Hawkins about his crimes in front of his fellow officers. Mangana, despite Clare's pleas, dons war paint and kills Hawkins and Ruse and is himself deeply wounded. Clare and Mangana flee to a beach where Mangana dances and declares himself a free man, while Clare sings a Gaelic folk song. In singing this song, the film returns to the first scenes where Clare was compelled to sing as a performance of subordination: now she sings in freedom and rebellion. Together, they watch the sunrise.

When Clare is faced with the opportunity to exact her revenge on Hawkins and decides not to follow through with this violence, the audience's expectations of a gratifying vengeance are thwarted. Clare rejects violence as a solution, and instead the ending of the film thematises the solidarity between Clare and Mangana. This narrative arc rejects the personal in favour of the political, signified by the alliance between Clare and Mangana. Conforming to Creed's formulation of 'revolt,' their alliance targets the entire patriarchal symbolic order, which is shown to be inextricable from the violence of settler colonialism (Creed, 2022, p. 53). Van Diemen's Land was notorious for being among the most brutal of the early Australian colonies, where women who committed trivial crimes were nevertheless sent to even out the gender imbalance.

The depiction of multiple acts of sexual violence in the film led to an attack on Kent at the Venice Film Festival, where a critic denounced her as a 'whore'; in reply, Kent argued that her film does not sexualise the rape scenes but rather focuses on the faces of the characters to highlight the soul-destroying nature of the violence (Kent, 2019, in Creed, 2022, p. 53). Alongside sexual violence, the film depicts the genocide of First Nations people without any euphemism—the violence is horrific, including hangings and beheadings. It is important that Australia's colonial violence be shown to be inseparable from Australia's continuing high rates of sexual violence—the two kinds of violence are effects of the same patriarchal and colonial logics.

Jennifer's Body: Playing With Genre

Jennifer's Body is a horror-comedy film directed by Karyn Kusama and written by Diablo Cody. It was made in 2009, so pre-dated #MeToo by several years, but anticipated some of the movement's concerns. The story begins when two best friends, Jennifer Check (Megan Fox) and Anita 'Needy' Lesnicki (Amanda Seyfried), go to their local dive bar in the small town of Devil's Kettle to watch an all-male band, Low Shoulder. During the performance, the bar burns down, and then the band members entice Jennifer into their van. They try to kill Jennifer, who instead becomes possessed by a demon and starts feeding on the boys in her town. The film was a flop at the box office, partly because it was marketed to the wrong audience—the young and uneducated boys and men who were the target audience of the basic rape-revenge film—but it has since become a cult classic (Blichert, 2021, p. 18).

Jennifer's Body begins with the tenet 'Hell is a Teenage Girl.' There are two ways to read this statement: first, the experience of being a teenage girl is hellish, or second, that the teenage girl is herself an agent of hell. As readers and viewers, we are more familiar with the former reading: indeed, we could say that the figure of the teenage girl is overdetermined as a figure of suffering. In contrast to this overdetermined, abject figure, we have Jennifer, who at the moment of abjection becomes a joyful agent of suffering. When Jennifer is enticed into the van by the band members of Low Shoulder, she is driven to a remote place and killed, as an audience would expect in the first part of a basic rape-revenge film; the film's title comes from Hole's 1994 track 'Jennifer's Body,' which tells the story of a woman who is abducted, murdered, and dismembered (Blichert, 2021, p. 21). But against these genre expectations, at the moment of her violation, Jennifer is not destroyed but rather turned into a demon with extraordinary powers. *Jennifer's Body* not only rewrites the figure of the violated adolescent girl, but the film does so in a comical, celebratory way, making fun of the earnest films and novels that usually centre this figure.

Although the scene in which Jennifer is killed by the band members is free of literal sexual violence, it is coded as rape. Describing the scene, director Kusama says,

> When we would test the film and when I would talk about the movie with executives, they would always describe the scene as 'the gang rape,' instead of as the sacrifice. . . . The scene mirrors . . . what the horror of sexual assault actually is, which is this complete inability to see a person.
> (Blichert, 2021, p. 13)

Before they kill her, the men laugh at and talk over Jennifer's sobs as she asks whether they are going to rape her. Constance Grady says of this scene:

> Watching . . . in 2018 brings up unavoidable echoes of Christine Blasey Ford's testimony about Brett Kavanaugh's alleged assault on her when she was a teenager, of the phrase 'Indelible in the hippocampus is the laughter.'
> (Grady, quoted in Blichert, 2021, p. 18)

Megan Fox, who plays Jennifer, says of that scene:

> Being mocked in such an excruciatingly flippant way pulled that performance out of me. I wasn't acting. Just reacting to being devalued.
> (Unterberger, 2019, n.p.)

When Jennifer protests her treatment, one of the band members says, 'We don't need to talk if you don't want to.' The fact that Megan Fox played Jennifer is significant. On 11 September 2009, the same day that *Jennifer's*

Body premiered at the Toronto International Film Festival, three crew members from Fox's previous movies (the *Transformers* series) published an anonymous letter that attacked her. Fox had publicly criticised the director of those films, Michael Bay, for his abuse and sexism on the set. In the crew's letter, which director Michael Bay published on his website, the anonymous men used a range of sexist tropes. They concluded that 'Megan really is a thankless, classless, graceless, and shall we say unfriendly bitch' and stated that they wished her character would be crushed to death in the opening scene of the next *Transformers* film (Blichert, 2021, p. 15). Fox was later dismissed from the franchise before the next *Transformer* film was made. The #MeToo movement evidenced that actresses who spoke out about sexual violence and harassment were collectively punished by being blacklisted and having their careers effectively ended. For example, Peter Jackson has stated that he decided not to work with Mira Sorvino and Ashley Judd on the *Lord of the Rings* trilogy because he received (untrue) warnings from the now-officially-a-sex-offender/criminal Harvey Weinstein (Rubin, 2017, n.p.).

Weaponising the Figure of the Violated Girl

At the point of her violation, Jennifer is not made abject, but rather transforms into a monster who needs to consume other people to stay alive. Frederick Blichert reads this transformation within a trauma framework, her subsequent violence also signifying a recurring trauma: Jennifer's originary trauma occurs at Devil's Kettle when she is killed, and this destruction of her humanity is referenced each time Jennifer acts out as an inhuman demon. In contrast, I believe that the film rejects the trauma framework: at the moment Jennifer changes from a violated body to a vengeful demon, the film exits a trauma narrative and replaces it with something else. The terms of this justice rely in part on the reversal of the positions of perpetrator and victim, but justice in the film relies on more than this reversal of roles, in contrast to the basic rape-revenge genre. After Jennifer's transformation into an actual, man-eating demon, Needy says, 'You're killing people.' 'No. I'm killing *boys*,' Jennifer replies, flipping the usual trope that justifies violence against girls and women—that girls are not fully human in the ways that boys and men are. When Chip's mom tries to give him 'ladies' pepper stray,' and Chip protests, his mother says, 'There's obviously a sicko out there who likes boys,' again reversing the trope of the girl who is always-already a victim. Jennifer is not a mindless monster, though, as she retains her own sensibility and agency. Her agency is mainly expressed through her love for her friend, Needy. In an early scene, Jennifer rejects her impulse to feed on Needy. Her humanity has not been destroyed; she is not a zombie or a mindless monster. Jennifer objectifies and consumes boys in a way that is comical as well as horrific. Needy tells her boyfriend, 'She's eating boys! They like make her really pretty and glowy . . . and her hair looks amazing. And then when she's hungry she's weak and cranky and ugly.'

The film makes fun of trauma discourse, including the candlelight vigils for the victims and over-the-top newspaper coverage. 'The whole country got a huge tragedy boner for Devil's Kettle,' Needy says, in voice-over, wryly commenting on the instrumentalisation of trauma stories. While the town celebrates the band members that attacked Jennifer, turning them into heroes, Jennifer's own violation is completely overlooked, as per usual. The film also rejects earnestness as the dominant tone of representing Jennifer's murder and her subsequent possession. Trauma stories are often didactic: they show the viewer or the reader how they must feel, and this feeling itself can stand in for justice. The film's push-back is not against trauma discourse in general but the overdetermined figure of the suffering girl framed through this discourse. This figure is the quintessential trauma victim, and it is as though her suffering or wound speaks for her. In this, she demonstrates Cathy Caruth's reading of the wound that has dominated trauma discourse from the 1990s:

> What the parable of the wound and the voice thus tells us . . . is that trauma . . . is always the story of a wound that cries out, that addresses us in the attempt to tell us of a reality or truth that is not otherwise available. This truth, in its delayed appearance and its belated address, cannot be linked only to what is known, but also to what remains unknown in our very actions and our language.
>
> (Caruth, 1996, p. 4)

Here, the wound is meant to speak for itself and in itself demand justice. The problem with this reliance on trauma discourse for justice is that the terms of justice are not articulated.

Framing Sexual Violence as Horror-Comedy

The town of Devil's Kettle—the world of Jennifer and Needy—is grounded in systemic misogyny, and this violence is represented in a realist way rather than as part of the horror story. Sexual violence is so quotidian, so accepted by everyone and by all our institutions that there is no point being earnest about it. At the film's opening scene at the bar, Jennifer talks casually to Needy about being sexually abused by a police cadet, Roman (Chris Pratt), who is an adult while she is underage. Needy describes the model of the van that Jennifer was abducted in as 'an '89 Rapist.' Needy says to her boyfriend Chip, 'They had one of those white molester vans with no windows. The back was all blacked out.' There is also humour in Jennifer's enjoyment of her monstrosity: 'I am a god,' Jennifer tells Needy, after she discovers that she can devour boys to increase her vitality, that she can immediately heal from any injury and, later in the film, fly. *Jennifer's Body* transforms the narrative figured by the violated girl from a trauma story where a girl's suffering can mainly attest to her own trauma and suffering, to something else. *Jennifer's Body* rewrites the figure of the violated girl by giving her extra-human and extra-judicial powers. The violated bodies that we do see belong to boys, which Jennifer, once in her demonic form, violates with relish. 'I need you frightened,' Jennifer says to her second boy victim. As in the film *The Exorcist* (1973), the demonic possession of a girl expresses social anxieties about the power of feminine sexuality, but *Jennifer's Body* subverts this trope by foregrounding the girl's body as a site of power. Unlike Reagan in *The Exorcist*, Jennifer's demon is never exorcised but instead is passed on to Needy when Jennifer is killed. Needy gets to keep the demon, and it does her good—by the end of the film, she's lost her neediness.

The film also forms a critique of social contract theories of law, showing how liberal socio-legal processes will not provide justice or protection from violence. *Jennifer's Body* takes the law's failure to adjudicate and end sexual violence for granted; it also takes for granted the social and cultural norms that perpetuate violence, which are so immovable, despite years of feminist activism, that Needy can only make jokes about rape vans. Given these legal, cultural, and social failures, this revenge film suggests we need something extra, something new. The new form of justice the film proposes is in the form of a contract. The contract the film proposes is in some ways the same that most rape revenge films propose: that since sex offenders cannot be controlled by legal or social norms, they need to be controlled by extra-legal, brute force. Sexual assault offenders can be considered to have entered into the terms of a new contract of violence, one that will be returned with equal or greater force. *Jennifer's Body* adds something extra, though, in that the agent of vengeance is not a cop, father, brother, or other human vigilante, or a sexualised, femme fatale version of the survivor, but a demonic force that enters Jennifer's body. Jennifer's suffering leads to powers that exceed her will; once Jennifer's powers are activated, her justice is not easily set aside, and when Jennifer dies, her powers are passed on to her friend Needy. We thereby have a continuing contract, rather than a single act of revenge, which we can think of as the foundation for a new social contract. Jennifer's body becomes the site not of subjugation but of a 'super agency'—she kills Needy's boyfriend and then Needy kills her but not without being bitten by Jennifer. Ultimately, however, Needy gets the best of both worlds—she isn't 'turned' fully into a demon, which means that she doesn't rely on killing in order to stay alive, but Needy is contaminated, or perhaps blessed, with demonic powers. After this transformation, Needy spends time in a mental institution, another trope of the traumatised, protesting, or rageful girl. But then Needy says, as voice-over: 'if you're bitten by a demon and you live, you just might absorb some of the demon's abilities. You just might get lucky for once in your miserable life.' Needy hovers, smashes through the prison window, and escapes in her bunny slippers. Returning to Devil's Kettle, she takes up the knife used to stab Jennifer and hitchhikes east. The girl hitchhiker, of course, is another trope of victimology—many horror and thriller films that show a hitch-hiker catching a ride are inevitably followed by scenes of the girl's violation and death. But the viewer knows this won't, and cannot, happen here, because of Needy's demonic powers—she intends to find Low Shoulder and presumably kill/punish them.

The Revenge Contract

The extra-judicial, underlying contract operating in *Jennifer's Body* refuses the abstractions of law and even justice, maybe even the abstraction of 'revenge' and instead asserts a transactional economy, based on bodies and their capacity for pain. The film rejects moral discourses—*rape is bad; rape is unjust*—as being beside the point. We know that rape is bad, but where has that judgment ever got us? Jennifer and Needy treat rape as background—it's like the weather. Ultimately, the film offers a Nietzschian view of morality and justice. *Jennifer's Body* diagnoses the problem of sexual violence as a problem of power and offers a contractual solution. In the 'Second Essay' of his book *Genealogy of Morals* (1887), Nietzsche provides a perverse account of social contract theory, one that is based not on abstractions of rationality, sovereignty, and law, but upon power relations produced through the materiality of bodies. This materiality—namely, the pain of bodies—is disguised by the language of abstractions such as morality. Nietzsche's conceptualisation of morality reveals that what is thought of as morality is actually power, and that pain and subjection are central to constituting authority. Nietzsche's method proceeds through an analysis of transactions, bodies, and codes. He shows that the moral domain is not separate from the social contract, but rather, that morality supports power relations. Nietzsche begins the 'Second Essay' with a description of 'nature's' paradox: 'To breed an animal with the right to make promises' (1887, p. 57). Nietzsche explains that this 'breeding' requires the production of conscience or responsibility. In turn, conscience requires memory (Nietzsche, 1887, p. 60), and the key is then revealed: that memory, which backs the contract, is activated through pain: 'all this has its origin in the instinct that realised that pain is the most powerful aid to mnemonics' (Nietzsche, 1887, p. 61). Reason itself—such as the decision not to commit a violent act for fear of the consequences—is an effect of either the experience or observation of pain implemented through punishment, which serves to assist memory. Nietzsche catalogues a number of spectacular punishments that have been implemented historically, concluding that 'with the aid of such images and procedures one finally remembers five or six "I will not's" in regard to which one had given one's promise so as to participate in the advantages of society' (1887, p. 62). The infliction of physical pain, then, is key to our ability to enter contracts, including the social contract that is said to represent the collective will of the people.

In this way, the suffering body insures all legal and political domains, which are in turn supported by moral discourses. This economy is highly gendered. The other side of this contract based on pain is the creditor's pleasure—'the pleasure of being allowed to vent his power freely upon one who is powerless' (Nietzsche, 1887, p. 65). The pleasure appealed to here is sadistic but is also disguised as being moral in nature, a way of conceptualising what is owed to oneself and what is owed to others. Pain—the original injury—becomes the occasion for this exchange, and then the subject of it. Pain produces consciousness of guilt, or 'bad conscience,' which is located 'in the very material concept [of] Schulden [debts]' (Nietzsche, 1887, p. 63). Debts that are incurred through the creditor/debtor relationship are insured by pain. Repayment is always possible, 'even if only through the pain of the culprit' (Nietzsche, 1887, p. 63) (emphasis in original). In *Essays Critical and Clinical* (1998), Deleuze reworks Nietzsche's understanding of the contract to think through debt not as a transcendental concept, but as inscribed between bodies. The implications of this embodied and specific creditor-debtor relation remains finite as a contained 'system of cruelty' (Deleuze, 1998, p. 128). Justice pays this debt of 'terrible signs that lacerate bodies and stain them' (Deleuze, 1998, p. 128), marking out what each person owes and what they are owed. Judgment condemns its debtors 'to an endless servitude [that] annuls any liberatory process' (Deleuze, 1998, p. 128) that justice might otherwise offer; in turn preventing 'the emergence of any new mode of existence' that is free from the forces of being judged (Deleuze, 1998, p. 135).

Nietzsche's use of the creditor/debtor fiction to explain obligation in contract provides an immanent critique to Enlightenment liberal social contract theories based on the free, rational individual. The social contract is not a way out of suffering, as argued by Enlightenment thinkers—rather, pain is necessary to, and instrumentalised in, its very formation. In reading *Jennifer's Body* through the creditor/debtor metaphor, the stakes of holding the position of creditor become clear: since an underlying economy of pain is already in operation, and liberal legal processes fail to adequately protect us from sexual violence, the film suggests that the way through sexual violence is to engage with the underlying sexual/social contract on its own terms. This points to the possibility of new terms of engagement, possibly even a new social contract, based not on abstraction but on the material principles of bodies and exchange, where a survivor-creditor is legally produced as a subject who is entitled to claim their debt. The girls' super-agency is marked in the film by the trope of demonic possession, but there are other ways—social and legal—to give girls super-agency. It's worth considering how this might be done, in law and in culture; for example, we could legally define sexual assault survivors as creditors. The film theorises what might happen if we were to give girls this greater agency within the framework of revenge.

Conclusion

The films examined previously are each unique in their approach, but they are exemplary in taking the scene and figure of the violated girl and then theorising new legalities by radically departing through a range of genres, narratives, and tropes. Their narratives take revenge seriously but also critique the simplistic notion of revenge. Acts of individual revenge will not lead to justice—rather, solidarity of the disempowered is the answer. First Nations people, other non-white people, women, LGBTQIA people, and the poor all need to join together. It reveals that the war against one is a war against all, and the only way forward is to fight together. They critique the inadequacies of the legal system and propose alternative forms of justice that operate outside traditional legal boundaries, but they also critique assumptions around these alternatives, including the possibilities of revenge and the limits of basing justice on individual agency. By incorporating elements of tragedy, forgiveness, comedy, and the radical reimagining of social contracts, they offer more complex and nuanced approaches to addressing harm. Although the transformation from suffering/victimhood to agency/empowerment is thematised, these films make clear that individual agency within existing structures is not an end-point; rather, it is a starting point for new, radical possibilities. These films subvert traditional revenge narratives by emphasising systemic and institutional complicity in sexual violence and theorising radical new legalities in their place. The chapter argues that while revenge is often viewed negatively, it can serve as the basis for a legitimate legal framework.

Bibliography

Bastién, A. J. (2021, January 21) 'Emerald Fennell Explains Herself.' *Vulture*. Available at: www.vulture.com/2021/01/emerald-fennell-promising-young-woman-interview.html (Accessed: 8 August 2022).
Berlant, L. (2021) *Cruel Optimism*. Durham: Duke University Press.
Blichert, F. (2021) *Extra Salty: Jennifer's Body*. New York: ECW Press.
Butler, J. (2016) *Frames of War: When Is Life Grievable?* New York: Verso.
Caruth, C. (1996) *Unclaimed Experience: Trauma, Narrative, and History*. Baltimore: Johns Hopkins University Press.
Crawley, K. 'Promising Young Woman: Ambivalence and Disappointment in Feminist Attachments to Law.' Paper presented at the 'Righteous Feminist Violence: The Cinematic Jurisprudence of Revenge' panel of the Law, Literature and Humanities of Australasia Conference, *Deux in Machina*, QUT, December 2023. See the review here: www.lawlithum.org/women-on-the-edge-of-justice-by-elizabeth-rajapakshe/
Creed, B. (2022) *Return of the Monstrous-Feminine: Feminist New Wave Cinema*, 1st ed. London: Routledge.
Deleuze, G. (1998) *Essays Critical and Clinical*. London: Verso.
Ebert, R. (1980, July 16) 'I Spit on Your Grave.' *RogerEbert.com*. Available at: www.rogerebert.com/reviews/i-spit-on-your-grave-1980 (Accessed: 8 August 2022).
The Exorcist (1973) Directed by William Friedkin [Film]. Los Angeles: Warner Bros.
Fennell, E. (2020a) 'Promising Young Woman Director Breaks Down That Brutal Twist Ending.' *Interview by Joey Nolfi, Entertainment Weekly*. Available at:

https://ew.com/movies/promising-young-woman-ending-explained/ (Accessed: 10 March 2022).
Fennell, E. (2021a, March 14) 'Promising Young Woman Grabs Rape Culture by the Balls.' *Interview by Jessica Baxter, Hammer to Nail.* Available at: www.hammertonail.com/interviews/promising-young-woman-zoom/ (Accessed: 14 March 2021).
Fennell, E. (2021b, January 4) '"Promising Young Woman": Inside Emerald Fennell and Carey Mulligan's Unflinching Revenge Flick.' *Interview by JohnBoone, ET.* Available at: www.etonline.com/promising-young-woman-interview-emerald-fennell-carey-mulligan (Accessed: 4 January 2021).
Gilmore, L. (1994) *Autobiographics: A Feminist Theory of Women's Self-Representation.* Ithaca: Cornell University Press.
Gilmore, L. (2001) *The Limits of Autobiography: Trauma and Testimony.* Ithaca: Cornell University Press.
Gilmore, L. (2017) *Tainted Witness: Why We Doubt What Women Say About Their Lives.* New York: Columbia University Press.
Gilmore, L. (2023) *The #MeToo Effect: What Happens When We Believe Women*, 1st ed. New York: Columbia University Press.
Glista, V. (2023) 'Miriam Toews' *Women Talking* and the Embodied Life of Feminist Nonviolence.' *Contemporary Women's Writing*, 17(1), pp. 95–109.
Grady, C. (2018, October 31) 'How Jennifer's Body Went from a Flop in 2009 to a Feminist Cult Classic Today.' *Vox.* Available at: www.vox.com/culture/2018/10/31/18008686/jennifers-body-megan-fox-karyn-kusama (Accessed: 8 August 2022).
Heller-Nicholas, A. (2011) *Rape-Revenge Films: A Critical Study.* Jefferson: McFarland & Co.
Henry, C. (2014) *Revisionist Rape-Revenge: Redefining a Film Genre.* New York: Palgrave Macmillan.
I Spit on Your Grave (1978) Directed by Meir Zarchi [Film]. Los Angeles: CineTel Films.
Jennifer's Body (2009) Directed by Karyn Kusama [Film]. Los Angeles: 20th Century Fox.
Kehler, G. (2020) 'Becoming Divine Women: Miriam Toews' Women Talking as Parable.' *Literature & Theology*, 34(4), pp. 408–429.
Kent, J. (2018) 'The Nightingale: Official Director's Statement.' *IMDb.* Available at: www.imdb.com/title/tt4068576/trivia (Accessed: 10 March 2022).
Kent, J. (2019, August 1) 'Jennifer Kent Doesn't Think The Nightingale Is a Rape-Revenge Story.' Interview by Rachel Handler, *Vulture.* Available at: www.vulture.com/2019/08/the-babadooks-jennifer-kent-on-the-nightingale.html (Accessed: 1 August 2019).
Kill Bill Vol 1 (2003) Directed by Quentin Tarantino [Film]. Los Angeles: 20th Century Fox.
Kill Bill Vol 2 (2004) Directed by Quentin Tarantino [Film]. Los Angeles: 20th Century Fox.
Kristeva, J. (1982) *Powers of Horror: An Essay on Abjection.* Translated by Leon S. Roudiez. New York: Columbia University Press.
Kristeva, J. (2002a) *Intimate Revolt: The Powers and Limits of Psychoanalysis*, vol. 2. Translated by Jeanine Herman. New York: Columbia University Press.
Kristeva, J. (2002b) *Revolt, She Said.* Edited by Sylvère Lotringer. Translated by Brian O'Keefe. Los Angeles: Semiotext(e).
LaChance, N. (2016, September 2) 'Media Continues to Refer to Brock Turner as "Stanford Swimmer" Rather than a Rapist.' *The Intercept.* Available at: https://theintercept.com/2016/09/02/media-continues-to-refer-to-brock-turner-as-stanford-swimmer-rather-than-a-rapist/ (Accessed: 8 August 2022).

Larsson, S. (2015) *The Girl with the Dragon Tattoo*, vol. 1. London: MacLehose Press.
Lehman, P. (2014) 'Don't Blame This on a Girl: Female Rape-Revenge Films.' In S. Cohan and I. R. Hark (Eds.), *Screening the Male: Exploring Masculinities in Hollywood Cinema*. London: Routledge, pp. 103–117.
Lilley, K. (1997) 'Living Backward: Slessor and Masculine Elegy.' In P. Mead (Ed.), *Kenneth Slessor*. St Lucia Imprint: University of Queensland Press, pp. 246–264.
Mead, R. (2022) 'Talk Therapy.' *The New Yorker*, vol. 98. New York: Conde Nast PublicationsInc.
Motha, S. (2015) 'As If—Law, History, Ontology.' *UC Irvine Law Review*, 5, p. 327.
Nietzsche, F. (1887) *Genealogy of Morals*. Frankfurt: Boni and Liveright.
The Nightingale (2018) Directed by Jennifer Kent [Film]. Sydney, Australia: Causeway Films.
Pfau, T. (2010) 'Mourning Modernity: Classical Antiquity, Romantic Theory and Elegiac Form.' In K. Weisman (Ed.), *The Oxford Handbook of the Elegy*. Oxford: Oxford University Press, pp. 246–264.
Projansky, S. (2001) *Watching Rape: Film and Television in Postfeminist Culture*. New York: New York University Press.
Rae, P. (2007) *Modernism and Mourning*. Lewisburg: Bucknell University Press.
Ramazani, J. (1994) *Poetry of Mourning*. Chicago: The University of Chicago Press.
Reichman, R. (2003) 'New Forms for Our New Sensations: Woolf and the Lesson of Torts.' *Novel: A Forum on Fiction*, 36(3), pp. 398–422.
Reichman, R. (2009) *The Affective Life of Law: Legal Modernism and the Literary Imagination*. Stanford: Stanford University Press.
Réti, Z. O. (2023) 'Film Genres after #MeToo: Promising Young Woman as a Rape-Revenge Film and a Rom-Com.' *Hungarian Journal of English and American Studies*, 29(1), pp. 189–206.
Revenge (2017) dir Coralie Fargeat. Paris: Rezo Films.
Rubin, R. (2017, December 15) 'Ashley Judd, Mira Sorvino Respond to Peter Jackson's Claims that Weinstein Blacklisted Them.' *Variety*. Available at: https://variety.com/2017/film/news/ashley-judd-mira-sorvino-respond-peter-jackson-weinstein-blacklist-1202645066/ (Accessed: 8 August 2022).
Russo, A. (2019) *Feminist Accountability: Disrupting Violence and Transforming Power*. New York: New York University Press.
Sacks, P. (1985) *The English Elegy: Studies in the Genre from Spenser to Yeats*. Baltimore: Johns Hopkins University Press.
Salter, M. (2013) 'Justice and Revenge in Online Counter-Publics: Emerging Responses to Sexual Violence in the Age of Social Media.' *Crime, Media, Culture*, 9, pp. 225–242. http://doi.org/10.1177/1741659013493918 (Accessed: 8 August 2022).
Stewart, M. (2015) 'As If—Law, History, Ontology.' *UC Irvine Law Review*, 5, p. 327.
Toews, M. (2018) *Women Talking*. London: Faber & Faber.
Unterberger, A. (2019, September 12) 'The Story of Low Shoulder from Jennifer's Body, the Funniest and Most Disturbing Fictional Indie Rock Band Ever.' *Billboard*. Available at: www.billboard.com/articles/columns/pop/8529738/low-shoulder-jennifers-body-fictional-band (Accessed: 8 August 2022).
Women Talking (2022) Directed by Sarah Polley [Film]. Los Angeles: Orion Pictures.

Chapter 4

Law and the Girl at the End of the World

Introduction: The Instrumentalised Child

The persistence of state violence against First Nations peoples is constituted through legal and political domains, as well as through particular stories, myths, and figures that are part of our colonial legacy. These include the stories we tell about so-called 'settlement,' and about the effects of colonialism on First Nations people. One of the most dangerous myths is that colonial law is justified in asserting jurisdiction over First Nations people, and one of the most dangerous figures in this context is the figure of the child. The figure of 'the vulnerable First Nations child' is an overdetermined figure in both legal and public imaginaries. The role of this figure in what we might think of more widely as Australia's imaginary of colonial authority—which transcends legal, political, and cultural domains—needs to be interrogated and challenged (see van Rijswijk, 2012, 2013, 2014, 2015a, 2015b, 2016b, 2017, 2018, 2019, 2021, 2023, 2024). The effect of the figure of 'the vulnerable First Nations child' can be explained through the concept of haunting, which points to a way of knowing that takes account of the role of the past in the present, as well as the relation between representation and materiality (Gordon, 2008). Haunting marks the resistant power of this figure of the child in case law, legislation, and more widely in the public imaginary. Haunting also marks the fact that the figure's presence and effects are not immediately transparent to us, despite the figure being so dominant. Brian Massumi explains haunting as an 'affective intensity,' which operates 'in excess of any narrative or functional line' (2002, p. 26). We can also think of haunting as marking the ways in which legal and cultural aesthetics affect judgment, beyond explicit reasoning and logic.

To say that state law is haunted by the figure of 'the vulnerable First Nations child' is also to point to the aesthetic, affective, and political effects of the continuing colonial imaginary of authority. 'Haunting' points to complex ways this figure shores up colonial legality, supported by law's own practices of representation. These practices include the ways in which law narrates the past and the present to itself, which in turn is an effect of colonial histories of loss and repression, as well as an effect of the politics of the colonial present.

DOI: 10.4324/9780429263675-4

The persistence of state violence against First Nations peoples is constituted through legal and political domains, as well as through the persistence of cultural imaginaries that are part of the colonial legacy. At the same time that we analyse these imaginaries, we need to pay attention to the ways in which communities are materially affected by the legal and social policies that are produced through 'the vulnerable First Nations child'—the ways in which real children, and real women and men, are harmed. We need to examine the gendered nature of twentieth and twenty-first century state colonial violence and connect historical with contemporary violence.

This chapter begins with a critical examination of law's violent imaginary formed around the figure of the First Nations child, moves through public responses to these harms (initiated by the state), and then looks to the counter-imaginary provided by a reading of Alexis Wright's novels, focusing on how the instrumentalisation of children is not only refuted but reimagined. Alexis Wright, a First Nations Waanyi novelist, uses the figure of the First Nations child—with a focus on the *girl*—to write against the violent myths of Australian state law.[1] I examine harm and its relation to authority in Wright's novels, which I argue together provide an exemplary, radical text that counters the imaginary of colonial authority. Each of Wright's novels—*Plains of Promise* (1997), *Carpentaria* (2006), *The Swan Book (2013)*, and *Praiseworthy (2023)*—challenges the relation of harm to questions of First Nations authority. In this counter imaginary, Wright rewrites law's narratives and figures and makes explicit that which the state has hidden in plain sight. This chapter begins by focusing on the figure of the child as described in legal cases and political discourses, but at all times it must be remembered that the child is necessarily racialised and gendered. The material nature of the child is essential to the critical work being done here and will be brought out in the development of the counter-imaginary. I will show how Wright's work deconstructs law's violent myths and figures and provides us with new frameworks of meaning—so that we can fully see the violence of our existing laws and so we can demand better laws in the future. This literature is so significant because it provides forms for what we would otherwise not see: first, that law is violent; and second, that law's violence is disguised through its myths and figures.

Legal narratives and figures, as well as what we might more widely think of as practices of representation, produce social, economic, and political realities. The imaginary is therefore an important area of intervention for social justice—exemplary novels, poems, films, and TV shows—can also be sites of

1 The phrases 'state law' and 'colonial law' are used interchangeably in this chapter to mark the current Australian legal system and to distinguish the particular legal system of Australian state, territory and federal governments from the multiple First Nations legal systems and relations that also operate within Australian territories (but continue to not be recognised by the state).

'doing law,' as this book has explored. This literary jurisprudence encourages a broader understanding of what constitutes 'law' and legal thinking. In this way, novels, poems, and films become sites where emergent imaginaries theorise new law, new ways of thinking, beyond the state-going against law's violence and also against the (frequently) violent imaginary of mainstream culture. In this tradition, Alexis Wright's novels provide us with alternative ways of legal thinking—in very real ways they show how we might create and 'do' law. Her novels reveal the fragility of categories and narratives of identity and truth upon which justice relies. Her novels undo the violent logics that our current laws take as axiomatic and reveals what it often disguised not only in law but in mainstream culture—the continuing violence of both our laws and our politics against First Nations children, which is still papered over with a story of 'best interests.' We see this violence in the continuing removal of First Nations children from their families and communities, and the related violence of Australia's carceral imagination, which has led to the over-incarceration not only of First Nation adults but of First Nations children as young as ten years old. Moreover, Wright's novels reveal the inter-connectedness of these different forms of brutality, stripping away any kind of sentimental feeling to show the very bleak reality of how cruel our laws are and how cruel our public cultures of feeling are towards our most vulnerable citizens. Her novels show that this violence is not only historical but very much located in the present—and that the public sentimentality of the Apology or *Bringing Them Home* or Reconciliation mean nothing if we cannot stop this violence in the present.

Wright's work also gives us hope and a way forward. Her fiction provides new frameworks, metaphors, and narratives to represent not only the injustice of the harms inflicted by the law against First Nations children but what should come next. Wright's oeuvre not only thematically deals with law's violence against First Nations children, it also reimagines law's frameworks through the point of view of vulnerable First Nations children, providing us with the most important focalisation through which we should be thinking and doing law, rethinking jurisdiction, and rethinking sovereignty.

The Aesthetics of Producing Colonial Authority: Past Harms

State law continues to assert and reinforce its authority over First Nations people in the ways it narrates the past in legal cases, legislation, and public projects. As the legal scholar Irene Watson argues, past and present violence against First Nations people has been read as 'beneficial,' as acts of 'saving [First Nations people] from themselves' (Watson, 2009, p. 1). Examining the history of state law and policy, the First Nations child emerges as a significant figure through which colonial violence was enacted. The Australian state has historically asserted authority and jurisdiction over First Nations people on the basis that it is addressing, preventing, or redressing *purported* harms to First Nations children. This figure has been the occasion for legal violence from the Aborigines Protection Acts of the twentieth century, which produced the harms suffered by the Stolen Generations,[2] to the Northern Territory Intervention in the twenty-first century.[3] Between 1995 and 1997, an Australian federal government agency, the Human Rights and Equal Opportunity Commission (HREOC), conducted an inquiry into the forcible removal of First Nations and Torres Strait Islander children from their parents (referred to as the Stolen Generations). HREOC examined widespread practices that had been carried out by both government and private organisations under the auspices of state and federal legislative regimes. HREOC's final report, *Bringing Them Home*, published in 1997, found that from approximately 1910 to 1970, between one and three of every ten First Nations or Torres Strait Islander children had been forcibly removed from their families, and that this had led to ongoing physical and psychological harms (HREOC, 1997, p. 308 onwards).

Bringing Them Home concluded that the forcible removal of First Nations and Torres Strait Islander children from their families and communities constituted cultural genocide under the United Nations Genocide Convention 1948 (ratified by Australia in 1949) as well as customary international law (HREOC, 1997, pp. 308–309). HREOC recommended the use of the United Nations' van Boven Principles for Victims of Gross Violations of Human Rights for survivors, including implementation of a full range of reparation measures, such as restitution, compensation, rehabilitation, satisfaction, and guarantees of not-repetition (HREOC, 1997, pp. 308–309). *Bringing Them Home* also recommended that a reparations scheme be established and that there be a national apology (HREOC, 1997, pp. 308–309). *Bringing Them*

2 Human Rights and Equal Opportunity Commission, *Bringing Them Home: Report of the National Inquiry into the Separation of Indigenous and Torres Strait Islander Children From Their Families* (Sydney: Commonwealth of Australia, 1997) ('*Bringing Them Home*'). Examples of earlier regulatory regimes include: the *Aborigines Protection and Restriction of the Sale of Opium Act 1897* (Qld), s 9, 11, 13; *Aborigines Protection Act 1886* (Vic); *Aborigines Act 1890* (Vic); *Aborigines Protection Act 1890 (WA)*; *Aborigines Protection Act 1909 (NSW)*; *Northern Territory Aborigines Act 1910* (SA) 1910; *Aborigines Act 1911* (SA).

3 *Northern Territory National Emergency Response Act 2007* (Cth) No. 129 (NTNERA); *Family, Community Services, Indigenous Affairs and Other Legislation Amendment (Northern Territory National Emergency Response and Other Measures) Act 2007* (Cth) No. 128; *Social Security and Other Legislation Amendment (Welfare Payment Reform) Act 2007* (Cth) No. 130; *Families, Community Services and Indigenous Affairs and Other Legislation Amendment (Northern Territory National Emergency Response and Other Measures) Act 2007* (Cth) No. 128; *Appropriation (Northern Territory National Emergency Response) Act (No. 1) 2007* (Cth) No. 126 and *Appropriation (Northern Territory National Emergency Response) Act (No. 2) 2007* (Cth) No. 127. I use the phrase 'the Northern Territory Intervention' or 'the Intervention' to refer to this regime.

Home thereby did important work in documenting 'the everydayness and bureaucratisation of genocide and of massive human rights violations in the liberal democratic state' (Orford, 2006, pp. 851–883). In tracing the past 'laws, practices and policies' that produced the Stolen Generations (HREOC, 1997, p. 3), the inquiry and the final report made a significant intervention into the silence of both the legal domain and the public sphere of that time. But despite the important recommendations made, no federal reparations scheme has ever been put in place.

The responses of both the legal system and the government to the state violence documented in *Bringing Them Home* are telling. Responsibility in the *Bringing Them Home* report was broadly textured, outlining the national and international legal frameworks that applied to the removals, but not focusing in detail on the actions or responsibilities of specific institutions and individuals. No criminal proceedings arose out of the findings. Further, the wide range of people who were responsible for the policies of child removal, and who were involved in child removals—including still-living public servants, legislators, politicians, police officers, heads of institutions, and government ministers—were not included in the process of acquiring the testimonies that formed a large part of the inquiry or of the subsequent report. Raimond Gaita argues that those authorities and their agents would have been guilty of genocide and should have faced trials: 'How can one say that genocide had been committed, yet only ask for an apology and compensation? How can you think genocide always to be a serious crime, yet find it unthinkable to call for criminal proceedings?' (Gaita, 2011, p. 44). Gaita also states that in Australia, such trials were 'literally unthinkable, and that they are so . . . is the most persuasive evidence that the significance of the crimes against [First Nations People] has not been fully appreciated' (Gaita, 2011, p. 45).

Bringing Them Home made clear that the state violence of child removal was based on false narratives centred on the figure of the 'vulnerable First Nations child.' The Report found that removals across different states and territories were justified through a range of legislative regimes, including 'protectionist' legislation that was specific to First Nations peoples[4] and more general welfare-based legislation (HREOC, 1997, pp. 22–34). In removing children, officials often relied on claims of abuse or neglect, evidence for which was either not required, or which was justified on the sole basis that the child was a First Nations child, or was living in poverty (HREOC, 1997, pp. 22–34). Other claims relied upon by the state were that children were removed on the basis that their parents consented to or even solicited

4 Examples of these regimes include the *Aborigines Protection and Restriction of the Sale of Opium Act 1897* (Qld), s 9, 11, 13; *Aborigines Protection Act 1886* (Vic); *Aborigines Act 1890* (Vic); *Aborigines Protection Act 1890 (WA); Aborigines Protection Act 1909 (NSW); Northern Territory Aborigines Act 1910* (SA) 1910; and *Aborigines Act 1911* (SA).

their removal, claims that have subsequently been proven to be false—for example, historians have documented that in many cases, this 'consent' was fraudulently manufactured or produced through duress (see van Rijswijk and Anthony, 2012; Luker, 2005). A great number of survivors of these removals gave evidence to HREOC that they had not in fact been vulnerable or neglected and that their parents did not consent to their removal (HREOC, 1997, pp. 22–42). *Bringing Them Home* documented the different ways in which the purported 'abuse' or 'neglect' of children was used as a ruse for the forced removal and assimilation of First Nations children. Many survivors have testified that they were sent to foster homes or institutions that were themselves violent and abusive, when their family of origin was not. Thus, children who had been safe in their own homes were sent to institutions and foster homes under these policies where they suffered significant harm.

Sexual violence was noted as one of the many harms caused to survivors, with a number of witnesses reporting sexual abuse during the course of the inquiry (HREOC, 1997, pp. 140–144). In *Bringing Them Home*, HREOC stated that 'children in every placement were vulnerable to sexual abuse and exploitation' (HREOC, 1997, p. 140). Despite not being directly asked about experiences of sexual abuse during the extensive interviews, out of sensitivity to interviewees' experiences, approximately 30% of women volunteered that they had experienced sexual abuse in foster families and 11% volunteered that they had experienced sexual abuse in institutions (HREOC, 1997, p. 141). However, sexual abuse and sexual harassment were not studied as a focus harm across survivors of the Stolen Generations (HREOC, Vol 2, p. 53). In another study of around 700 care-leavers—including Forgotten Australians, members of the Stolen Generations and Former Child Migrants who resided in institutions including children's homes, orphanages, and other forms of out-of-home-care between 1930 and 1989—most participants (96.7%) experienced some form of maltreatment. Emotional, physical, and sexual abuse frequently co-occurred, and around 41% of participants in the study experienced all forms of maltreatment (physical abuse, sexual abuse, verbal abuse, emotional abuse, witnessing violence, bullying, neglect, and other). Other forms of maltreatment included inadequate food and clothing, humiliation, exposure to extreme weather, and solitary confinement (Fernandez et al., 2016, p. 112).

The Royal Commission into Institutional Responses to Child Abuse in 2015 (the Commission) illuminated the specific, material ways that a vast number of Australian institutions failed to protect children from sexual abuse (van Rijswijk, 2016a). The Commission had strong powers to call people to give evidence and also had significantly more flexibility in how that evidence was given, compared to common law processes. Some of the case studies concern institutions also described in Bringing Them Home: these include Case Study 7 (Parramatta Training School for Girls and the Institution for Girls in Hay), Case Study 17 (Retta Dixon Home), and Case Study 19 (Bethcar

Children's Home). But the Commission's focus on institutions meant it could not include evidence from foster homes (noted as having a 30% abuse rate in *Bringing Them Home*) and other non-institutional settings. And despite its documentation of sexual abuse, the Commission did not take an intersectional approach to gender and race—in turn failing to capture the ways in which this sexual violence is not epiphenomenal, that it cannot be separated from the colonial violence of forcible separation and state violence.

Following the failure of the state to implement key recommendations of *Bringing Them Home*, some Stolen Generations survivors brought claims at common law. But there have only been a handful of cases concerning harms arising from the Stolen Generations, and only one of these has succeeded.[5] In these cases, harms are framed as personal or individual, disconnected from wider state policies of assimilation, which included the forceful removal of communities from their land, and the targeting of language and culture, all of which were direct attacks on the sovereignty of First Nations peoples. This narrow framing is made necessary through the forms of common law, which insist on individuation and only recognise limited harms and responsibilities (van Rijswijk and Anthony, 2012). These absences regarding questions of authority in the Stolen Generations cases mean that no connection is made in the legal archive between past and present state harms against First Nations peoples. One of the most significant barriers to these claims succeeding has been the tendency of courts to interpret past actions of the state as having been carried out with the 'best interests' of First Nations children in mind. In other words, courts took the beneficial intentions of the state at face value, regardless of evidence to the contrary (van Rijswijk and Anthony, 2012). The reading of beneficial state intention in these cases relies on an underlying narrative that the state is acting in good faith in deciding how to prevent harm and that these decisions are effective. However, evidence concerning both past and present state interventions has demonstrated that these decisions are not made in good faith, and they mostly cause more harm than good (for examples and analysis, see Genovese, 2011; O'Connor, 2001; Cunneen and Grix, 2004; Buti, 2008, 2008–2009; Hocking and Stephenson, 2008; Luker, 2005; van Rijswijk and Anthony, 2012). In turn, most courts have not examined the racist, harmful assumptions behind the legislative frameworks and state policies, which were based on the violent principle of assimilation. The

5 The High Court denied claims for compensation in *Kruger v Commonwealth* (1997) 190 CLR 1 ('*Kruger*'), and the Federal Court denied claims in *Cubillo v The Commonwealth [No 2]* 112 FCR 1 ('*Cubillo*'). The Western Australian Supreme Court recently denied a claim for compensation in *Collard v The State of Western Australia* [No 4] [2013] WASC 455. *South Australia v Lampard-Trevorrow* (2010) 106 SASR 331 (*'Lampard-Trevorrow'*), where the court dismissed the State's appeal against the decision of Gray J in *Trevorrow v South Australia (No 5)* (2007) 98 SASR 136 (*'Trevorrow'*), has been the only successful Stolen Generations case (hereafter referred to as the '*Trevorrow* cases').

harm-prevention narrative, marked by the phrase 'best interests,' therefore occludes the role of state violence and its genocidal effects.

The question of responsibility for suffering raises the key question of who will be the authority that is empowered to determine responsibility for harms. In other words, the adjudication of harms implicitly raises the question of sovereignty. But sovereignty is not marked at all in the Stolen Generations cases. Rather than seeing forcible removal as part of the state's wider refusal to acknowledge First Nations sovereignty and authority, and acknowledging that policies of assimilation were a violent assault against their authority, courts have distanced specific acts of state actors from the context of these general policies of assimilation, and further, defined the state's intentions as beneficial. Claiming a role merely in the adjudication of harms taking place in First Nations communities, the state asserted its jurisdiction; the use of state authority in this way in turn inflicted harms on those communities, but this violence was disguised as being in the 'best interests' of First Nations children.

The Colonial Imaginary

The figure of 'the vulnerable First Nations child' is a focal point for the aesthetic, affective, and political effects of the continuing colonial imaginary of authority. Stolen Generations' testimonies, which have been shaped to centre this figure, have been one of the main domains through which the Australian public has encountered state violence against First Nations people. At the same time that Stolen Generations' testimonies have been part of important grassroots projects to address the gaps and refusals of law and public life, the testimonies have also been instrumentalised by state narratives that were counter-productive to the achievement of justice for the Stolen Generations. Public testimony is also the main form through which the public has made sense of the political and juridical claims that arise from the Stolen Generations' experiences. However, these encounters have occurred largely through the sentimental genre (see e.g., Kennedy (2011)), and even, in Robert Meister's terms, through the genre of 'melodrama' (2011). The consequence of the public encountering these testimonies in the public domain in the sentimental mode is that the political and juridical claims of the Stolen Generations are sidelined: people encounter the testimonies in a 'bystander' role, rather than as responsible actors (Meister, 2011). Often, the effect of a sentimental encounter has been produced by state design, as fragments from testimonies have been selected and instrumentalised in public meta-narratives that emphasise particular elements of the Stolen Generations' experiences rather than their full complexity as in the national Apology, described next.

Bringing Them Home was a didactic text—one of its main purposes was to educate the mainstream public regarding the experiences of the Stolen

Generations, and the responsibilities that arose through this suffering. It was clearly aimed at eliciting empathic responses from the public in ways that were compatible with the state's narrative that these harms were in the past, and that they could be healed through reconciliation processes. Rosanne Kennedy (2011) argues that a didactic training of the Australian public began with the Council for Reconciliation, and continued through the inquiry by HREOC, and its subsequent report, *Bringing Them Home*, as well as through the activities of the National Sorry Day Committee. Kennedy describes the Sorry Books Campaign of the late 1990s as 'a popular reconciliation movement' and argues that, far from Australians' responses of personal apology being spontaneous or 'intuitive,' the Sorry Books had the effect of a didactic movement that 'educated' ordinary Australians on their moral obligation to respond—and on the forms their response should take (Kennedy, 2011, p. 265). Kennedy compares this response to what Lauren Berlant has described in the context of the United States, as 'a popular belief in national sentimentality, a rhetoric of promise that a nation can be built across fields of social difference through channels of affective identification and empathy' (Kennedy, 2011, pp. 49, 53). Here, sentimentality serves as a conduit through which widespread subaltern suffering is brought into the dominant public sphere, framing it at the heart of national unity; privileged national subjects internalise the suffering of marginalised or disenfranchised citizens as their own (2011, pp. 49, 53).

The effect of public sentimentality is that a certain affect or empathy is felt, without that affect, or the underlying suffering, leading to juridical or political justice (in the form of the reparations recommended by HREOC, for example). *Bringing Them Home* was the medium through which testimonies of suffering circulated, prompting their audience to identify merely empathically with that suffering (Kennedy, 2011, p. 259). Encountered in this way, the testimonies led to a form of national feeling that had little to do with the material experiences of suffering and which did not lead to political or legal calls for justice. The Apology made by then Prime Minister Kevin Rudd in 2008 is one such example. The Apology did not acknowledge the full degree of the damage caused by removal policies to individuals and to First Nations communities through the destruction of cultural practices, identity, and language. The Apology was the ideal moment when a federal reparations scheme should have been announced and thereafter implemented, but reparations were not mentioned. Instead, the Apology emphasised the discursive justice aspect of responses to the Stolen Generations and implied that the state's apology signified closure of past injustices, and a shift to a focus on a fair future.

Most significant, Prime Minister Rudd's Apology built on the didacticism of *Bringing Them Home* by providing a powerful lesson from state to public in how to interpret the Stolen Generations' experiences. In his speech preceding the formal Apology, Rudd drew on the testimony of a member of the Stolen Generations, instrumentalising select elements of her life story as a First Nations girl who was removed from her family so that it corresponded to the state-sanctioned framework of reconciliation and fit within a sentimental, resolvable narrative (see also Frow, 2001; Reilly, 2009; Mookherjee et al., 2009). Stating that Lorna 'Nanna Nungala' Fejo's story was one of many thousands of stories of forced separation, Rudd emphasised the role of suffering in grounding the need for a response:

> There is something terribly primal about these firsthand accounts. The pain is searing; it screams from the pages. The hurt, the humiliation, the degradation and the sheer brutality of the act of physically separating a mother from her children is a deep assault on our senses and on our most elemental humanity. . . . These stories cry out to be heard; they cry out for an apology. Instead, from the nation's parliament there has been a stony and stubborn and deafening silence for more than a decade.
>
> (Rudd, 2008, n.p.)

Rudd then proceeded to tell Nanna Fejo's story by focusing on her as a child, rather than, for example, examining the ways her stolen childhood has affected her throughout her adulthood. Rudd deployed the subjective third person point of view in his retelling of Nanna Nungala Fejo's story. Focalising his speech through a childlike point of view, and using short sentences and simple vocabulary to evoke a child's experience, Rudd recounted Nanna Fejo's early life, before her removal, taking on a position of innocence and naivety. Recalling Nanna Fejo's earliest childhood days in the late 1920s, Rudd described a small girl living with her family and her community in a bush camp just outside Tennant Creek in the Northern Territory:

> She remembers her earliest childhood days living with her family and her community in a bush camp just outside Tennant Creek. She remembers the love and the warmth and the kinship of those days long ago, including traditional dancing around the campfire at night. She loved the dancing. She remembers once getting into strife when, as a four-year-old girl, she insisted on dancing with the male tribal elders rather than just sitting and watching the men, as the girls were supposed to do.
>
> (Rudd, 2008, n.p.)

Rudd then related the scene of removal, again using short sentences and simple words to evoke the point of view of a child:

> But then, sometime around 1932, when she was about four, she remembers the coming of the welfare men. Her family had feared that day and

> had dug holes in the creek bank where the children could run and hide. What they had not expected was that the white welfare men did not come alone. They brought a truck, two white men and an First Nations stockman on horseback cracking his stockwhip. The kids were found; they ran for their mothers, screaming, but they could not get away. They were herded and piled onto the back of the truck. Tears flowing, her mum tried clinging to the sides of the truck as her children were taken away to the Bungalow in Alice, all in the name of protection.
>
> (Rudd, 2008, n.p.)

She was taken to a mission, and Prime Minister Rudd took up her story there:

> She stayed at the mission until after the war, when she was allowed to leave for a prearranged job as a domestic in Darwin. She was 16. Nanna Fejo never saw her mum again. After she left the mission, her brother let her know that her mum had died years before, a broken woman fretting for the children that had literally been ripped away from her.
>
> (Rudd, 2008, n.p.)

Rudd then recalled this encounter with Nanna Fejo:

> As I left, later on, Nanna Fejo took one of my staff aside, wanting to make sure that I was not too hard on the First Nations stockman who had hunted those kids down all those years ago. The stockman had found her again decades later, this time himself to say, 'Sorry.' And remarkably, extraordinarily, she had forgiven him.
>
> (Rudd, 2008, n.p.)

In this recounting, Nanna Fejo's particular experience becomes an allegory for the reconciliation of the nation—all losses are remedied by the return to family, all losses are now in the past, and most important, there has been forgiveness and resolution through the speech act of saying 'sorry.' The stockman's apology is graciously accepted, anticipating and modelling the response that Rudd hopes for his own, national Apology. This is a familiar pattern in the shaping and reception of these testimonies—writing of *Bringing Them Home*, Anne Orford argues that the report's narrative begins with the transgressions of violence and removal and ends with the resolution of obligations, and with stable families, 'where all are sorted back into their proper places and all debts are paid' (Orford, 2006, pp. 870–871). She notes that many people found that there was no home to return to and that they could not recover their old identity or community, so that 'the text is haunted by the stories of children who cannot go home' (Orford, 2006, p. 871). These losses that cannot be recovered are present in the testimonies but are not prominent in the report's final recommendations (Orford, 2006, p. 872).

Indeed, the genocidal practices, and colonisation in general, have set in motion losses that can never be recovered.

Rudd's Apology proceeded to describe a future that 'embraces all Australians.' It flattened out history and asserted that First Nations and non-First Nations Australians were equal in both the past and the future. A number of clauses in the Apology opened with reference to the future, and there were a number of statements that gestured towards the closing of the past, symbolically, with the discursive act of Apology. The framing narratives in both the Apology and in *Bringing Them Home* focus on the scene of a child's removal from their family and community, whose significance depends upon subsequent legal or social recognition (Orford, 2006, pp. 870–871). This has the effect of separating the event of removal from its ongoing context and creates a false distance between removal and the wider policies of past and present. Policies regarding the Stolen Generations are better understood as a series of ongoing practices (see Orford, 2006; Haebich, 2000). Considering the ways in which the child has instrumentalised in these transitional justice projects opens up critique on wider state and cultural myths, whose juridical forms and aesthetics have overdetermined the possibility of justice for subjects of state-inflicted violence and trauma. Narratives of the continuing rupture of First Nations lives are important—narratives that show the ways in which this suffering is not 'historical' for those who have survived, but present-day, and interrelated with current structural racism and gendered harms.

The Production of Colonial Authority in the Present

Perhaps the most literal example of the overdetermination and instrumentalisation of the figure of the 'vulnerable First Nations child' can be seen in the Northern Territory National Emergency Response, known as 'The Intervention.' The Intervention was implemented in 2007 through a set of laws that permitted the seizure of local community land leases by the federal Liberal government, the deployment of the army into Northern Territory communities, the use of extra police powers, and the quarantining of welfare benefits. This regime ended in 2012, when it was replaced by a similar set of laws implemented by the federal Labor Government, rebranded as the *Stronger Futures* legislation.[6] The occasion for The Intervention was the publication

6 When the Northern Territory Intervention came to the end of its five-year period in July 2012, it was immediately replaced by the *Stronger Futures in the Northern Territory Act 2012* (Cth) (No. 100) and related laws: *Stronger Futures in the Northern Territory Act 2013* (Cth) (No. 184); *Social Security Legislation Amendment Act 2012* (Cth) (No 102). These laws will operate for a ten-year period: Stronger Futures s 118. Stronger Futures is broken up into a number of Parts that administer aspects of the lives of First Nations citizens in the Northern Territory. 'Tackling alcohol abuse' (Part 2) is aimed at 'reducing alcohol-related harm to those First Nations people'; 'Land reform' (Part 3), is 'aimed at facilitating the granting of rights and interests,

of the *Little Children are Sacred Report* (Wild and Anderson, 2007, 'The Report') following an inquiry commissioned by the Territory's *Inquiries Act* in August of 2006.[7] The Board of Inquiry into the Protection of First Nations Children from Sexual abuse was tasked to, among other things, 'examine the extent, nature and factors contributing to sexual abuse of First Nations children, with a particular focus on unreported incidents of such abuse' and to 'consider how the NT Government can help support communities to effectively prevent and tackle child sexual abuse' (Wild and Anderson, 2007, p. 4). The subsequent report found that child sexual abuse was 'an issue of urgent national significance' (Wild and Anderson, 2007, p. 22). A number of earlier reports had also found that child abuse and violence against women were significant problems in First Nations communities in the Northern Territory (see Cunneen and Libesman, 2002 and government reports on New South Wales, Queensland, and Western Australia).[8]

The language of The Intervention legislation refers to First Nations welfare and well-being (for example, the purpose of the *Northern Territory National Emergency Response Act* was 'to improve the well-being of certain communities in the Northern Territory'). However, The Intervention, and subsequent *Stronger Futures* legislation introduced measures that went well beyond the issue of child abuse, to affect land rights, welfare benefits, and access to services. The first recommendation of the Board of Inquiry was to emphasise 'the critical importance of governments committing to genuine consultation with First Nations people in designing initiatives for First Nations communities' (Wild and Anderson, 2007, p. 21), but this principle was not carried through in the subsequent legislation, or in the subsequent

and promoting economic development'; 'Food security' (Part 4), and some miscellaneous matters (Part 5) are also covered. The legislation includes income management schemes, and provisions for the suspension of parents' welfare payments if children's attendance rate at school is considered unacceptable (*Social Security Legislation Amendment Act 2012* (Cth) (No 102) Sch 2.). I use the term 'Stronger Futures' to refer to this regime.

7 The Board of Inquiry into the Protection of First Nations Children from Sexual Abuse was established on 8 August 2006 ('the Inquiry').

8 Chris Cunneen and Terri Libesman, *A Review of International Models for Indigenous Child Protection*, A report prepared for the NSW Department of Community Services (2002); Human Rights and Equal Opportunities Commission (HREOC), *Ending Violence and Abuse in First Nations and Torres Strait Islander Communities—Key Issues: An Overview Paper of Research and Findings by the Human Rights and Equal Opportunities Commission, 2001–2006* (Sydney: HREOC, 2006); NSW First Nations Child Sexual Assault Taskforce, *Breaking the Silence: Creating the Future, Addressing Child Sexual Assault in First Nations Communities in NSW* (Sydney: NSW Premier's Department, 2006); Queensland Crime Commission and Queensland Police Service, *Child Sexual Abuse in Queensland: The Nature and Extent: Volume 1. Project Axis* (Brisbane, 2000); S Gordon, K Hallahan and D Henry, *Putting the Picture Together, Inquiry into the Response by Government Agencies into Complaints of Family Violence and Child Abuse in First Nations Communities* (Perth: Department of the Premier and Cabinet Western Australia, 2002).

iterations of government policy. The report also noted the roles of poverty, poor health, and poor employment opportunities in producing violence and included recommendations to support Northern Territory communities by providing additional resources, such as provision for community consultation, family support services, education, employment, and housing, but most of these recommendations were not implemented in the subsequent legislation either. 'The vulnerable First Nations child' became a dangerous figure in the imaginaries of both state jurisdiction and the public domain, through which the scope of 'legitimate' violence by the state becomes overly broad. This feeds into the enduring colonial story in Australia that the state has a unique (and exceptional) role in adjudicating harms suffered by First Nations communities in ways that are different from law's adjudication of the harms of non–First Nations communities. In these legislative regimes and their surrounding public debates, the suffering, such as that documented in the *Little Children are Sacred Report* (Wild and Anderson, 2007), is explained as an effect of aberrant community and family structures. Law's reading excludes the complex effects of continuing colonisation, and the intergenerational effects of past traumas caused by the state, well documented in Stolen Generations legal cases and the *Bringing Them Home* report (HREOC, 1997). Although the system has officially ended, its ideology lives on in other forms, as discussed in later parts of this chapter. A narrative of harm-prevention has been used to justify a legislative response that provides for, simultaneously, both the withdrawal of state services to First Nations communities that non-First Nations Australians take for granted, and the introduction of techniques of colonial-type governance. Claiming a role merely in the adjudication of harms taking place in First Nations communities, the state asserts its jurisdiction and thereby inflicts harms on those communities and, in doing so, disguises its own violence. The 'vulnerable First Nations child' becomes a dangerous figure in law's imaginary, a key trope through which the scope of seemingly 'legitimate' violence by the state becomes overly broad, and a figure that also limits the subsequent adjudication of acts of the state—for example, supporting reasoning such as that of the court in *Kruger*, which found that state acts carried out under the Aboriginals Ordinance 1918 (NT) were not genocidal because they were carried out with good intentions, in the 'best interests' of First Nations people. These problems concern law's categories and logics, but they also concern law's practices of representation—the genres, figures, and narratives that constitute and are legible to law.

Alexis Wright's Radical Imaginary as a Critique of Colonial Authority

In this section, I argue that Alexis Wright's novels provide an exemplary and radical critique of colonial authority, countering the imaginary of colonial authority. Each of Wright's novels, including *Plains of Promise* (1997), *Carpentaria* (2006), *The Swan Book* (2013), and *Praiseworthy* (2023), challenges the relation of harm to questions of First Nations authority. This counter-imaginary rewrites law's narratives and figures, revealing what the state has hidden in plain sight. The focus on the figure of the child, as described in legal cases and political discourses, is crucial, bearing in mind that the child is necessarily racialised and gendered. Wright's work deconstructs law's violent myths and figures, offering new frameworks of meaning to expose the violence of existing laws and demand better laws in the future. Wright's literature is significant as it brings to light the fact that law is violent and its violence is disguised through myths and figures. Temporality is key here—in Wright's work we see the continuous presence of First Nations sovereignty through the forms of the Dreamtime; in contrast, Wright's novels represent the continuous *harm* caused by the colonial order. In the colonial imaginary, both First Nations sovereignty and harm to First Nations people are discrete events that are relegated to the past, reflecting the teleology of the coloniser. Wright radically reimagines this imaginary; her work is generative and involves undoing and remaking, shedding light on the liminal figure of 'the girl' that is caught up in narratives signifying ruptures of extremity and the violence of the everyday.

Thematically, *Plains of Promise* addresses the Stolen Generations, while the later novels speak to questions of harm in relation to sovereignty (*Carpentaria*), and the state's treatment of the First Nations child (*The Swan Book* and *Praiseworthy*). Together, all four of Wright's novels provide a developed counter-imaginary to the state's continuing assertions of authority over First Nations people based on the figure of 'the vulnerable First Nations child.' I argue that Wright's work provides a way of thinking through elements of the imaginary of colonial authority—not only this authority's juridical and political aspects, but as it manifests in cultural representations, and in the public imaginary. These novels connect that which has been disconnected or omitted in law. A central point, which will be examined later, is that First Nations law has tended to be interpreted as a form of myth or folklore, or as a marker of 'culture,' rather than as a source of authority in its own right. Wright directly takes on this issue of representation, implicitly arguing that this de-centring of First Nations authority as a matter of acknowledgement and genre is central to the ways in which the state—and the public—have used the occasion or perception of harm to intervene in First Nations communities. The interpretation of First Nations law as being cultural, rather than authoritative, supports the underlying racialised and colonial logic for state intervention: in removing children from communities, states do not need to acknowledge that they are breaching First Nations sovereignties and laws.

Contemporary Violence Against the First Nations Child

Wright's novels highlight what socio-legal research has demonstrated: that despite an ideology of child protection, First Nations children continue to be removed from their families at alarming rates and experience disproportionately high rates of imprisonment, harm, and suicide. Sixteen years have elapsed since Kevin Rudd, the former Prime Minister of Australia, issued a formal Apology to the Stolen Generations, but contemporary data indicates that the practice of First Nations child removal by the state, though implemented through different law and policies from the past, nevertheless continues at an alarming rate. This trend not only persists but has seen a notable increase: in fact, the most recent *Closing the Gap Report*—the third Annual Data Compilation Report monitoring progress under the National Agreement on Closing the Gap—found that, in the decade following Rudd's National Apology, there has been a *doubling* in the instances of child removal.[9] The National Agreement on Closing the Gap, specifically through its twelfth target, has set the goal of reducing the number of First Nations children in out-of-home care by 45% by the year 2031. But the most recent Closing the Gap report, published in July 2023, starkly indicates that progress toward this target is not on course (Closing the Gap, 2023). Furthermore, the 2023 Family Matters report, issued by the Secretariat of National First Nations and Islander Child Care (SNAICC), reveals that over 22,000 First Nations children are currently living in out-of-home care environments across Australia. This figure represents a rate of removal that is 10.5 times higher for First Nations children compared to their non–First Nations peers. Additionally, First Nations children constitute 42% of the out-of-home care population, despite only accounting for 5% of the overall child population in Australia. In 2024, Shine Lawyers filed Complaints in the Australian Human Rights Commission against the Department of Communities in Western Australia, alleging the Department has been removing First Nations children from their families discriminatorily and against the Department of Communities and Justice (NSW). The firm alleges that widespread racial discrimination across a number of State governments has resulted in the unlawful and unjust removal of First Nations children into State care, and in the failure to reunify those children with their families. Class Actions Special Counsel, Caitlin Wilson, said the foster care system has been 'flooded' with First Nations children who

9 See SOCIO-ECONOMIC OUTCOME AREA 12, 'First Nations and Torres Strait Islander children are not overrepresented in the child protection system,' Australian Government Productivity Commission, *Closing the Gap Annual Data Compilation Report July 2023*, www.pc.gov.au/closing-the-gap-data/annual-data-report/report. (Viewed 12 February 2024). See also Larissa Behrendt. (2017). After the Apology. Sydney: Ronin Films. www.roninfilms.com.au/feature/16485/after-apology.html. (Viewed 12 February 2024).

the firm alleges should never have been removed from their families and/or have been isolated from their families, community, and culture once placed into State care.[10] This is despite continuing, robust research concerning the problem of removal. For example, in late 2019, the *Family is Culture Report*, commissioned by NSW Department of Communities and Justice, involved a three-year process involving the forensic review of the case files of 1,144 First Nations children who had been removed from their homes. A First Nations Reference Group was established, which engaged with First Nations communities, received submissions and analysed data.[11] The production of a comprehensive 434-page report, encompassing 126 recommendations, marked a significant milestone in the effort to address the issue of First Nations children being placed into care. These recommendations, if enacted, hold the potential to markedly diminish the incidence of First Nations children entering the child-care system. Despite the urgency and the critical nature of these recommendations, the department responsible for their implementation has chosen to postpone any legislative changes. These reports suggest a slow advancement on some of the recommendations, especially reforms aimed at establishing essential independent oversight mechanisms within the system.

The Voice referendum of 2023 was important in marking a first, small step in the recognition of First Nations sovereignty. This, and the Uluru Statement from the Heart, called for Australians to engage with critical issues faced by First Nations and Torres Strait Islanders. Sadly, the Voice referendum failed. Shortly after the defeat, Opposition Leader Peter Dutton and Senator Nampijinpa Jacinta Price, two figures who vocally opposed the Voice, attempted to pass a senate motion for a royal commission into child sexual abuse in First Nations communities. Fortunately, this motion was rejected parliament, but its underlying ideology was in line with the Northern Territory Intervention and the historical Protection Acts.

Suicide significantly contributes to premature mortality among First Nations people, particularly in younger age groups. According to data from the National Mortality Database and the Australian Bureau of Statistics Causes of Death reports from 2018 to 2022, the percentage of deaths by suicide is highest among younger First Nations people. For those aged 0–24 years, almost a quarter of all deaths (22.0%) were due to suicide. In the 25–44 age group, 19.2% of all deaths were by suicide, while for those aged 45–64, the rate was 2.3%, and for those aged 65 and older, it was 0.2%. The suicide death rate per 100,000 population was highest among First Nations

10 www.shine.com.au/service/class-actions/first-nations-child-removal-class-action. (Viewed 12 February 2024).

11 NSW Department of Communities and Justice. (2019). *The Family is Culture Report*. https://dcj.nsw.gov.au/children-and-families/family-is-culture.html. (Viewed 12 February 2024).

people aged 25–44 years, at 50.0 deaths per 100,000 population, followed by those aged 45–64 years (23.4), 0–24 years (16.0), and 65 years and over (9.9). Among First Nations people aged 0–24 and 25–44, suicide rates were more than three times higher (3.1 each) compared to non-First Nations Australians.[12]

Plains of Promise: Undoing State Law Through the Lens of Gendered Harm

Formally, Wright's fiction exceeds the realist genre, asserting not only alternative claims to truth from legal and social narratives, but also challenging the modes in which truth claims are made. Wright's novels work to escape the 'colonising spider's trap door' of colonial representation practices, which implicitly assert an exclusive claim to truth (Wright, 2007, p. 90). Literary claims for social justice relating to the Stolen Generations have been pursued in Australia largely through the genres of life writing and autobiography (see Brewster, 1996; Ferrier, 2008), whereas Wright's novel *Plains of Promise* is not only fictional but highly stylised. *Plains of Promise* thematically addresses the harms suffered by the Stolen Generations, but also connects these harms to broader questions of First Nations sovereignty and law. Set in the 1950s, *Plains of Promise* tells the story of a mother and her young child, Ivy Koopundi, who are both forcibly removed to St Dominic's Mission in northern Queensland. The missionary, Errol Jipp, immediately separates the child from her mother, leading to the mother's absolute despair: 'Her heart stopped dead' (Wright, 1997, p. 13). Disturbed by her grief, Jipp imprisons the woman in the 'black hole,' the prison cell at the Mission (Wright, 1997, p. 38). When she is released, Ivy's mother soaks herself with kerosene before walking into a campfire, leaving Ivy entirely alone and vulnerable to Jipp, who repeatedly rapes her. The novel describes the terrible suffering of Ivy and her mother, but the novel also connects this suffering to wider political and legal frameworks, making personal suffering an issue of sovereignty. The novel opens with a description of an invasive tree that grows on the mission's grounds:

> The First Nations inmates thought the tree should not have been allowed to grow there on their ancestral country. It was wrong. Their spiritual ancestors grew more and more disturbed by the thirsty, greedy foreign tree intruding into the bowels of their world. The uprising fluid carried away precious nutrients; in the middle of the night they woke up gasping for air,

12 Australian Institute of Health and Welfare (AIHW). (2024). Suicide and intentional self-harm. Available at: www.aihw.gov.au/suicide-self-harm-monitoring/summary/suicide-and-intentional-self-harm (Viewed: 8 March 2024).

> thought they were dying, raced up through the trunk into the limbs and branches, through the tiny veins of the minute leaves and into the flowers themselves.
>
> (Wright, 1997, p. 4)

This metaphor for violent invasion provides an opening framework for harm that connects the psychological and physical harms suffered by members of the Stolen Generations to the history of invasion and to the ongoing colonial violence that denies First Nations people their laws and sovereignty. In the adjudication of harms suffered by members of the Stolen Generations, such as in the cases of *Cubillo* (2000) and *Trevorrow (2007*, 2010), such harms were framed as only personal and disconnected from questions of law and sovereignty. In contrast, in *Plains of Promise*, First Nations jurisdiction is asserted from the start: the removal of children is immediately connected to the question of 'their' ancestral country; the presence of the invasive tree is a breach of First Nations laws and is 'wrong.' The invading tree is 'thirsty, greedy, foreign' and it intrudes into the 'bowels' of the First Nations world, parasitically carrying away their 'precious nutrients.'

Halfway through the novel, there is a moment of ambivalent healing that is figured through the land, rather than interpersonally: 'the land turned into a brilliant carpet of bright shades of green moments after the rain finally stopped. . . . The land rejoiced. The words of the world whistled by in an endless murmur of repeated rhythms' (Wright, 1997, p. 80). *Plains of Promise* deals with characters who suffer, but the evolution of these characters is not framed through the trauma narrative of personal healing and resolution. Rather, the removal of First Nations children is shown to go to the heart of First Nations law, and to offend First Nations sovereignty. The novel ends in tragedy, figured through the loss of land and animal life that signifies the violation of First Nations laws:

> Over time . . . the waterbird's children's children's child went mad, because she lost her daughter in a terrible place. And the secret of the lake was lost because the crows were too interested in evil things and could not control the waterbird's madness.
>
> So the great lake dried up and is no more.
>
> (Wright, 1997, p. 304)

Carpentaria: The Aesthetics of Colonialism and Sovereignty

This practice of foregrounding First Nations authority when dealing with themes of harm is further developed in Wright's subsequent novels, *Carpentaria, The Swan Book*, and *Praiseworthy. Carpentaria* was awarded the Miles Franklin Award on 21 June 2007—the day the Northern Territory

Intervention commenced. *Carpentaria* is set in the Gulf of Carpentaria, in a small town the First Nations community call Desperance. The white bureaucrats refer to it as Masterton. *Carpentaria* opens with a paragraph in which 'innocent little Black girls' call upon the apocalypse in a Biblical register, and in all capitals:

> *THE BELLS PEAL EVERYWHERE.*
>
> *CHURCH BELLS CALLING THE FAITHFUL TO THE TABERNACLE WHERE THE GATES OF HEAVEN WILL OPEN, BUT NOT FOR THE WICKED. CALLING INNOCENT LITTLE BLACK GIRLS FROM A DISTANT COMMUNITY WHERE THE WHITE DOVE BEARING AN OLIVE BRANCH NEVER LANDS. LITTLE GIRLS WHO COME BACK HOME AFTER CHURCH ON SUNDAY, WHO LOOK AROUND THEMSELVES AT THE HUMAN FALL OUT AND ANNOUNCE MATTER-OF-FACTLY, ARMAGEDDON BEGINS HERE.*
>
> (Wright, 2006, p. 1)

The mayor of Desperance, Stan Bruiser, has been voted the 'citizen of the year . . . for ten straight years' (Wright, 2006, p. 34) despite it being commonly known that he is a brutal man who rapes First Nations women. Constable Truthful, the town's policeman, is also a sexual predator. Literary scholars have noted the significance of readings of land in *Carpentaria* to developing a literary imagination outside the colonial state (see Devlin-Glass, 2008; Brewster, 2010; Ravenscroft, 2010). Laura Joseph reads the emphasis on region in *Carpentaria* as a technique to move beyond the nation state, 'doubling' the world of the national imaginary with that of the colonial 'underworld' and making possible new readings of power and history that are produced through colonial specificities—making possible, too, a futurity based outside national myths (Joseph, 2009a, 2009b).[13] It is important to think through the consequences of this reimagining for questions of law, sovereignty, and responsibility—state law is not the only authority acting on this territory. *Carpentaria* refuses both the time and geography of the nation-state and its laws. Rather, the law of the state is shown to operate alongside First Nations authorities that ultimately challenge and subjugate the authority of state law. The law of the Waanyi people and the Waanyi land inheres in the figure of a serpent, whose covenant 'permeates everything' (Wright, 2006, p. 11).

First Nations authority is innately bound to and generated by the land. *Carpentaria* ends with a violent uprising of this land, which calls up an

13 For a reading of Wright's concept of land as a challenge to capitalist logics, see Gleeson-White (2019).

apocalyptic weather event that destroys the white settlement, and brings about the re-assertion of the Waanyi nation's Dreaming (Wright, 2006, p. 519). The natural apocalypse that destroys Desperance and its colonial authority proves at the same time that First Nations law is alive. Law's song is the source of the renewal and hope at the end of the novel: 'It was a mystery, but there was so much song wafting off the watery land, singing the country afresh' (Wright, 2006, p. 519). In contrast to colonial law's reading of authority, it is not First Nations sovereignty but the white state that is revealed to have been historically contingent and that is extinguished. This is a powerful reversal of the colonial Native Title cases, in which a foundational, historical event is said to end First Nations sovereignties in favour of the settler state. This is a significant reversal, too, of the common law's reading of the land as a passive object of law's categories of title and a reversal of the absences of the Stolen Generations cases, where First Nations Dreaming is marked as cultural rather than authoritative, and the harms of child removal are divorced from the harms of sovereign violation. In Australia, Native Title has been the main domain in which First Nations sovereignty is encountered (and then displaced) by Western law. In Native Title cases, state law has read First Nations sovereignty as finite and as superseded; law refusing to entertain the possibility of a plurality of sovereignties and laws (Motha, 2005, p. 108). At best, First Nations law is recognised as having been supported by a sovereignty that once existed, but which has no authority now (*Yorta Yorta First Nations Community v the State of Victoria* (2002), [43] per Gleeson CJ, Gummow and Hayne JJ). Shaunnagh Dorsett and Shaun McVeigh suggest that following the *Yorta Yorta* case (2002), it seemed clear that '[d] espite the use of the phrase "traditional laws and customs," there can only be one legal system' (Dorsett and McVeigh, 2005, p. 12). Following these failed encounters between First Nations and non-First Nations laws, First Nations authority becomes coded not as law, but as 'custom' (Dorsett and McVeigh, 2005, p. 12).

One of the significant interventions of Wright's novels is to question the status of what is known as 'Dreamtime,' a term that is deeply misunderstood in mainstream culture (see Devlin-Glass, 2008; Ravenscroft, 2010). In the context of the cultural reception of *Carpentaria*, Alison Ravenscroft notes there has been a tendency for readers and critics to deaden the potential of the Dreaming form by referring to it as a work of 'magic realism.' The term 'magic realism' itself is 'very much the product of a certain white Western critical strategy' in which 'magic' and 'realism' are 'taken to be two distinct, even oppositional, representational codes' that reference 'two distinct worlds or cultures—that of the coloniser and the colonised subject respectively' (Ravenscroft, 2010, pp. 195–196). Under this term, First Nations truth is interpreted 'as if it were a version of the colonisers' own, only a lesser one: less rational, less logical . . . mythic and magical'—that is, as possessing a less authoritative relation to 'reality' (Ravenscroft, 2010, pp. 195–197; Devlin-Glass, 2008; Ravenscroft, 2010). In *Carpentaria*, Wright uses the elemental authoritative force of the Dreamtime to overturn/flood colonial law. This is not signifying the binary of nature/artifice, which is a colonial logic that deadens the power of the Dreaming. Rather, the novel's ending signifies an alchemical remaking that re-establishes First Nations sovereignty.

The Swan Book: Undoing the Figure of the First Nations Child

Wright's third novel, *The Swan Book*, is a dystopic history of Australia's future, focalised through a teenaged First Nations girl, Oblivion Ethylene, nicknamed 'Oblivia.' It is 2088, and the world is post-apocalyptic, following catastrophic climate change and widespread violence. Millions of people have left the global north, crossing the seas in boats—'countless stateless millions of sea gypsies looking for somewhere to live' (Wright, 2013, p. 23), most of whom will die at sea. Oblivia lives in the Northern Territory, Australia, within 'the world's most unknown detention camp' (Wright, 2013, p. 40). Her home is a rusted boat on the periphery of a First Nations community that has been pushed onto a swamp and surrounded by government razor-wire. Oblivia is deliberately mute, refusing to speak since she was gang-raped by members of her own community. Her ongoing trauma is figured as a vicious 'cut snake virus' that has invaded her mind and which she can neither fight nor eliminate (Wright, 2013, p. 1). She is trying to 'regain sovereignty over [her] own brain,' and the plot of the novel is based on her 'quest' to regain this sovereignty (Wright, 2013, p. 4). Wright puts the female First Nations child at the centre of political and legal claims, thereby radically challenging state law's frameworks of both personal injury and First Nations sovereignty.

Oblivia epitomises the figure of 'the vulnerable First Nations child.' Through the character of Oblivia, Wright 'undoes' this figure, challenging the related colonial narratives and aesthetics that underpin state law. As in *Carpentaria, The Swan Book* foregrounds the role of narrative and figuration in assertions of jurisdiction over the 'truth.' In *The Swan Book*, state law is only one authority operating on the land, alongside a number of intersecting First Nations authorities, but in contrast to the ending of *Carpentaria*, colonial law is winning. The novel depicts an Australian landscape 70 years into the future, which is still subject to a violent application of state law—the Northern Territory Intervention is not only still in force, its policies have been heightened. A number of First Nations communities that have been invaded by the state army, including Oblivia's, which is determined 'to intervene and control the will, mind and soul of the First Nations people' (Wright, 2013, p. 47). A minority of First Nations sovereignties have been cynically recognised by the state, in return for assimilation. Warren Finch, the novel's first Indigenous President of Australia, is described as being one of the 'well and truly yes people' (Wright, 2013, p. 111). Although growing up close to Oblivia's community, Finch's people are very different from her—they go along with state rule and are given concessions by the state to apply some of their own laws in exchange for assimilation. Finch's 'First Nations Government Nation' has grown 'prosperous' from 'saying yes, yes, yes to anything on offer—a bit of assimilation, a bit of integration, a bit of giving up your own sovereignty, a bit of closing the gap' (Wright, 2013, p. 116). Finch's traditional authority as a senior lawman is recognised when he takes Oblivia from her home and claims her as his wife, blowing up her swamp as he leaves. The story then follows Oblivia to a violent southern city, where Warren Finch makes her Australia's First Lady.

Harm in *The Swan Book* is worked through an understanding of how representation has operated, and continues to operate, in the context of colonisation. To imagine harm fully, the book requires us to go beyond an individual victim to include the 'mind' of colonisation, of land, and of sovereignty. Wright's novel opens up an alternative reading of Australian authority and sovereignty to the reading made possible under colonial law and mainstream culture. This alternate reading explains the production of sovereignty not only through territory but also through past and continuing harms. 'Land,' as it has been produced both materially and discursively through law, is innately connected to past and present personal harms inflicted on First Nations people, as well as to harms to their laws and sovereignty. Australian legal concepts of property and title have been produced through the processes of colonisation—through the harms inflicted on First Nations people and through harms inflicted on the land itself. Law's focus on land as 'property,' focusing on the technicalities of title and interests, and the reduction of sovereignty to matters of territory, means that land's relation to this historical violence and harm is disguised. The harms of assimilation, including those suffered by the Stolen Generations, are adjudicated separately from Native Title claims regarding land and title, although they are innately imbricated. These occlusions mean that the connection between past and present state practices regarding First Nations subjects are also more difficult to see. The state's practices of both targeting First Nations sovereignty, and then omitting this violence from the legal record, are apparent in past legislation that asserted a particular authority over First Nations people, based on law's claim to offer protection to First Nations children—policies that also went to the heart of First Nations sovereignty and to First Nations rights to land. The *Bringing Them Home* report documented the twentieth century legal and political practices in which children were forcibly removed from their families and communities, with the effect that their connections to First Nations language, law, culture, and the land were weakened and sometimes completely lost. This legal violence, and these omissions, are also present in contemporary legal regimes.

The genre of state law is aggressive realism (van Rijswijk, 2019): the state asserts its authority with respect to a purported reality that it claims it alone can access and adjudicate. Outside the novel, in the public debates and in the second-reading speeches behind the Northern Territory Intervention and Stronger Futures legislation, an imaginary of harm was organised through the figure of 'the vulnerable First Nations child,' and a tale of First Nations violence was told, which the state asserted it alone can and should resolve—without the need to recognise and consult with First Nations authorities and laws. In contrast to the genre of aggressive realism that belongs to state law and the colonial imaginary, *The Swan Book* demonstrates a critical self-consciousness regarding its status as representation. This representational plurality is emphasised by *The Swan Book*'s use of multiple genres. There are realist details and descriptions, but there are also multiple excesses to this mode. The fantastical is evoked as the child Oblivia sleeps inside a Eucalyptus tree for ten years, like 'Rip van Winkle' (Wright, 2013, p. 7), and a pet monkey is abandoned after 'predicting colossal wars that started to frighten the life out of everyone' (Wright, 2013, p. 40). The dystopic is represented by the violent upending of the nation's weather patterns: the weather has 'flipped sides, swapping southern weather with that of the north' (Wright, 2013, p. 18); and black swans have migrated to the north of Australia, where they have never lived before. The epic is evoked as refugees are led from a European mountaintop by a holy white swan, who whispers 'a greeting of good day and good fortune' (Wright, 2013, p. 28). The swan guides the refugees to the water and across the seas. The swan is a dominant motif of the book—figuring unlikelihood and impossibility, and also echoing the many problematic myths of rape in the western literary canon: Ovid in *Metamorphoses* addresses Zeus/Jove's rape of Leda in passing in only a single line: 'and Leda, lying under a swan's wing' (VI.153). In Yeats' 'Leda and the Swan,' the violation sets in motion the birth of four offspring, including the 'terrible beauty' Helen, and the state violence occasioned through her: 'A shudder in the loins engenders there/The broken wall, the burning roof and tower/And Agamemnon dead Being so caught up.'

As a 'little First Nations kid' (Wright, 2013, p. 2), Oblivia holds a position of representational complexity within the dominant Australian imaginary. Given the legal and political history of the figure of 'the vulnerable First Nations child,' it is impossible for a mainstream audience to hear the story of Oblivia's rape, which was committed by members of her own community, as anything other than a narrative of community or familial dysfunction. Similarly, First Nations children become legible in law mainly as an occasion for law's intervention and jurisdiction but are not legible on their own terms. *The Swan Book* writes against these representational tactics of colonialism. Oblivia's rape is never represented as a scene; the individuals who committed the violence are never identified or brought to justice, and Oblivia's rape as such is never resolved. Oblivia's story does not fall within the genre of a trauma or healing narrative, in which rupture is remedied. Instead of telling the story of a 'rape,' the novel depicts a futuristic, dystopic world where the consequences of colonialism—to First Nations people, to the environment—are taken to their logical conclusion. It is not that the sexual violence inflicted on Oblivia is less important than these other harms, but that a narrative of interconnecting environmental, political, and legal harms is needed to explain Oblivia's suffering: 'like any other long-standing conflict around the world, one act of violation becomes a story of another' (Wright, 2013, p. 20). To tell the story of her rape as a distinct event, the novel argues, would not only demonstrate a misunderstanding of the nature of harms—particularly the interrelation of sexual violence with colonialism, poverty, and structural racism—and it would also reinforce law's habit of instrumentalising sexual violence in law's own violence against First Nations people.

The concept of 'the sovereignty of the mind,' which is central to *The Swan Book*, represents harm to the person as something that cannot be separated out from harm to land, animals, languages, sovereignties, cultures, and laws. It is striking that the novel represents harm as a question of 'sovereignty' and makes sovereignty central to the harms suffered by the child Oblivia. In contrast, Australian law has obscured the role of sovereignty in both the infliction and adjudication of harms to the child. The novel's reframing of sexual violence takes place in the context of it also reframing state law. The world of *The Swan Book* is animated by multiple laws and authorities. The swans move around the country, 'following stories for country that had been always known to them' because 'Swans had Law too,' and they have their own 'Law scriptures' (Wright, 2013, p. 86). The tree that is Oblivia's refuge is 'a sacred tree where all the stories of the swamp were stored like doctrines of Law left by the spiritual ancestors' (Wright, 2013, p. 36). The landscape is permeated by 'law spirits' who 'scrutinise' the country (Wright, 2013, p. 40). The country has 'law music,' brought up by 'old powerful chants' (Wright, 2013, p. 86). Law is innately bound up with the materiality of the landscape. This aliveness of First Nations authority—the capacity of First Nations legal knowledge to thrive as an ongoing source of new law—is exactly what is denied in cases such as *Mabo* (1992) and *Yorta Yorta* (2002). The living First Nations laws are also denied in the Stolen Generations cases, which focus on the 'beneficial intentions' of the state, rather than on the damage caused to First Nations authority through the state's actions. The novel's thick description of intersecting authorities and laws produces a version of Australia that is plural and postnational.

The Swan Book refuses law's temporality and law's teleology—for example, law's way of artificially segregating past trauma from contemporary violence. The novel rejects plot as an organising structure and reworks the trope of the apocalypse to subvert the colonial approach to narrating harm. *The Swan Book* is held together through a connected, elegiac recounting of losses, the novel's multiple points of view expressing a polyphony of harms.

The novel begins with the violent internal displacement of First Nations people, and these harms are connected to those of a blighted Europe, where 'whole herds of deer [are] left standing like statues of yellow ice while blizzards stormed' (Wright, 2013, p. 17). The Europeans who flee this disaster by boat become 'the uncharted floating countries of condemned humanity' (Wright, 2013, p. 17) and die at sea, '[m]en, women and children captured forever in the ghost nets of zero geography' (Wright, 2013, p. 17). Among the European refugees is 'the maddest person on Earth,' Aunty Bella Donna of the Champions (Wright, 2013, p. 11), a rare survivor who walks deep into the interior of Australia to find Oblivia, and who cares for her for some time. In an effort to stay sane, Oblivia befriends thousands of black swans who have come to live in the swamp, drawn there by their own law. The novel shifts from the connected elegiac consciousness of a dying world population to the point of view of the land, which is falling away. Plagues of rats, owls, butterflies, and locusts flourish and then are cut down; droughts begin to kill Australia's coastal areas, while floods overwhelm the continent's centre. *The Swan's Book* rewrites 'the apocalypse' as a trope of harm. The apocalypse has emerged as a significant figure in contemporary cultural and political life, signifying the vanishing point of history, and marking a moment in which harm has begun to exceed the explanatory capacity of humanist frameworks.[14] But *The Swan Book* rejects the exceptionalism of apocalyptic logic. *The Swan Book* brings the apocalypse into civic institutions and everyday life, representing harm less as an exceptional, rupturing event, and more as continuous with racism, dispossession and assimilation, gender violence, state law, and family structures. We are located in a post-apocalyptic landscape but are missing the 'eventfulness' of an apocalypse. Following the apocalyptic devastation, land is itself a grieving subject: 'It was land screaming with all of its life to the swans' (Wright, 2013, p. 328). Harm is the beginning of elegiac relations between beings, and between beings and the land, and harm is a site of authority. The landscape is sublime, excessive, rebellious, and law-making. When the ecology changes, the narrator asks whether it is Law, 'doing something to Country' (Wright, 2013, p. 319). When the plagues begin, the 'law spirits' begin travelling the country, trying to 'keep the balance' (Wright, 2013, p. 317). Animal life and land are agents who suffer, make law, attest to a different authority from that of the state. But the land is dying, despite

14 The emergence of the apocalypse and post-apocaplyse as important contemporary tropes can be seen in the popularity of fiction kicked off by Cormac McCarthy's novel *The Road* in 2006, the proliferation of literature, films and television programs based on the figures of the vampire and the zombie, and the increased popularity of genres such as dystopia and bleak science fiction that predicts the end times through environmental collapse or technical singularity. Related to this concept are recent theorisations of the 'posthuman,' particularly the 'Anthropocene era,' which posits that humans are no longer merely biological agents but have now become 'geological agents' who shape the future planet.

its ability to animate laws, and the swans and their law also die. To understand Oblivia's suffering means to mourn land and animals, laws, language, and culture and also to understand that land, animals, and laws mourn. The argument of *The Swan Book* is that these harms cannot be isolated: the rape of women and children is connected to state practices of incarceration and punishment, to poverty, abuse of the rule of First Nations law, and to forced assimilation. The failure of law to register the interconnectedness of these harms is part of law's violence. Through this extended development of the trope of the continuing apocalypse, Wright explodes the teleology the colonial state uses to absolve itself of responsibility in the present.

The Swan Book employs a number of genres, and one of its dominant genres is the anti-elegy. As an anti-elegy in the modernist tradition, Wright's novel provides a metaphor of harm and responsibility that reorganises time, destabilises colonial law's claims to authority over the adjudication of harms, and queries law's claim to authority over First Nations' legal systems and sovereignties. *The Swan Book* connects harms, and uses the anti-elegy genre to take the framework of harm beyond the personal, to include the violent histories that have produced colonial legal concepts including 'land,' 'sovereignty,' and even 'law' itself—histories and contexts that are separated and obscured under colonial law. *The Swan Book* provides a domain in which to critique, encounter, and re-vision colonial legal imaginaries of harm. Moving the framework of harm beyond the person weakens law's violent jurisdictions and loosens law's aggressive representational practices that go to the heart of colonial legal authority. We need such a twenty-first century, decolonising jurisprudence that rethinks legal relation through a new model of harm—one that reorganises the category of personal harm by contextualising the human in relation to First Nations' perspectives on law, land, and sovereignties. This jurisprudence needs to comprehend the specific histories through which colonial law has enacted judgment and through which law continues to act.

As discussed in Chapter 3, we can think of law as having a classical elegiac structure: law figures harm as being located primarily in the person, as having occurred in the past, and as being capable of resolution. Thomas Pfau argues that the elegiac is '*the* defining characteristic of aesthetic production in Modernity,' a mode that increasingly influenced literature, art, and theory from the mid-eighteenth century onwards (Pfau, 2010, p. 548; emphasis Pfau's). Pfau locates the power behind this elegiac sensibility in the mourning of ideality, arising through modernist disenchantment, especially with those practices of representation that supported Enlightenment logics and rationalities (Pfau, 2010, p. 549). The significance of the modernists' response to the elegiac is also due, Pfau argues, to modern temporality, which, with its teleological approach, institutes clear 'programmatic breaks' with the past, bringing about what Walter Benjamin described as 'homogenous [and] empty' time (Benjamin, 1968, p. 264). Modern time (including the time of colonial law) is nothing more than 'a causal connection between various moments' (Pfau, 2010, p. 549; Benjamin, 1968, p. 264). The modernist anti-elegy undoes this teleological, colonial logic. The classical elegy was reworked by modernists as they sought new frameworks and metaphors to respond to the violence of modernity, especially the rupturing event of the Great War, which made existing representational forms seem redundant.[15] From Walter Benjamin's angel of history, to Freud's theories of shock and psychoanalysis, and on to the transitional justice processes after World War II, legal and literary writers throughout the twentieth century sought new forms to understand and adjudicate modern violence.[16]

With its continuous-present temporality and its refusal to offer a resolution, the anti-elegy provides an alternative way to frame harm to that of the colonial imaginary. Structurally, final closure is refused, and instead of loss being transcended or redeemed, the reader continues to be immersed in loss, inhabiting a state of 'resistant mourning' (Rae, 2007, p. 14). *The Swan's Book*'s anti-elegy disrupts law's teleological narrative of violence through an engagement with 'the apocalypse' as a trope of harm, not only revealing law as a particular genre, but also its purported claim over past/present/future. *The Swan Book*'s anti-elegy considers how representation has operated, and continues to operate, in the context of ongoing colonisation, and it engages the modernist project of challenging Enlightenment categories and histories of representation. Representations of state law, of army violence, of rape, of harms to asylum seekers, and of environmental damage—all concerns of *The Swan Book*—are heavily mediated by the histories of western representational practices. The novel reveals and critiques these practices. The category of 'person'—the Enlightenment individual—is opened up, so that personhood—in this case, Oblivia's suffering subjectivity—is represented as an effect of land and law, as well as of human violence. The novel foregrounds questions that are occluded by the law, including the relationship of past harms to the present; the connection of harms to the land to harms to the person; and law's role in causing harm when it responds to suffering. This broader perceptual framework challenges law's violent assertions of authority based on its claims to have an exclusive jurisdiction over the harms of First Nations people.

One of Wright's stated aims is to represent the continuing harms suffered by First Nations people—to describe the 'the living hell' of many First Nations lives (Wright, 2002, p. 15). As an anti-elegiac text, The *Swan Book* leaves the psychoanalytic model of trauma behind. The attack on Oblivia's mind's sovereignty is figured as a 'virus' (Wright, 2013, p. 1)—interconnected, infectious, mutable, and uncontainable—in contrast to the

15 On the roles of legal and literary modernism in responding to the harms of modernity, see Reichman, 2003.

16 See e.g., (Reichman, 2009; Felman, 2002; van Rijswijk, 2012).

structural aesthetic of the psychoanalytic trauma paradigm, in which suffering is contained within the person, and can be resolved within the individual. Oblivia says, 'If you want to extract a virus like this from your head—you can't come to the door of its little old-fashion prairie house with passé kinds of thinking' (Wright, 2013, p. 2). In the late twentieth century, trauma theorists such as Shoshana Felman, Dori Laub, and Cathy Caruth extended the psychoanalytic framework of trauma beyond the individual psyche to account for the collective and intergenerational trauma of events such as the Holocaust.[17] These theorists emphasise the role of representation in responding to trauma and, in particular, the role of the literary domain in finding new forms and frameworks to make suffering legible, emphasising the ways in which the representational work of witnessing articulates historical losses. However, these theories and responses do not fully account for the harms of dispossession caused by the history of settler colonialism and through continuing colonial techniques. The harms of colonisation call for different kinds of legal and ethical responses from those modelled on rupturing, traumatic events such as war: clear events with a start and a finish.

The Swan Book provides a domain in which to critique, encounter, and re-vision legal imaginaries of harm. Moving the framework of harm beyond the person weakens law's violent jurisdictions, and loosens law's aggressive representational practices that go to the heart of law's authority. These deconstructive, anti-elegiac practices can themselves be thought of as essentially decolonial in mode, 'locating the very possibility of reading and writing in an *impossible* desire for presence, completion, and coherence' (Lilley, 1997, p. 247, emphasis mine). We need a twenty-first-century jurisprudence that rethinks legal relation through a new model of harm—one that reorganises the category of harm and comprehends the specific histories through which law has enacted judgment, and through which law continues to act. This strategy is imperative if we are ever to develop a jurisprudence of legal relation and authority in continuing colonial contexts.

Praiseworthy (2023): The Figure of the Paedophile

Alexis Wright's most recent novel, *Praiseworthy* (2023), is also concerned with state violence against First Nations communities based on false claims of harm to First Nations children, focusing especially on the psychological violence inflicted on First Nations communities through the figure of

17 See (Felman, 2002; Caruth, 1996; Laub and Felman, 1992). Dominick LaCapra queries the universalisation of trauma as history in *Writing History, Writing Trauma* (2001) and *Representing the Holocaust: History, Theory, Trauma, History and Memory After Auschwitz* (1996).

the child. *Praiseworthy* and *The Swan Book* use the Northern Territory Intervention as a metonym for continuing state violence against First Nations people that is based on the figure of the vulnerable First Nations child. Each novel marks the continuing present of the Intervention, which has officially ended but whose underlying ideology lives on under different guises. Praiseworthy is a hot, dry town on the Gulf of Carpentaria where the persecution of First Nations people converges with the global crisis of climate collapse. The novel begins as a 'monument of haze' settles over the town (Wright, 2023, p. 4), portending an impending ecological apocalypse and the furore of the ancestral spirits of Country. According to one of the ten oracles who narrate the novel, this toxic haze is the accumulation of ancient stories and fury, 'the tragedies in the epical pyres of life' (Wright, 2023, p. 22). The haze serves as a tangible symbol of the ecological and social crises that the townspeople face, highlighting the deep interconnections between environmental harm and the loss of sovereignty under colonial rule. The novel evidences the violence against a community stripped of its collective autonomy and subjected to the oppressive forces of colonialism; it is particularly interested in representing how the psyche of First Nations people is damaged by this violence.

The novel's modes of representation far exceed realism. In addition to the genre of The Dreaming, Wright draws on Western genres as disparate as science fiction, horror, epic, classical myth, romance, and melodrama to represent the continuing violence of colonialism. *Praiseworthy* is an epic story and also a satire, a deep critique of the Northern Territory Intervention as well as a cautionary tale about suffering, including youth suicide and climate change. The novel is propelled by a wry sense of humour: central character Widespread (also known as Planet and Cause Man Steel) is determined to save the environment by establishing a long-haul transport conglomerate using feral donkeys, while the community's mayor Ice Pick is so pro-assimilation, his skin and eyes have turned white. The novel begins 'Once upon a fine time for some people in the world'—an assertion that there are different realities in the world, for the powerful and less powerful—differences that are mirrored in the different modes of representation (Wright, 2023, p. 5). The story is set during the Howard Government's Intervention commencing in 2008, but the story is not confined to this singular historical moment—the temporality of the novel is non-linear and complex. It is set in the continuing time of the Intervention but also references contemporary political and social realities (Donald Trump; Tiktok). The book's ten parts circle back in time, revisiting events and past language as different versions of the truth come to light, layering both time and language. The suicidal act whereby the young Aboriginal Sovereignty walks into the ocean is a particular focus, an event that is returned to again and again. There is no linear movement out of this event, no resolution or final meaning made of it.

The story focuses on the Steel family, who live at the periphery of Praiseworthy on disputed Native title land. Cause Man Steel is the patriarch of the family and harbours a vision to end fossil fuel dependency and foster First Nations financial independence from the colonial government, but the townspeople regard him as a nuisance. Embarking on a quixotic journey, Cause Man Steel takes to the road in a decrepit Ford. His mission is to supplant Qantas, Australia's flagship airline, with an innovative transport network powered by the country's five million feral donkeys. His wife, Dance Steel, seeks escape from Cause's foolishness by immersing herself in the beauty of butterfly dances and by conducting online searches on how to repatriate her First Nations/Chinese family to China. The Steels have two sons: Aboriginal Sovereignty is a 19-year-old dancer, and Tommyhawk is 8 years old, a 'government-indoctrinated robotic type of kid fascist' who spends his life on the internet, obsessing about the 'infestation' of paedophilia the media claim is rampant in his community (Wright, 2023, p. 81). Tommyhawk dreams of being taken away 'into the white world before he too was molested' (Wright, 2023, p. 83). Brainwashed by the media, Tommyhawk fixates on scenes of imagined sexual abuse and predation. He believes Praiseworthy is overrun with 'paedophile cockroaches living on First Nations communities and preying on First Nations children' (Wright, 2023, p. 120) and that his brother is one of them. Tommyhawk is unable to distinguish fantasy from reality and becomes obsessed with the idea that the minister for First Nations affairs—'the swivel-throned Golden Hair Mother'—will adopt him and take him away from Praiseworthy, where he will live with her 'like a prince in Parliament House' and be 'assimilated to the level of being rich white" (Wright, 2023, p. 124). He constantly texts the minister, begging her to rescue and adopt him to save him from his fate of being prey to paedophiles. Tommyhawk has internalised the brutal racist ideologies of the twentieth and twenty-first centuries, suspecting that he has been adopted into his First Nations family as 'a kind of Stolen Generation in reverse' (Wright, 2023, p. 124). He attempts to set his plan in motion by reporting his 17-year-old brother, Aboriginal Sovereignty, to the police for statutory rape, after Aboriginal Sovereignty marries his 15-year-old girlfriend in accordance with traditional law: 'Tommyhawk had hotmailed the police about how Aboriginal Sovereignty was raping an underage girl' (Wright, 2023, p. 196). Tommyhawk turns on his brother as a direct result of government and media propaganda:

> This is what the government is saying. Not me saying it. It was all in the newspapers. I even know the hotline. We got it at school. . . . I reckon you are one of those paedophiles. You are? Your girlfriend is underage? She still goes to school. The police will be coming for you, you know?
>
> (Wright, 2023, p. 192)

Tommyhawk's action makes Praiseworthy a lightning rod for claims of paedophilia, with dire consequences for the entire community. Like many First Nations boys and men, Aboriginal Sovereignty is targeted by the state as a rapist and paedophile. The police arrive to beat Aboriginal Sovereignty, and then he walks into the ocean. Tommyhawk stands on the shore and watches him go, Tommyhawk's mind 'eaten alive by a thought a virus, a pandemic, where every First Nations child was at risk' (Wright, 2023, p. 204). Feeling that he is right, Tommyhawk feels no grief watching Aboriginal Sovereignty commit suicide. Aboriginal Sovereignty's disappearance becomes a big news story on First Nations youth suicide, and a government task force is sent to find his body.

Praiseworthy shifts the focus of *The Swan Book* from the figure of the violated First Nations girl to the figure of the First Nations man who is defined in the national legal and social imaginary as her abuser. The fates of the two children in *Praiseworthy*, Aboriginal Sovereignty and Tommyhawk, are determined by two epidemics sweeping through the town: one epidemic is fabricated (the so-called epidemic of First Nations paedophiles who, according to the mainstream media, are predators in their own communities) and the other epidemic is real but not taken seriously by the colonial Australian government (the epidemic of suicides of First Nations children). In Tommyhawk's painful subjectivity, written in excruciating, realist detail, we see the effects of colonial psychic violence on First Nations children, driven by the fascist ideology of government and media, which has created a fantasy of harm:

> There was a total miserere outpouring from all sorts, in the new world psalm of those who were desperately turning themselves blue in the face with worrying about First Nations children being attacked by paedophiles and neglected by their parents, and jumping up and down in their tracks, and lurching at one another to be the top dog of all the argy-bargy facts, to dominate the frenzied media about loving First Nations children more than their parents loved them. There was bugger-all need for stitching real facts together in the complete osmosis of First Nations men being rampant prowlers of First Nations communities to get their molesting hands on the little children.
>
> (Wright, 2023, p. 83)

This persistent, relentless barrage of violence sends Tommyhawk mad: 'He reasoned that if he was to be raped by paedophile parents who did not love him, if that was the future, why was he still here' (Wright, 2023, p. 88). Tommyhawk, whom his father, Cause Man, labels an 'assimilationist fascist,' is a symptom of colonial violence (Wright, 2023, p. 68). He becomes consumed by his obsession with the figure of the paedophile, who he sees as real and omnipresent. Tommyhawk has internalised the mainstream racist violence of the colonial state and media and in turn inflicts this violence against himself and his own community. Wright explains in her novel that Tommyhawk's fears of being abused were unsurprising in a child:

> born into the shrill of a nation constantly yelling at the top of its voice about how to fix up the black problem. . . . It was easy for him to believe he was living in a typical First Nations community plagued by paedophiles and being cared for by misopedists, by children-hating parents. . . . Hatred was not a strong enough word for how he felt about his parents.

Tommyhawk's interiority is brutal; his psychology is a living hell. At 8 years old, he believes 'All sexual depravers were out to get him' (Wright, 2023, p. 191). His child's mind is full of grotesque and violent images that have originated not *de novo* from his imagination but from governmental policy and racist media coverage: '*Filthy penises. Stick it anywhere. Into little girls. Sicko*' (Wright, 2023, p. 193). He packs his bag, ready to leave his family, waiting for the government to send the army in to protect him (Wright, 2023, p. 197).

In contrast to the imagined harm caused by fictional paedophiles, Praiseworthy is enduring an actual epidemic of youth suicide. This reality is represented with absolute sorrow, Wright describing the quotidian way in which

> on these perfect youth suicidal nights of Praiseworthy, where wind comes in the afternoons, blows the dust out to see, trading lightly through the water, another child of Praiseworthy was leaving the butterfly country. . . . He was going to the dream country like those other lost children disappearing over weeks and months, being led away by the hand.
>
> (Wright, 2023, p. 178)

Tommyhawk, only 8 years old, thinks 'of how he would kill himself like the other children, of what it felt like to be walking like a zombie through the air with your feet above the ground' (Wright, 2023, p. 200). He 'became obsessed with ways of committing suicide' (Wright, 2023, p. 200). Still a young child, he is yet

> a seasoned witness to a string of kid deaths. You could say he was an expert unbiased observer of this kind of tragedy, kind of like the aspiring first world viewing the third world committing suicide at its expense. The first time he saw a kid die he just felt that somehow this did not happen. It affected him less each time he saw it happen. He could not help it, and he had become fascinated with the idea of some of his friends committing suicide.
>
> (Wright, 2023, p. 216)

Is there anything bleaker than an 8-year-old child fantasising about the suicide of his friends? In Tommyhawk, we see the epitome of psychological harm to children produced by state violence in the name of the child.

The Figure of the Australian Cop

The cop is a figure of both violence and ridicule in Wright's novels. In *Carpentaria*, the town's cop is called Constable Truthful—even though he is deeply corrupt and a sexual predator. He torments the Phantom family's youngest daughter, Girlie; he continuously coerces her into having sex with him by threatening to harass her family if she refuses. He is also punished: one night, Truthful dreams of hearing a knock at his door, but when he answers, no one is there. Turning around, he sees the police station filled with First Nations people whose grey skin is covered with greenish sea slime. Frightened, Truthful checks on his three young prisoners, only to find that the boys have hanged themselves and are dead. Days later, Desperance residents report a terrible stench of death emanating from the police station. The corrupt town mayor, Bruiser, goes to investigate and finds Truthful still there, bringing meals to the boys and putting their dead bodies to bed each night.

In *Praiseworthy*, when Tommyhawk becomes obsessed with paedophiles, Wright describes a psychological state where 'the police cars roar . . . through the streets of his . . . brain' (Wright, 2023, p. 77). Tommyhawk gives in 'to the cop in his head and call the cops on [Aboriginal Sovereignty] . . . knowing full well what they will do. And they do it properly, beating this kid to within an inch of his life.' Tommyhawk then emails the police to dob his brother in, and the police come searching for Aboriginal Sovereignty. They find him at school, where his teacher tries to protect him, protesting, 'Can't you see he is just a boy?' Aboriginal Sovereignty has just turned seventeen, but the police claim that 'He's a man' (Wright, 2023, p. 359) and drag him away.

Mykaela Saunders, a Koori/Goori and Lebanese writer, has written a brilliant meditation on the figure of the cop in the Australian cultural imaginary, arising from reflections on her own experience of reading *Praiseworthy*. Saunders observes that the cop is a dominant figure in the Australian imaginary:

> From 1788, when Sydney was magically conjured on stolen Dharug land, Australia has always been a nation of cop-lovers, evident in its love of heavy-handed, paternalistic laws, enacted by both large-scale military interventions as well as its smaller-scale culture of policing and dobbing on thy neighbours.
>
> (Saunders, 2023, n.p.)

Saunders points out that the first police in Australia were 'snitches and lags'—the penal colony relied on people policing each other, and some of them were willing to do so, for whatever relative benefit that would give them (Saunders, 2023, n.p.). Saunders suggests that in *Praiseworthy*, Wright provides a harrowing answer to the question of

> What would happen if a community of assimilationist-minded First Nations people became cops to each other? Everyone would start dobbing on everyone else, and even children would police each other too.
>
> (Saunders, 2023, n.p.)

The cop is the ultimate figure of colonisation, and for a First Nations child to inhabit the cop's point of view means we are at the limit point of colonial dystopia.

Conclusion: Undoing the Imaginary of Colonial Authority

At the end of *Carpentaria*, the apocalypse enacted by the land and its law washes away colonial violence and the contingent sovereignty of the colonial state, bringing about the resurgence of First Nations authority. The ending of *The Swan Book* is a lot more pessimistic. *The Swan Book* denies closure and reads as a text that is working through the ethics and legalities of a world that has left 'eventfulness' behind. Rather than its characters fighting to resolve a traumatic event, they are immersed in the continuing violence of political, social, and environmental crisis. Rather than harms and losses being resolved, they heighten as the novel progresses. The main characters die: Bella Donna dies; Warren Finch is assassinated; all the swans Oblivia has loved are taken; and finally, Oblivia moves back to the swamp where she originated, holding the broken body of the last remaining swan. Then time shifts again, and she appears as a haunting figure who may or not be still living and who is only glimpsed from time to time. She is still possessed by the virus. The novel ends:

> There is a really big story of that ghost place: a really deadly love story about a girl who has a virus lover living in some lolly pink prairie house in her brain. . . . Swans might come back. Who knows what madness will be calling them in the end?
>
> (Wright, p. 364)

The Swan Book does not offer redemption or even judgment; it closes with a still-apocalyptic world and the call of a haunting, unmoored 'madness.' It recounts losses in registers alternatively mournful, comedic, vengeful, and horrific. In the end, Oblivia fails to regain sovereignty, leaving her, and the world, in a state of continuing loss. Law figures harm as having occurred in the past, as something to be resolved and put behind us, and has no framework for organising responsibility for ongoing harms. Quasi-judicial, transitional justice processes have tried to find new forms to respond to harm, but they have also been criticised for the ways in which they separate the past from the present. For Meister, the main tropes of these processes, including reconciliation, transition and redemption, have an affective logic that is about 'buying more time' for beneficiaries, buying more time 'after evil' but 'before justice' (Meister, 2011, p. 70). Orford contends that transitional justice processes are 'centrally concerned' with time; she argues that the *Bringing Them Home* report produces a narrative of closure, a view of 'a unified past and a shared future within the liberal democratic nation-state' (Orford, 2006, pp. 880–881). In contrast, forms of *The Swan Book* provide metaphors to frame harms as both proximate, dispersed, and continuing, rather than as distant, eventful, and in the past. *The Swan Book* leaves resolution as an open question and demands ways of relating to harm in the present. It suggests a way to meet harms that focuses on process, contingency, and possibility, in contrast to law's genre of aggressive realism, which fails to take into account its relation to representation, or question its assertions of an exclusive access to reality. The novel marks an unhopeful futurity that acts to 'resist the mourning time of "moving on"' (Cooppan, 2009, p. 63) doing the work of refusing the time of state imaginaries.

In *The Swan Book*, no final authority judges or resolves the extensive suffering represented in the novel. This failure to resolve harms is a refusal, too, of the time of the colonial state. Wright's novels represent time as extending beyond colonisation and its laws—the temporality of Dreamtime revealing this historical period to be relatively short and exceptional in the larger picture of Australian temporalities. *The Swan Book* figures an apocalyptic present-future in which people need to think through the ethics and politics of a situation of continuing harm, a situation that cannot be resolved until colonialism ends. *The Swan Book* rejects the teleological time of law, as well as national temporalities of reconciliation and transitional justice, which insist on resolution and a firm break with the past. For the dominant legal and public affective responses to the Stolen Generations, the removal of First Nations children ends in reconciliation, with both suffering and responsibility located in the past. State time precludes a continuing time of responsibility, as well as a mode of encounter with First Nations authority regarding these harms.

Praiseworthy also ends with a continuing apocalypse. Further, the narrative arc is not linear but circular: the key harm of the novel, the death of Aboriginal Sovereignty, is returned to again and again, and each time is given different meaning. When the police come searching for him, they find no evidence that Aboriginal Sovereignty has actually died, and yet there is no evidence that he is living, either; the mystery of his disappearance becomes the novel's fixation: 'nobody could say what it was that happened to Aboriginal Sovereignty, or what it meant' (Wright, 2023, p. 312). The tone is not always earnest, though: there is a subversive, carnivalesque scene where the 'corpse hunters' who come looking for Aboriginal Sovereignty are attacked by Cause Steel's horde of 5 million asses (Wright, 2023, p. 317), evoking the carnivalesque. The carnivalesque refers to a literary mode that subverts and liberates the assumptions of the dominant genre through humour and chaos. It embodies the spirit of carnival, characterised by a temporary suspension of hierarchical rank, privileges, norms, and prohibitions (Bakhtin, 1984; Stallybrass and White, 1986). *Praiseworthy* overturns the colonial legal order, and law's genre of aggressive realism, through carnivalesque tactics including the use of collective bodies (e.g., the horde of donkeys that chaotically clash with the police) and by breaking down the barriers between self and world (self/animal, spirit/material). Aboriginal Sovereignty becomes a powerful idea for his community. The novel ends: 'Of course, the spirit of Aboriginal Sovereignty never dies, for you cannot destroy what was infinitely existing in the law of Country that always is, and always will be governing itself' (Wright, 2023, p. 754).

Wright's novels offer not only thematic answers to questions of justice but also a method for examining the forms, devices, and habits through which these truths are represented in both legal and cultural contexts. Motha and van Marle note that the liminal space of critique at the intersection of law, aesthetics, and politics provides a domain for developing critique through literary forms and for exploring the role of the imaginary in responding to legal and political problems (van Marle and Motha, 2013, p. 17). They distinguish their version of liminality from one that merely characterises it as a midpoint, marking the degree to which one mode shares commonality with another (van Marle and Motha, 2013, p. 35). Instead, they view liminality as occupying the space and time of traversal, emphasising the importance of keeping that transformative zone open (van Marle and Motha, 2013, p. 25). This form of liminality is not about transcendence but about ambivalence and uncertainty; it is not about abstraction but about historically grounded specificity (van Marle and Motha, 2013, p. 128). This domain offers a means of representing and criticising dominant forms, both in terms of the substance of those dominant claims and the ways in which those claims are made. By moving the framework of authority beyond that of state law, we can weaken law's violent jurisdictions and loosen the aggressive representational practices central to law's authority. When law's assertion of singular jurisdiction is placed alongside First Nations laws, genres, narratives, and figures, its authority is challenged and contextualised. In the liminal space of law and literature, legal worlds can be diagnosed and described differently. This space provides an opportunity to chip away at the singularity of law's authority and begin the significant task of delineating responsibility in ways that acknowledge and encounter the multiple authorities operating in Australian times and places. These authorities exist in spite of, within, and outside the nation form, offering a richer, more nuanced understanding of justice and law's role in society.

As the occasion for continuing legal violence, the haunting figure of 'the vulnerable First Nations child' persists—with serious legal, political, and material effects. In response, we should put the First Nations child at the centre of our jurisprudence—Ivy Koopundi (*Plains of Promise*), Bala (*Carpentaria*), Oblivia (*The Swan Book*), and Tommyhawk (*Praiseworthy*) should be the subject position and voice of legal critique. The *abstract* figure of the child does harm—in the name of this child, our contemporary laws remove *actual* First Nations children from their families, incarcerate actual children as young as ten in 'facilities' so brutal that Dickens could incorporate them into his novels without there being any dissonance. Wright's novels make this figure *particular and material*—gendered, raced, classed, and located in a specific time and space. In Ivy's, Bala's, Oblivia's, and Tommyhawk's quests for justice and in their failures, we hear them as the voice and subject-position of legal critique. Wright's novels are thereby contributing to an emergent transnational, interdisciplinary jurisprudence that seeks to remake our legal worlds.

Bibliography

Books and Articles

Amnesty International (2009) *Discriminatory Aspects of the NTER Yet to Be Addressed*. Available at: www.amnesty.org.au/news/comments/20169 (Accessed: 15 October 2014).

Anaya, J. (2010) *Observations on the Northern Territory Emergency Response in Australia Report by the United Nations Special Rapporteur on the Situation of Human Rights and Fundamental Freedoms of Indigenous People*. Geneva: United Nations.

Anthony, T. (2018) '"They Were Treating Me Like a Dog": The Colonial Continuum of State Harms Against Indigenous Children in Detention in the Northern Territory, Australia.' *State Crime*, 7(2), pp. 251–277.

Attwood, B. (2001) 'The Stolen Generations and Genocide: Robert Manne's in Denial: The Stolen Generations and the Right.' *Aboriginal History*, 25, pp. 163–172.

Bakhtin, M. (1984) *Rabelais and His World*. Translated by H. Iswolsky. Bloomington: Indiana University Press.

Benjamin, W. (1968) *Illuminations*. Translated by H. Zohn, Edited by H. Arendt. New York: Schocken.

Black, C. (2010) *The Land Is a Source of Law: A Dialogic Encounter with an Indigenous Jurisprudence*. London: Routledge-Cavendish.

Black, C. (2011) 'Maturing Australia through Australian Aboriginal Narrative Law.' *The South Atlantic Quarterly*, 110(2), pp. 347–362.

Borrows, J. (2002) *Recovering Canada: The Resurgence of Indigenous Law*. Toronto: University of Toronto Press.

Brewster, A. (1996) *Aboriginal Women's Autobiography*. Sydney: Oxford University Press in association with Sydney University Press.

Brewster, A. (2010) 'Indigenous Sovereignty and the Crisis of Whiteness in Alexis Wright's Carpentaria.' *Australian Literary Studies*, 25(4), pp. 85–102.

Buti, A. (2008) 'The Stolen Generations Litigation Revisited.' *Melbourne University Law Review*, 32(3), pp. 382–421.

Buti, A. (2008–2009) 'Reparations, Justice Theories and Stolen Generations.' *University of Western Australia Law Review*, 34, pp. 168–189.

Caruth, C. (1996) *Unclaimed Experience: Trauma, Narrative and History*. Baltimore: John Hopkins University Press.

Chakrabarty, D. (2000) *Modernism and Empire: Writing and British Coloniality 1890–1940*. Edited by N. Rigby and H. J. Booth. Manchester: Manchester University Press.

Chakrabarty, D. (2007a) *Modernism and Colonialism: British and Irish Literature, 1899–1939*. Edited by R. Begam and M. Moses. Durham, NC: Duke University Press, Durham.

Chakrabarty, D. (2007b) *Provincialising Europe*. Princeton: Princeton University Press.

Chakrabarty, D. (2009) 'The Climate of History: Four Theses.' *Critical Inquiry*, 35(2), pp. 197–215.

Cooppan, V. (2009) *Worlds Within: National Narratives and Global Connections in Postcolonial Writing*, 1st ed. Stanford: Stanford University Press.

Crofts, P., and van Rijswijk, H. (2020) 'Picnic at Hanging Rock: Coming of Age as a Girl in the Gothic Colonial Institution.' In K. Weinert, K. Crawley, and K. Tranter (Eds.), *Law, Lawyers, and Justice: Through Australian Lenses*. London: Routledge, pp. 106–128.

Cunneen, C., and Gri, J. (2004) *The Limitations of Litigation in Stolen Generations Cases (Research Discussion Paper no. 15)*. Canberra: Australian Institute of Aboriginal and Torres Strait Islander Studies.

Cunneen, C., and Libesman, T. (2002) 'A Review of International Models for Indigenous Child Protection." *A Report Prepared for the NSW Department of Community Services*. Sydney: University of New South Wales Department of Community Services.

Devlin-Glass, F. (2008) 'A Politics of the Dreamtime: Destructive and Regenerative Rainbows in Alexis Wright's Carpentaria.' *Australian Literary Studies*, 23(3), pp. 392–407.

Dimock, W. C. (2006) *Through Other Continents: American Literature Across Deep Time*. Princeton: Princeton University Press.

Dorsett, S., and McVeigh, S. (2005) 'An Essay on Jurisdiction, Jurisprudence, and Authority: The High Court of Australia in Yorta Yorta (2001).' *Northern Ireland Legal Quarterly*, 56(1), pp. 12–32.

Felman, S. (2002) *The Juridical Unconscious: Trials and Traumas in the Twentieth Century*. Cambridge, MA: Harvard University Press.

Fernandez, E., Lee, J., Blunden, H., Mcnamara, P., Kovacs, S., and Cornefert, P. A. (2016) *No Child Should Grow Up Like This: Identifying Long Term Outcomes of Forgotten Australians, Child Migrants and the Stolen Generations*. Sydney, NSW: University of New South Wales.

Ferrier, C. (2008) '"Disappearing Memory" and the Colonial Present in Recent Indigenous Women's Writing.' *Journal of the Association for the Study of Australian Literature*, Special Issue, pp. 37–55.

Frow, J. (2001) 'Discursive Justice.' *The South Atlantic Quarterly*, 100(2), pp. 331–348.

Gaita, R. (2000) *A Common Humanity: Thinking about Love and Truth and Justice*. London: Routledge.

Gaita, R. (2011) 'Literature, Genocide, and the Philosophy of International Law.' In *Crime, Punishment, and Responsibility*. Oxford: Oxford University Press.

Genovese, A. (2011) 'Metaphor of Redemption, Myths of State: Historical Accountability in Luhrmann's Australia and Trevorrow v South Australia.' *Griffith Law Review*, 20(1), pp. 67–90.

Gleeson-White, J. (2019) 'Valuing Country.' *Griffith Review*, 63 (Writing the Country). Available at: www.griffithreview.com/articles/valuing-country/.
Gordon, A. F. (2008) *Haunting and the Sociological Imagination*, Minneapolis: University of Minnesota Press.
Haebich, A. (2000) *Broken Circles: Fragmenting Indigenous Families, 1800–2000*. Perth: Fremantle Arts Centre Press.
Hocking, B. A., and Stephenson, M. (2008) 'Why the Persistent Absence of a Foundational Principle? Indigenous Australians, Proprietary and Family Reparations.' In F. Lenzerini (Ed.), *Reparations for Indigenous Peoples*. Oxford: Oxford University Press, pp. 477–522.
Human Rights and Equal Opportunity Commission (HREOC) (1997) *Bringing Them Home: Report of the National Inquiry into the Separation of Aboriginal and Torres Strait Islander Children from Their Families*. Canberra: HREOC.
Intervention Rollback Action Group (2009) *Rollback the Intervention*. Available at: http://rollbacktheintervention.wordpress.com (Accessed: 15 October 2014).
Joseph, L. (2009a) 'Dreaming Phantoms and Golems: Elements of the Place Beyond Nation in Carpentaria and Dreamhunter.' *Journal of the Association for the Study of Australian Literature: JASAL*, pp. 1–22.
Joseph, L. (2009b) 'Opening the Gates of Hell: Regional Emergences in Carpentaria and Dreamhunter.' *Southerly*, 69(2), pp. 66–80.
Joseph, L., and van Rijswijk, H. (2020) 'Going Bunta on Western Law: Violent Jurisdictions, Melodrama, and the Australian Carceral Imaginary in Wentworth.' In K. Weinert, K. Crawley, and K. Tranter (Eds.), *Law, Lawyers, and Justice: Through Australian Lenses*. London, UK: Routledge, pp. 275–288.
Kennedy, R. (2008) 'Subversive Witnessing: Mediating Indigenous Testimony in Australian Cultural and Legal Institutions.' *Women's Quarterly Studies*, 36(1/2), pp. 58–75.
Kennedy, R. (2011) 'An Australian Archive of Feelings.' *Australian Feminist Studies*, 26(69), pp. 257–279.
Kennedy, R. (2012) 'Humanity's Footprint: Reading Rings of Saturn and Palestinian Walks in an Anthropocene Era.' *Biography*, 35(1).
LaCapra, D. (1996) *Representing the Holocaust: History, Theory, Trauma, History and Memory After Auschwitz*. Ithaca: Cornell University Press.
LaCapra, D. (2001) *Writing History, Writing Trauma*. Baltimore: John Hopkins University Press.
Laub, D., and Felman, S. (1992) *Testimony: Crises of Witnessing in Literature, Psychoanalysis and History*. New York: Routledge.
Lilley, K. (1997) '"Living Backward": Slessor and Masculine Elegy.' In P. Mead (Ed.), *Kenneth Slessor*. Brisbane: University of Queensland Press, pp. 246–264.
Luker, T. (2005) "'Postcolonising' Amnesia in the Discourse of Reconciliation: The Void in the Law's Response to the Stolen Generations.' *Australian Feminist Law Journal*, 22, pp. 67–88.
Manderson, D. (2012a) 'Crocodile Tears.' *Indigenous Law Bulletin*, 7(10), pp. 8–11.
Manderson, D. (2012b) *Kangaroo Courts and the Rule of Law: The Legacy of Modernism*. London: Routledge.
Manderson, D., and van Rijswijk, H. (2015) 'Introduction to Littoral Readings: Representations of Land and Sea in Law, Literature, and Geography.' *Law & Literature*, 27(2), pp. 167–177.
Massumi, B. (2002) *Parables for the Virtual: Movement, Affect, Sensation*. Durham, NC: Duke University Press.
McCarthy, C. (2006) *The Road*. New York: Vintage Books.
Meister, R. (2011) *After Evil: A Politics of Human Rights*. New York: Columbia University Press.

Mookherjee, N., Rapport, N., Josephides, L., Hage, G., Todd, L. R., and Cowlishaw, G. (2009) 'The Ethics of Apology: A Set of Commentaries.' *Critique of Anthropology*, 29(3), pp. 345–366.
Motha, S. (2005) 'The Failure of "Postcolonial" Sovereignty in Australia.' *Australian Feminist Law Journal*, 22(1), pp. 107–125.
Napoleon, V. (2004) 'By Whom and by What Processes Is Restorative Justice Defined and What Bias Might This Introduce?' In H. Zehr and B. Toews (Eds.), *Critical Issues in Restorative Justice*. New York: Criminal Justice Press, pp. 33–45.
Napoleon, V. (2005) 'Aboriginal Self Determination: Individual Self and Collective Selves.' *Atlantis: A Women's Studies Journal*, 29(2), pp. 31–46.
O'Connor, P. (2001) 'History on Trial: Cubillo and Gunner v The Commonwealth of Australia.' *Alternative Law Journal*, 21(1), pp. 27–31.
Orford, A. (2006) 'Commissioning the Truth.' *Columbia Journal of Gender and Law*, 15(3), pp. 851–883.
Pfau, T. (2010) 'Mourning Modernity: Classical Antiquity, Romantic Theory and Elegiac Form.' In K. Weisman (Ed.), *The Oxford Handbook of the Elegy*. Oxford: Oxford University Press.
Rae, P. (2007) *Modernism and Mourning*. Lewisburg: Bucknell University Press.
Ravenscroft, A. (2010) 'Dreaming of Others: Carpentaria and Its Critics.' *Cultural Studies Review*, 15(2), pp. 194–224.
Reichman, R. (2003) '"New Forms for Our New Sensations": Woolf and the Lesson of Torts.' *Novel: A Forum on Fiction*, 36(3), pp. 398–422.
Reichman, R. (2009) *The Affective Life of Law: Legal Modernism and the Literary Imagination*. Stanford: Stanford University Press.
Reilly, A. (2009) 'How Sorry Are We? The Limits of the Apology to the Stolen Generation.' *Alternative Law Journal*, 34(2), pp. 97–101.
Rudd, K. (2008, February 13) 'Apology to Australia's Indigenous Peoples.' *Hansard*.
Saunders, M. (2023, June 5) 'Think of the Children!' *Sydney Review of Books*. Available at: https://sydneyreviewofbooks.com/review/praiseworthy/ (Accessed: 11 December 2023).
Stallybrass, P., and White, A. (1986) *The Politics and Poetics of Transgression*. Ithaca: Cornell University Press.
van Marle, K. (2013) 'Liminal Landscape—Law, Literature and Critique in Post-Apartheid South Africa.' In K. Van Marle and S. Motha (Eds.), *Genres of Critique*. Stellenbosch: Sun Press.
van Marle, K., and Motha, S. J. (Eds.) (2013) *Genres of Critique: Law, Aesthetics and Liminality*. Stellenbosch: Sun Press.
van Rijswijk, H. M. (2012) 'Neighbourly Injuries: Proximity in Tort Law and Virginia Woolf's Theory of Suffering.' London: *Feminist Legal Studies*, 20, pp. 39–60.
van Rijswijk, H. M. (2013) 'Stolen Generations: Online Testimonies as Sources of Social Justice: Towards an Ethics of Encounter.' *Australia and New Zealand Law and History E-Journal*, 2013(10), pp. 1–13.
van Rijswijk, H. M. (2014) 'Archiving the Northern Territory Intervention in Law and in the Literary Counter-Imaginary.' *The Australian Feminist Law Journal*, 40(1), pp. 117–134.
van Rijswijk, H. M. (2015a) 'Encountering Law's Harm Through Literary Critique: An Anti-Elegy of Land and Sovereignty.' *Law and Literature*, 27(2), pp. 237–252.
van Rijswijk, H. M. (2015b) 'Towards a Literary Jurisprudence of Harm: Rewriting the Aboriginal Child in Law's Imaginary of Violence.' *Canadian Journal of Women and the Law*, 27(2), pp. 311–335.

van Rijswijk, H. M. (2016a) 'Interventions into the Feeling of Popular Justice: Australia's Stolen Generations, the Problem of Sentimentality, and Re-Encountering the Testimonial Form.' In C. Sharp and M. Leiboff (Eds.), *Cultural Legal Studies: Law's Popular Cultures and the Metamorphosis of Law*, 1st ed. Abingdon: Routledge, pp. 71–94.

van Rijswijk, H. M. (2016b) 'Introducing Complicity into the Australian Imaginary: The Bethcar Case Study in the Royal Commission into Institutional Responses to Child Abuse.' *Australian Humanities Review*, 59, pp. 223–246.

van Rijswijk, H. M. (2017) 'Encountering Aboriginal Legalities Through a Literary Jurisprudence of Suffering.' In *Challenges to Living Together: Transculturalism, Migration, Exploitation, and a Semioethics of Human Relations*. Milan, Italy: Mimesis, pp. 323–332.

van Rijswijk, H. M. (2018) 'From Sentimentality to Sadism: Visual Genres of Asylum Seeking.' In D. Manderson (Ed.), *Law and Visual Representations: Technologies and Critique*. Toronto: University of Toronto Press, pp. 189–209.

van Rijswijk, H. M. (2019) 'Feminist Genres of Violence and Law's Aggressive Realism.' In *Routledge Handbook of Law and Theory*. London, UK: Routledge, pp. 329–346.

van Rijswijk, H. M. (2021) 'Harms of the Stolen Generations Claimed Under the Flag: Contesting National World-Making Through Literature.' In A. Wagner (Ed.), *Flags, Color, and the Legal Narrative: Public Memory, Identity, and Critique*. Berne, Switzerland: Springer, pp. 593–603.

van Rijswijk, H. M. (2023) 'Law and the Aboriginal Girl: Gender, Genre, and Violence.' In A. Wagner (Ed.), *Intersemiotic Perspectives on Emotions: Translating Across Signs, Bodies, and Values*. London, UK: Routledge, pp. 130–144.

van Rijswijk, H. M. (2024) 'The Drover's Wife the Legend of Molly Johnson: Leah Purcell's Reclaiming of a Colonial Fetish.' In D. Manderson and S. Chalmers (Eds.), *Special Issue Colonial Legal Imaginaries | Southern Literary Futures, Law and Literature*, 36(2), pp. 265–283.

van Rijswijk, H. M., and Anthony, T. (2012) 'Can the Common Law Adjudicate Historical Suffering? Evaluating South Australia v Lampard-Trevorrow (2010).' *Melbourne University Law Review*, 36(2), pp. 618–655.

Waldram, J. (2015) 'The Traumatised Aboriginal.' In *Revenge of the Windigo: The Construction of the Mind and Mental Health of North American Aboriginal Peoples*. Toronto: University of Toronto Press, pp. 212–236.

Watson, I. (2009) 'In the Northern Territory Intervention: What Is Saved or Rescued and at What Cost?' *Cultural Studies Review*, 15(2), pp. 45–60.

Watson, N. (2011) 'The Northern Territory Emergency Response—Has It Really Improved the Lives of Aboriginal Women and Children?' *Australian Feminist Law Journal*, 35, p. 147.

Wild, R., and Anderson, P. (2007) *Little Children Are Sacred: Report of the Northern Territory Board of Inquiry into the Protection of First Nations Children from Child Sexual Abuse*. Darwin: Northern Territory Government.

Wright, A. (1997) *Plains of Promise*. Brisbane: Queensland University Press.

Wright, A. (2002) 'Politics of Writing.' *Southerly*, 62(2), pp. 10–20.

Wright, A. (2006) *Carpentaria*. Artarmon: Giramondo.

Wright, A. (2007) 'On Writing Carpentaria.' *Heat*, 13, pp. 79–95.

Wright, A. (2013) *The Swan Book*. Artarmon: Giramondo.

Wright, A. (2023) *Praiseworthy*. Artarmon: Giramondo.

Yeats, W. B. (1924) 'Leda and the Swan.' In R. J. Finneran (Ed.), *The Poems of W. B. Yeats: A New Edition*. London: Macmillan Publishing Company.

Zizek, S. (2010) *Living in the End Times*. New York: Verso.

Case Law

Collard v The State of Western Australia [No 4] [2013] WASC 455.
Cubillo v The Commonwealth [No 2] 112 FCR 1.
Cubillo v Commonwealth of Australia (2000) 103 FCR 1.
Kruger v Commonwealth (1997) 190 CLR 1.
Mabo and Others v Queensland (No. 2) [1992] HCA 23.
Members of the Yorta Yorta Aboriginal Community v The State of Victoria 2002 [2001] FCA 45.
South Australia v Lampard-Trevorrow (2010) 106 SASR 331.
Trevorrow v South Australia (No 5) (2007) 98 SASR 136.
Yorta Yorta Aboriginal Community v The State of Victoria [2002] HCA 58.

Legislation

Aboriginals Protection and Restriction of the Sale of Opium Act 1897 (Qld).
Aborigines Act 1890 (Vic).
Aborigines Act 1911 (SA).
Aborigines Protection Act 1886 (Vic).
Aborigines Protection Act 1890 (WA).
Aborigines Protection Act 1909 (NSW).
Northern Territory Aboriginals Act 1910 (SA).
Social Security Legislation Amendment Act 2012 (Cth).
Stronger Futures in the Northern Territory Act 2012 (Cth).
Stronger Futures in the Northern Territory Act 2013 (Cth).

Index

FSC
www.fsc.org
MIX
Papier | Fördert
gute Waldnutzung
FSC® C083411

Kolibri 360 GmbH
Ferdinand-Jühlke-Straße 7
99095 Erfurt, Deutschland
produktsicherheit@kolibri360.de